LOVE YOUR NEIGHBOUR

LOVE YOUR NEIGHBOUR

The Bible and Christian Ethics
Today

PAUL BRETT

DARTON, LONGMAN AND TODD
London

First published in 1992 by
Darton, Longman and Todd Ltd
89 Lillie Road, London SW6 1UD

© 1992 Paul Brett

ISBN 0–232–51995–1

A catalogue record for this book is available
from the British Library

The Scripture quotations are taken from the New Jerusalem Bible,
published and copyright 1985 by Darton, Longman and Todd Ltd
and Doubleday & Co. Inc., and used by permission of the publishers

Cover: stained glass window in Lincoln Cathedral
depicting the parable of the Good Samaritan.
Photograph by Sonia Halliday; design by Pat Craddock.

Phototypeset in 10½ /12½ Bembo by Intype, London
Printed and bound in Great Britain
at the University Press, Cambridge

For Judy,
Anna, Tom and Alex,
and Milly,
who are teaching me about love.

Contents

Preface

This book began as a series of Bible studies on social issues prepared for the parish of St Mary's Becontree, Dagenham, in east London. Fourteen house groups used the twelve leaflets I had written for them in two separate courses during 1988 and 1989, and they were excited by the experience. Other parishes heard about the course and asked for copies too. Eventually the leaflets were distributed to all 500 parishes in the Diocese of Chelmsford through the diocesan mailing system. They have been widely used by all sorts of groups.

This edition is a completely re-worked and expanded version of that course, designed to bring the material to a much wider audience. Stories from real life have been added, together with more up-to-date facts and figures and selected details from the tradition of thinking about Christian ethics. At the end of each of the main sections, the themes that emerge from the material presented and discussed are linked with contemporary ethical questions. I have not hesitated to express opinions, sometimes controversial, and to suggest attitudes and action for today.

THE AIM OF THIS BOOK

Three objectives have been uppermost in my mind in writing this book. Firstly, I have wanted to identify and draw out everything I could find in the Bible that seems to speak about human behaviour. This book is, first of all, about the **Bible** and Christian ethics. I have tried to present the material in a

popular and easily readable form. I have also tried to summa-
rize the bare bones of a great deal of scholarly discussion
about the passages mentioned, and to present those interpretations of it that seem to me to be most accurate and most
helpful, even though not everyone will agree with them
on every occasion. This book is not, therefore, a complete
discussion of every moral issue. It does not consider matters
on which the Bible is silent. To justify this I can only plead
that to cover every subject fully would take far more than
one volume. A Bibliography at the end suggests additional
books to take the reader further than I have been able to do,
and to offer other insights.

In preparing this book I have been surprised at the amount
of material about ethics that there is in the Bible, and which
is frequently overlooked in the Bible study, the teaching and
the preaching that goes on in the Church. We have mostly
been taught to think of the Scriptures as a record of the
history of salvation, as a quarry from which Christian doctrine can be hewn, and as a source for material for worship.
We have mostly seen it in spiritual terms as the story of
creation, fall, redemption and future hope.

This approach has effectively blinded many Christians to
the **further** questions about how we ought to treat each
other both in the community of the Church and in the world
as a whole. A preoccupation with doctrine and with liturgy
has obscured ethics. And yet Christians are to love God
and to love their neighbours. The Bible, as the foundation
document of our religion, is as much about 'works' as it is
about faith. Looking at the Bible as a rich source of ideas
about human behaviour has been an 'eye-opener' for me, and
I hope it will be so for the reader as well.

For some, the sheer quantity of bible texts quoted in these
pages may seem daunting. At one stage I wondered whether
it might have been better to quote less and to discuss at
greater length. But in the end I felt that it would be more
useful to present as much of the Bible as I could within the
space available. Selection always involves imposing some
preference on the material and I have wanted to let the Bible
tell its **own** story as far as possible.

The difficult issues faced here cannot, of course, be fully assessed on the basis of texts alone. Questions about human behaviour need to be seen in the context of the Christian vision and the Christian gospel as a whole. Our approach to human sexuality, for example, is not just determined by a handful of verses from Genesis, Romans and 1 Corinthians. Discussion about the role of women is not confined to texts where women are specifically mentioned. As someone has put it: women too are **sons** of God. What has been written about sons applies to daughters as well. Christian behaviour as a whole is closely linked with Christian belief and with Christian character. Specific texts about questions of morality need to be seen in this wider context if we are to gain the full picture.

Again I can only justify the approach I have taken by suggesting that the texts which explicitly mention the topics considered in this book are the essential starting point. It is my hope that readers who have not yet begun to explore these things will start here and then go on to discover further, deeper insights elsewhere.

Secondly, I have wanted to provide something that can readily be used for group study in the Church. The material is, therefore, ordered with this in mind. Each of the sixteen main sections, although grouped under six general themes – sex, community, economy, environment, politics, life and death – can be read and studied independently. Together with the first and last chapters, a six-month study course of as many as eighteen sessions could be undertaken. Alternatively a selection of appropriate sections could provide a course of any convenient length to suit any particular group.

This arrangement has led to some repetition in some places. The creation stories, for example, have something to say under more than one heading. They are quoted, therefore, and the appropriate insights drawn from them, wherever they are relevant. The significance of some passages is enhanced by their use in different contexts in this way.

Thirdly, I have wanted to show that the Bible is relevant for ethics today, in spite of widespread views to the contrary. Some Christians think, for example, that the Bible is too time-bound in a culture long since vanished to be of much use now, or too specific to particular situations in Jewish and early Christian history to have any general application. Others think that it proposes ways of behaving that are inappropriate, even offensive. Man is to subdue the earth? Adulterers are to be stoned? Women are to submit to men? Personal possessions are to be sold and the money given to the poor? All authority comes from God and must be obeyed? Surely, people think, a book that says things like that cannot be taken seriously today! But these proposals should not be ripped from their context. All is not what it seems at face value, and this book reveals why.

Some readers may feel that I have too often appeared to impose modern views on ancient material in order to make it 'relevant'. My primary intention, however, has been to face the text as it is and to see what it does actually say. In some cases, as will become clear, subsequent Christian tradition has itself imposed partial or distorted interpretations on the material – on sex or on the environment, for example. What are thought to be 'traditional' understandings are not necessary biblical, nor are they right when looked at with the benefit of modern understanding. Other interpretations are often possible, and I have wanted to bring these out for consideration too.

It has also been my intention to bring the Bible and the tradition into dialogue with today's problems and to let the one speak to the other. Christians need to find ways of living that are both ancient **and** modern. If the Bible does not speak effectively to our contemporary situation we miss out on much of its power. I have tried to show that what underlies the ancient rules and conventions is of abiding worth, but that it may need to be expressed in different forms in different times. I try to point to this under the heading **Themes** at the end of each section.

ACKNOWLEDGEMENTS

In quoting from the Scriptures I have used the New Jerusalem Bible (NJB) throughout. In a few places I have also referred to the Authorised or King James Version (AV), the Revised Version (RV), and the recently published and excellent Revised English Bible (REB), where these translations seem to be more accurate or more illuminating. Where I have quoted from books in the Apocrypha, printed in the main body of the Bible in the NJB but separately in most other versions, I have made this clear.

Throughout the text I have mostly put the books of the Bible in the familiar order, even though this does not always accord with the dates when they are thought to have been written or compiled. I have done this, not to prejudge questions about dating, but to make it easier for readers to follow. In any case the Bible is also a work of literature as a whole, and it is not without significance that the books have been put in a particular order, and that some verses precede or follow others on the same or contrasting themes.

Some readers may not be familiar with the word 'Yahweh' used in the NJB. This is simply a transliteration of the name of the God of Israel – Yhwh in Hebrew – usually rendered 'the LORD' in other English versions.

For other quotations I have adopted the Harvard referencing system. This gives author, date and page number in brackets in the body of the text, and avoids the awkwardness of having to flip over the pages to the end of the chapter, or even to the end of the book, to discover what is being quoted. Full details of each publication are then given in the Bibliography at the end.

I write as an English Anglican, and occasionally this shows, but I have quoted sources from the United States, Germany, Switzerland and Latin America as well as from Scotland and England, and I have referred to Catholic and Evangelical publications. Theology and ethics are increasingly international and inter-denominational, and I welcome the richness of insight that this affords.

Grateful thanks are due to those who have helped me

produce this book. The Bishop of Chelmsford granted me sabbatical leave during which the bulk of the text was written. The Cambridge Federation of Theological Colleges and the Cambridge University Divinity Faculty gave me permission to use their libraries. Rupert Hoare, Principal of Westcott House, Richard Higginson, Lecturer in Ethics at Ridley Hall, Andrew Linzey, Director of Studies at the Centre for the Study of Theology in the University of Essex, and a number of other friends read drafts and made many helpful comments. Philip Woods, Enid Gear, Jenny Robinson and Maureen Ball, colleagues in the Social Responsibility department of the Diocese of Chelmsford covered for me during my absence at a difficult time, and then kept other demands at bay while I brought the text to its finished form. Without the help of all these this book could never have been written, or finished on time. Thanks are also due to Mary Jean Pritchard, Editorial Director of Darton, Longman and Todd, for encouraging me by accepting this book for publication before it had even been written.

Above all I am grateful to my wife Judy and our children for their tolerance as I buried myself in the study upstairs and got on with what our six-year-old called 'Daddy's story'.

THE READERSHIP

Who is this book for? It is my hope that it will be really useful in many contexts. I would like it to used by Bible study groups and house groups, by those who arrange adult confirmation classes, Lent courses and discussion groups of every sort, and by those who run religious education classes in schools. I would like it to find a place on the desks of clergy and preachers, theological students, RE teachers and of all Christian people who want to know 'what the Bible says' about ethics.

I would also like this book to be read like a novel – with excitement, the reader unable to put it down, eager to turn the page to discover what happens next. With this in mind there is even a slight twist to the tale towards the end!

Above all I would like Christian people to **live** the Christian life more fully. In the end this is what really matters. God has called us to love him and to love our neighbours. There is no more important task. If this book helps **you** to do these things better, it will have served its purpose.

PAUL BRETT
Easter 1992

1.

MAKING MORAL DECISIONS

Children growing up ask endless questions. The word 'Why?' is one of the most popular in the vocabulary: 'Why must I tell the truth?' 'Why shouldn't I hit Anna when I want to?' 'Why can't I take Tom's engines without asking?' And finding the right answers is not always easy – for children or for adults.

For Christian people one way of trying to answer these questions is to appeal to the will of God. We can say that he doesn't want us to lie, or to hurt other people, or to steal. It is God's will that we should love each other, as he loves us. But what does this involve? It won't mean much to small children, and it may not mean much to adults at first. This book sets out to try to answer this question.

LOVING THE NEIGHBOUR

Jesus was once asked which was the first of all the command-ments, and his answer came in words that have become famous. *'You must love the Lord your God,'* he said, *'with all your heart, with all your soul, with all your mind and with all your strength.'* And the second commandment, he continued, is this, *'You must love your neighbour as yourself'*. The story is told with small variations in each of the first three Gospels (Mk. 12:28–34; Mt. 22:34–40; Lk. 10:25–28).

In stating these two commandments Jesus is in fact quoting from the Hebrew Scriptures – the words about loving God come from Deuteronomy (6:5), and about loving the neigh-bour from Leviticus (19;18). He is quoting what his hearers

1

already know. But he puts the two commandments together in a striking and powerful way. For him they are two sides of the same coin.

The implications of these commandments are far-reaching. Jesus, for example, tells his followers to love even their enemies (Mt. 5:43–45; Lk. 6:27). For Matthew, the whole Law and the Prophets hang on them (22:40). Paul declares, *'To love the other person is to fulfil the law'*. All the other commandments are *'summed up in this single phrase: You must love your neighbour as yourself'* (Rom. 13:8–10; Gal. 5:14). There is no doubt that in touching these words we touch the heart of the Christian gospel.

Among the most famous of all Paul's words are those of the great hymn to love in 1 Corinthians. *'If I speak without love,'* he writes, *'I am no more than a gong booming or a cymbal clashing . . . Love is always patient and kind; love is never jealous; love is not boastful or conceited, it is never rude and never seeks its own advantage, it does not take offence or store up grievances. Love does not rejoice at wrongdoing, but finds its joy in the truth. It is always ready to make allowances, to trust, to hope and to endure whatever comes. Love never comes to an end . . . As it is, these remain: faith, hope and love, the three of them; and the greatest of them is love'* (13:1–13).

The basis for the life of love is not just obedience to Jesus' command, nor even responding to the emotional appeal of Paul's words, it is God's love for us. In 1 John, the theme is put like this: *'My dear friends, let us love one another, since love is from God . . . Whoever fails to love does not know God, because God is love. This is the revelation of God's love for us, that God sent his only Son into the world that we might have life through him . . . If God loves us so much, we too should love one another . . . Let us love, then, because he first loved us . . . Whoever loves God, must also love his brother . . .'* (4:7—5:4). Here John is talking about love between believers. It is central and fundamental within the Christian fellowship. It is just as important in the world as a whole, for we are to love the stranger as well as the brother and sister in faith.

In Luke's version of the story in which the two commandments are stated, the lawyer goes on to ask, *'And who is my neighbour?'* The parable of the good Samaritan is Jesus' answer (10:29–37). It is one of the best known and best loved stories in the Gospels: the man on his way to Jericho, the bandits, the priest and the Levite who pass by on the other side, and then the Samaritan who is *'moved with compassion'* and who gathers him up, takes him to the inn and pays for his care. The neighbour is the unexpected person, the outsider, the one who does not belong to our own community or even our own faith. This is the one the Christian is to love, the stranger. And the neighbour is also the one who shows compassion, who goes out of his way to help those in need. That is how the follower of Jesus is to act.

The story also suggests that love for others, whoever they are, is more than sentiment, a matter of goodwill or warm feeling alone. It is practical, concerned with the relief of physical and mental suffering. It is time-consuming and costly. It has to do with our families, our communities, our society. Love is at the heart of Christian life. It is the basis of all that is good.

To put it in other words, and to put it rather starkly, a Christian spirituality that is entirely inward-looking, concerned with the individual alone, spiritual in the narrow sense, or entirely upward-looking, focusing solely on God in all his majesty, is inadequate. It must also be outward-looking, concerned with the neighbour, if it is to be complete. James puts this well: *'If one of the brothers or one of the sisters is in need of clothes and has not enough food to live on, and one of you says to them, "I wish you well; keep yourself warm and eat plenty", without giving them these bare necessities of life, then what good is that? In the same way faith, if good deeds do not go with it, is quite dead'* (2:14–17).

Christian love finds expression in action as well as in attitudes, and both are necessary. What we think about things matters; it helps to mould our character and our behaviour, and it provides a reasoned basis for our actions. And how we behave matters, too. We need action grounded in love and love expressed in action. Words and deeds also go together like two sides of a coin.

Love is the foundation of Christian ethics and the motive

3

for Christian living. But this love – *agape* in Greek – is more than just affection, or friendship, or some form of sexual attraction. These involve an assessment of value on my side and yours. Christian love, by contrast, regards everyone equally. In *Agape*, the American theologian Gene Outka defines it as 'a regard for the neighbour which in crucial respects is independent and unalterable . . . The regard is for every person *qua* human existent' (Outka 1972: 9). Christian love is what I owe you purely because you are another person like me. There is a fundamental element of equality involved; we are to love our neighbours **as ourselves**.

This is why Christian love can be required of us. We can't be friends with everyone, nor fall in love with everyone, but God can command us to show equal regard to all alike. Christian love affirms the dignity and the value of every person. In *Justice and the Social Order*, the Swiss theologian Emil Brunner puts it like this: 'It is not a love which judges worth, but a love which bestows worth' (Brunner 1945: 114).

Love and Justice

Equal regard for all sounds impossible. How can it be put into practice? The American theologian Reinhold Niebuhr, who cut his teeth as an ethical thinker among the car workers of Detroit, thinks it **is** impossible in the real world of actual human communities. In *An Interpretation of Christian Ethics*, he describes this love as the 'quintessence of the character of God' (Niebuhr 1979: 24). For him the nearest we can get to it is justice.

The relationship between love and justice needs a little thought. Justice means giving people what is due to them. It is about fair relationships between persons and groups in society, and it may involve penalties when one treats another unfairly. There is no affection, or preference, in justice; it is impartial. Justice is about the claims we can have on one another. Without it we cannot begin to live together in communities or in society. Love, however, is what we offer, not what we can claim. It can be partial. There are no conditions attached to it. We do not deserve love. It comes to us as a gift. It can be generous and affectionate, extravagant even. In *Theology of Culture*, the American philosopher Paul Tillich brings the two together in a nice phrase. Love is 'the ground, the power, the aim of justice', he writes, so that 'love without justice is a body without a backbone' (Tillich 1959: 145). Justice is the stiffening that enables social relationships to stand and to survive.

In *Situation Ethics*, on the other hand, the American ethicist Joseph Fletcher, far from saying that the one is partially expressed in the other, declares that they are identical. 'Justice', he writes, 'is love distributed, nothing else' (Fletcher 1966: 87). But this makes love too cold, too calculating, too impersonal. Brunner puts it well: 'Love can only do more, it can never do less, than justice requires . . . The demand of justice can be satisfied, the demand of love never' (Brunner 1945: 117–118). In *Christianity and Social Order*, the former Archbishop of Canterbury William Temple sums up the importance of love in the Christian life and its relationship to justice like this: 'It is axiomatic that Love should be the predominant Christian impulse, and that the primary form of Love in social organization is Justice' (Temple 1976: 78).

At the end of the story of the good Samaritan Jesus says to the lawyer, *'Go, and do the same yourself'*. To follow Jesus is to care for others. Love is the foundation for our action in the world, and its source or origin is the love of God for us. We are to be channels through which his love flows into the world, and active agents of love in response to his command. Christian love is for all. There is no question of deserving it. It is both private and public, concerned with persons and their relationships, as well as with the structures and systems of society. It implies an equal regard for everyone. Justice is the least that it requires.

SCRIPTURE, TRADITION AND REASON

What, then, must we do to love our neighbours? What does justice require? How are Christian moral decisions to be made? These are the fundamental questions of Christian ethics. Traditionally, within the Anglican way of thinking at least, three elements have long had pride of place: Scripture, tradition and reason. I want to look briefly at each of these, in order to lay a foundation for all that follows.

The Bible

What is the Bible? It is not a book so much as a library of books. Its contents were written over a period of some 1,600 years. Much of the material was originally passed on orally as one generation told another the stories that formed their history and helped to shape their sense of identity. In the Hebrew Scriptures – I shall call them this, instead of the Old Testament, out of respect for the Jewish and the Muslim faith communities who also value these writings – there is ancient legend, together with codes of law, liturgical material for use in worship, history and varying interpretations of it, poetry, wisdom literature, prophecy and social comment, and visionary material about the future. All through there is a strong sense of Israel as a 'covenant community' under God, and of the obligations that follow from this relationship.

In the Christian Scriptures – the New Testament – there is the story of Jesus and the various attempts to interpret its significance, together with the history of the earliest Christian communities. There is theological thinking, some of it still in the process of being worked out, as well as further apocalyptic or visionary material about the future. All through there is a strong sense of the Christian Church as an 'eschatological community' living in the last days before the return of the Lord and the end of all things. There is a sense, too, of the Church as a fragile 'fellowship' struggling to find its identity in a hostile and uncomprehending world, Jewish, Greek and Roman.

Over the last 200 years or so scholars have subjected the Bible to the closest possible examination to try to discover the original texts, for this is not always clear, as well as their meaning in the original context. It is likely, for example, that there are four separate sources within the Torah, the first five books of the Law. In Genesis there are two creation stories with different emphases in them. Leviticus, though it is placed before Deuteronomy, may have been compiled much later in time. The prophetic books may have been the product of schools of prophets rather than the words of single individuals.

The four Gospels also show traces of dependence on other sources. Mark was probably written first, and Matthew and Luke copied from him, as well as using material of their own and other sources. Paul may not have written Ephesians and Colossians, or 1 and 2 Timothy or Titus. The thought is more developed and the background situation apparently later in time than that of the other letters attributed to him. But they are 'Pauline' in that they stand within the tradition of thinking that is clearly his.

All through the Bible the hand of editors is frequently to be found as earlier material is taken up, re-stated and re-interpreted for new religious, political and social situations. These editors approached the tradition that came to them with fidelity but also with creative imagination. The texts helped to shape the communities that received them, and the communities themselves shaped the texts as they used them and passed them on to others.

The Bible is a classic work of literature as well as a collection of material from many different sources. It has layers of construction and meaning that need to be carefully disentangled and understood in relation to each other. To take it at its face value alone is to miss much of what it actually has to say.

This point can be made by a comparison. In the National Gallery in London there is a large painting by Holbein called 'The Ambassadors'. A note on the wall indicates that it was painted in 1533 and depicts two men surrounded by 'symbols of their wealth and interests' – astronomical and scientific apparatus, a globe, musical instruments, a lute. On the floor between the two figures is an object looking like a French loaf stretching up at an angle towards the right. If you look sideways at it you can see that it is an elongated skull. In common with others of the period the picture points to the mortality of life. Riches and culture do not last for ever.

But the casual observer, taking the picture at its face value, will entirely miss further layers of meaning waiting to be discovered. The richly-dressed figures are those of a bishop, recently appointed but not yet consecrated and not in episcopal clothes, and a diplomat. They are standing on a pavement close in design to one round the shrine of Edward the Confessor in Westminster Abbey. They have come to London after Henry VIII's divorce from Catherine of Aragon and at the time of his secret marriage to Anne Boleyn. They have come to suggest, unsuccessfully as it turns out, that the Pope might approve this marriage if certain other liaisons are arranged for his family. The figures look calm and dignified, but underneath there is a high degree of political and social tension. One of the lute strings has snapped.

At one level the picture records the visit of two powerful men, but at another it is a record of a delicate diplomatic negotiation. At other levels it is a comment on religious reform, on Church and state, on the machinations of public life, and even on the exploitation of women for political purposes determined by men. In *Holbein*, the art historian John Rowlands concludes that the picture reflects 'in a discreet way the sitters' earnest concern over the religious crises facing Christendom' (Rowlands 1985: 86).

What does the picture 'mean'? It means all these things, and it speaks the truth, even though the two men may never have stood in the Abbey to have this snapshot taken for the family album. The Bible is at least as richly layered, and as powerful in its comment, as a picture by any famous painter.

The Bible deals with eternal truths that have influenced lives in the past, and can still do so today. As we read it and study it, using all the insights of the 'historical-critical' method developed by scholars, we experience a moral claim on us to regard what we read as authoritative for us, too, in our quite different setting. We read it not only to discover what happened then, but also to discover what ought to happen **now**.

In *Liberating Exegesis*, the theologians Christopher Rowland and Mark Corner quote Rudolph Bultmann, one of the most formative German thinkers in the development of the critical approach to the Bible. Bultmann asks, 'Are we to read the Bible only as an historical document in order to reconstruct an epoch of past history . . . ? I think our interest is really to hear what the Bible has to say for our actual present, to hear what is the truth about life and about our soul' (Rowland and Corner 1990: 72).

The Bible can help us to interpret life today in all its complexity. We are not to escape from life into the world of faith, but precisely the opposite, to enter into life assisted by the tradition of faith which we inherit from the past.

The Christian Tradition

Interpreting the significance of the Bible for Christian ethics is not something we start from cold. We enter into a tradition. Our interpretations will be shaped by those of the past, though we do not need to be constrained by them. It is worth looking at the way this tradition has developed, even if only in the briefest way.

In *The Changing Continuity of Christian Ethics, Volume 2, The Insights of History*, the Scottish Baptist R. E. O. White paints the picture. In the first and second centuries of the Christian era the Church found itself part of the Roman Empire. Slavery, infanticide, the cheapening of life generally, religious prostitution, all this and more seems to have been commonplace. In such a context it is easy to see why the Church sought at first to withdraw from the world. The theme of endurance, of resisting sensuality, of caring for its own members became important in early ethical thinking. Later a strong desire to imitate the life of Christ found expression in the monastic commitment to poverty, chastity and obedience to authority. In those first few centuries there was even a double standard: the world-renouncing life of asceticism for some and lower, more mundane standards for others.

The development of Christian ethics, however, took a significant step forward in the fifth century with Augustine,

9

Bishop of Hippo in north Africa. In words that have become famous he declared, 'Love God and do what you will', and 'Love, and you cannot but do well'. These words were not a recipe for licence, but a way of saying that love of God and love of neighbour belong together. 'Our love of our neighbour', Augustine continues, 'is a sort of cradle of our love to God' (White 1981: 100,105).

Towering above other theologians, and some 800 years later, was Thomas Aquinas. The tradition of thinking that stretches back to him, Thomism as it is called, is still of fundamental importance in Roman Catholic moral philosophy. Aquinas based his ethical thinking on natural law, which human reason can discover on its own, and behind which lies the divine law. The primary precept of this natural law, he writes, is 'that good should be done and pursued and evil avoided'. On this he continues, 'are founded all other precepts of the law of nature' (White 1981: 127). Aquinas stresses the importance of disposition, or motive. He discusses the natural virtues: temperance, courage, justice, prudence, and the theological virtues: faith, hope and love. To these he adds three intellectual virtues: wisdom, knowledge, intuition.

By the time of the Reformation, however, critical voices were being raised. Ethics had become too legalistic, too dependent on reason, and too much concerned with the individual. The relationship between 'works' and 'faith' needed to be examined more fully. In Germany Martin Luther turned to Scripture and experience. 'A man cannot do good', he writes, 'before he is made good' (White 1981: 160). The experience of justification by faith alone leads to the knowledge of what is right. It is God's gracious gift. Luther speaks of the two kingdoms, sacred and secular, the kingdom of God's right hand and of his left, in which different standards may apply.

In Switzerland John Calvin looked beyond personal spirituality to the creation of a sanctified society. The experience of salvation releases a great moral energy. The Christian delights in obedience to God and charity flows from this. 'Let a man be what he may,' he writes, 'he is still to be loved because God is loved' (White 1981: 196). For a while Geneva became a model of a disciplined Christian society under the sovereign law of God. But the Reformation was a time of great ferment and of questioning of authority. The world was changing fundamentally under the influence of science, industry, secularism and social revolution.

From then on there are many names to mention. In England Richard Hooker looked to Scripture, tradition and reason together as the basis for Christian ethics. Bishop Butler turned to conscience for authority. A growing number of Puritans lived disciplined, earnest and hard-working lives in the spirit of Calvin. Quakers relied on the inner light in people, and with their desire for perfectionism went a powerful social concern.

The dispute about the nature of Christian ethics, and their place in the Christian life, stirred up by the Reformation is well summarized by White. On the one hand he writes, 'The Calvinist denial of any natural goodness, or capacity for right choice, of any inward light of conscience, or reason, capable of perceiving truth or morality, destroys moral responsibility'. But on the other he continues, 'The rationalists' insistence upon man's natural moral capacity, through reason, conscience, or the Christ within, destroys the necessity for the gospel' (White 1981: 264).

This same dilemma is still around today in the suspicion some Christians have of 'good works' and of Christian involvement in political and social action, both by individuals and by the Church corporately. The questions remains: Can we live the good life with the help of reason alone, or does it depend on faith? And what sort of action does faith prompt?

In England in the eighteenth and nineteenth centuries Christian concern for the state of society grew. Public morality was as important as private morality. John Wesley, for example, preached the need for charity in very practical terms. F. D. Maurice used the term 'Christian socialism' and spoke about the kingdom of Christ in a corporate sense. The Christian Social Union was formed concentrating on industrial and economic matters.

In America at the beginning of the twentieth century the Baptist pastor Walter Rauschenbusch wrote passionately about the kingdom of God. A leader of the 'social gospel' movement, he wanted to Christianize the social order. Rein-hold Niebuhr brought this idealism down to earth with his emphasis on 'Christian realism'. In England William Temple wrote about 'Christian social principles'. In Germany Dietrich Bonhoeffer spoke of 'Christian worldliness'.

In the international Roman Catholic community successive Popes issued a growing series of encyclical letters about social issues, touching on such matters as the condition of the working classes, the dignity of the person, the importance of the family, the freedom of the individual, the promotion of the common good, the proper use of wealth and work.

The tradition of thinking about Christian ethics has been powerfully developed since the days of the early Church. Christian thinkers have been bold in their use of the tradition, and we can be so, too, today.

The Use of Reason

In distinguishing Scripture, tradition and reason it would be wrong to suggest that they are independent of each other. Scripture itself is a collection of the earliest elements of the tradition. It is part of the tradition. It reveals God's will. It contains the Christian revelation, which reason alone could never have produced. But human reason is the faculty that enables us to interpret the Scriptures and the tradition so that they can illuminate current concerns. Reason is an essential element in Christian ethics. The insights of philosophy play their part in the pursuit of what is good and true.

In the Roman Catholic tradition, for example, the concept of natural law has been central. God has created the world in such a way that certain types of behaviour 'go with the grain' of nature, and we can discover them just by using our powers of reasoning. No special religious insight is needed to know the value of preserving life and not destroying it, of doing to others the good you would like them to do to you, of respecting property, and caring for the weak and the needy. The Christian would say, simply, that God has made it so. Natural law expresses his will in creation.

Some thinking about sexual behaviour, or about contra-

12

ception, for example, is rooted in ideas about natural law. If the natural purpose of sex is considered to be procreation, then sexual activity that is not intended for this end, or that tries to prevent procreation, is against the natural law. Ethical thinking about war is also often based on natural law thinking. In a violent world war can be kept within bounds only if its intention, its conduct and its outcome are just. Reasoning alone can produce the answer in particular cases. But natural law is a difficult concept, and conclusions reached on its basis in one generation do not always seem so reasonable in another.

Other philosophical ideas have also played an important role in ethical thinking. Human behaviour can be assessed in terms of acts, or consequences, or intention. When the right thing to do is unclear, we can balance one possibility against another, and take the better or the safer course.

In *The Good and the True*, the Christian philosopher Michael Langford describes some of these ideas. Particular courses of action can be judged to be good 'in themselves'. They are right in an absolute sense, regardless of motive or outcome.

The eighteenth-century German philosopher Immanuel Kant, for example, formulated certain principles, or maxims, that were true whatever the circumstances. 'When you act,' Kant writes, 'act only in a way in which you can consistently will all other people to act.' On this basis suicide is wrong because it cannot possibly be made a universal requirement. It would be the end of human life on this earth. A second principle is this: 'Always treat every person as an end in himself or herself and never merely as a means' (Langford 1985: 13,18). Nazi experiments on human beings were wrong because they clearly broke this rule. People today often object to being 'used' by others for ulterior purposes, voicing this same objection of principle. Such things, we say, are **intrinsically** wrong.

Other philosophers, however, have looked more towards the consequences of human action in order to decide whether it is right or wrong. An action is good, not in itself, but if its consequences are good. The nineteenth-century philosopher

John Stuart Mill is particularly associated with this approach. His philosophy of utilitarianism seeks 'the greatest happiness of the greatest number' (Langford 1985: 8).

Most government legislation, for example, is utilitarian: the more people who are helped by tax cuts, or by social security benefit increases, or by training schemes, the better. Utilitarianism encourages individual choice and initiative, but it does not particularly encourage people to bear one another's burdens, or to care for the poorest, or to go in for self-sacrifice, values that appeal to the Christian mind. It has even been used to justify the continuation of slavery, for some happiness was increased by it. But a concern for the consequences of human action plays an important part in almost all ethical thinking.

Sometimes ethical principles conflict, whatever their basis. To shoot to kill is wrong, but to do so to prevent an attacker going for a child with an axe may be right. In this situation we choose the 'lesser of two evils', or in other situations of uncertainty, the 'greater of two goods'.

In complicated cases like this the principle of 'double effect' can often help us to sort out what to do. A particular action may have more than one effect: a primary one, which is what we intend to achieve by it, and a secondary one, which we may not intend. The use of a condom within marriage, for example, to prevent the passing on of Aids in sexual intercourse, contracted, say, from an infected blood transfusion, may be acceptable to strict Catholics, even though the secondary effect – preventing contraception – is not. A good primary intention is not necessarily invalidated by a bad secondary consequence.

In practice most actions are good or not in **relation** to other factors. Relativism plays an important part in almost all ethical thinking, too. Absolute standards sound good, but they break down in the face of actual experience. Pastoral concern for particular persons requires us to temper the absolute with the relative. In practice we can only do the best we can in the circumstances, and pray for forgiveness when we fail to get it right.

If the truth be told, however, most ethical decisions are

14

made, more often than not, on purely emotional grounds. We talk about what 'feels' right. Ernest Hemingway puts it in a nutshell: 'What's good,' he writes, 'is what I feel good after, and what's bad is what I feel bad after' (Fletcher 1966: 54). Or we act on intuition. People often say, 'You just know what's right'. Although it may have deeper origins in our reason or our emotions, an intuitive decision about what to do comes to us in a flash, without any lengthy process of argument or any struggle with principles and rules.

Reason and emotion both play a part in ethical decision-making, but there are other influences as well. The communities we belong to, for example, are clearly crucial in shaping character and the behaviour that flows from it. Family influence, upbringing, education, class, culture, environment, social conditioning, the 'system' all influence our behaviour in various good, and not so good, ways. The Church can play an important role here as a community in which moral issues are explored and Christian character is formed.

Principles and Practice

Where, then, does the study of the ethical material in the Bible and the subsequent tradition of reflection on it, and the use of human reason lead us? How can we put all this into practice? Are there any principles, or guidelines, to help us decide what Christian behaviour actually is in this or that situation?

In *Christianity and Social Order*, William Temple tries to set out a way of moving from basic theological principle towards practical policy for everyday life. He begins by defining two primary principles: 'God and his Purpose' and 'Man: his Dignity, Tragedy and Destiny'. From these he develops three derivative Christian social principles: 'Freedom', 'Social Fellowship', and 'Service'. They are to be regulated in social life, Temple continues, through love and justice (Temple 1976: 58–80).

But principles as general as this are hard to apply. The government in our own day, for example, may decide to increase interest rates in order to dampen down spending on

15

credit, to keep prices down and to reduce inflation. Or it may decide to reduce interest rates in order to encourage industry to borrow, to re-equip and to create more prosperity and more jobs. But it is not at all clear which course of action is the better, or which is more loving or more just.

Here the idea of 'middle axioms', or middle principles, is helpful. In *Church and Society in the Late Twentieth Century*, the ethicist Ronald Preston describes what these principles are and how they work. Middle axioms are ethical statements that lie somewhere between general principles 'which cannot be disputed because they have no specific content', on the one hand, and detailed recommendations about what should be done, on the other, where 'the issues are too involved and the details too uncertain to warrant such a prescribed conclusion' (Preston 1983: 142, 143).

Middle axioms bridge the gap between the general, too vague for anyone to disagree with, and the particular, too detailed and too divisive to gain any wide support. They can bring theologians and those concerned with 'technical' matters together. Private morality and public morality, Catholic and Protestant, religious and secular can meet in common action based on considered principle. Middle axioms can keep Christian ethics in touch with reality. They avoid the problems that arise from trying to 'apply' unchanging moral principles to particular cases with results that fail to offer any real help.

William Temple sets out a number of middle axioms. He writes: 'Every child should find itself a member of a family housed with decency and dignity, so that it may grow up as a member of that basic community in a happy fellowship unspoilt by underfeeding or overcrowding, by dirty and drab surroundings or by mechanical monotony of environment.' He goes on to state five other principles in similar vein on education, income, worker participation in industry, leisure, and liberty and to give his support to a seventh on the use of the earth's resources. Temple concludes, 'The aim of a Christian social order is the fullest possible development of individual personality in the widest and deepest possible fellowship' (Temple 1976: 96–97).

Middle axioms certainly suggest the direction in which public policy should go. They provide what the American theologian James Gustafson has called 'anchors and compasses' for Christian ethics (Preston 1983: 147). They offer a benchmark against which activities or policies that are not acceptable to the Christian moral conscience can be judged.

Some Christians argue that this is as far as the Church should go with its comment on public affairs, leaving the rest to individual action. But a more radical approach has been developed by liberation theologians, arising out of the oppressive political and economic situation in Latin American countries. They argue that Christians must stop sitting on the fence, seeing both sides of every issue and uttering generalizations. The Church needs to find a 'prophetic word' to society. Christians should take sides in the conflicts of life. They should show a bias in favour of the poor and the disadvantaged, so that they may be liberated from all that oppresses them.

In *Toward a Christian Political Ethics*, the Argentinian theologian José Miguez Bonino picks up the theme of liberation in the Bible and declares, 'God acts in righteousness when he establishes and reestablishes right relationships, restoring those who have been wronged in their legitimate claims as members of the covenant. Such action is the equivalent of "salvation". When God liberates Israel, when he protects the unprotected, when he delivers the captive or vindicates the right of the poor, he is exhibiting his justice' (Bonino 1983: 85).

The ancient story of the exodus from Egypt, of liberation from slavery, has been of fundamental importance to the Jewish community, and still is so today. The theme continues in the drama of Jesus, crucified but risen again to new life. Freedom from the slavery of sin is a fundamental concept in Christian theology. When those ancient events, told and retold in story form, find a parallel in human situations today, they given oppressed and exploited people a powerful sense of hope. It is in the practical struggle for justice and dignity for all that Christian love finds its true expression, and God's will is realized.

17

BRIDGING THE GAP

But is all this helpful to Christian people today? Love, foundations, motive, Scripture, tradition, reason, principles, axioms, liberation all sound so academic, so theoretical, so much in the realm of ideas. How can all this become part of **our** story in the city, the suburbs, the small town, the country village, where people in Britain mostly live out their ordinary lives? How, in other words, can we bridge the gap between the world of the Bible and reasoned reflection on it, and the world of today?

An example will help to point the way forward. I remember being at a conference of industrial chaplains – not a group of people habitually given to pious spirituality – and discovering a powerful way of using the Bible. We sat in small groups of five or six around the hall, studying Mark's version of the healing of the paralytic man: a large crowd listening to Jesus, four men bringing the man on a stretcher and lowering him through an opening in the roof, Jesus forgiving his sins on the basis of his friends' faith, the scribes arguing about blasphemy, Jesus telling the man to pick up his stretcher and go off home, and the astonishment of the crowd (2:1–12).

In our groups we took up the parts in the drama. We became the crowd watching what happened, or the owners of the house being broken up by strangers, or the man and his friends knowing only that they had to get to Jesus, or the scribes worried about theological niceties, or Jesus himself fed up with the religious establishment of his day. When we came to confront each other in these roles, uproar ensued. We lived these roles ourselves, and added our own dialogue and emotion. It was a moving experience. On a hillside in Derbyshire our story and the paralytic man's story became fused together, and we found healing too.

In *Transforming Bible Study*, the American theologian Walter Wink puts his angle on this 'experiential' method of Bible study. He brings the rational, logical, left side of the brain together with the emotional, artistic, right side in encounter with the text. This more 'wholistic' approach, using reason and emotion, can revolutionize Bible study. 'The payoff', he writes, 'is not information but transformation' (Wink 1990: 90).

Wink goes on to suggest a long list of exercises which engage 'the other side of the brain': role-play, telling the stories in paint or clay, mime, dance, poetry, reading the stories alongside similar ones from today. By methods such as these, as well as the more familiar academic study of the Bible, the word becomes incarnate, it gets 'into the substance of our living' (Wink 1990: 12).

The chapters of this book that follow try to echo something of this method. Each section begins with a story from actual human experience. Before looking at passages about marriage, for example, I introduce you to Shirley and Richard, and Stephen and Elaine. Before considering the relationships between parents and children, I tell you about Louise and Andrew and the worry they had over little Evie.

In each section, too, there are facts and figures about employment and unemployment, for example, or the ecological crisis, taken from official reports and other secular sources. The government publication *Social Trends* is particularly helpful here. Published annually in an updated form, it contains a great deal of statistical information about many aspects of British life. The contents page indicates the breadth of its concern. There are details on population, households and families, education, employment, income and wealth, expenditure and resources, health and personal social services, housing, environment, leisure, participation, law enforcement, transport (Central Statistical Office 1992: 2).

Then there is a review of all, or almost all, the references in the Hebrew and the Christian Scriptures that seem to bear on the subject of each section, drawing out the themes that these passages illustrate and tracing the development in thinking from one group of books in the Bible to another. Although it has not been possible, or sensible, to quote every reference to the poor, for example, or to animals, or to ancient battles, there is a fuller account here of the ethical material in the Bible than is to be found, perhaps, in any other single convenient volume. I have felt it to be more important to confront the texts in all their fullness, and their repetition, than to be selective and to consider fewer passages at greater length.

In most of the sections there is then a brief, sometimes extremely brief, look at some of the things that have been said by later theologians about these matters. For reasons of space I have not been able to do more than hint at the rich and varied tradition of two thousand years of reflection on the subjects considered.

Finally, in each section, I have tried to set out the main themes that emerge and to 'read across' from them into the situations we face today. Here insights from the past fuse with contemporary problems. Past and present 'ring bells' with the other, in such a way that principles, and in some cases specific policies, emerge to guide Christian behaviour in the modern world.

This is no simplistic taking texts at their face value, but a more subtle process of exploring what is of underlying importance in the ethical material in the Bible, and seeing what it suggests for policy and practice now. In some cases, the results are surprising. Quite liberal, even permissive, lines of action seem to receive support from the Bible. I have tried to bring ancient texts and modern problems together and to go wherever this process seems to lead. Although this book, as its sub-title suggests, is primarily about the Bible and Christian ethics today, tradition and reason play an important part in it too.

So now to the substance of the book. I turn first to matters of sexual relationships, and then to questions of family and community life. Then I look at economic questions, at wealth and poverty, and at the environment. Next I look at political matters, at the state and at dealing with violence. Then I turn to matters of life and death, abortion, embryo research, euthanasia. The last chapter offers some pointers to the practical implications of all this for the life of the Church today.

Finally there are suggestions for a study course using this material, and questions for discussion by church groups. Some of the questions are deliberately provocative in order to encourage a good discussion. The book concludes with a

Bibliography listing the publications I have found most helpful in preparing this material, so that the many matters raised here, and all too inadequately discussed in these pages, can be followed up elsewhere.

2.

INTIMATE RELATIONSHIPS

We are persons. It may seem obvious to say this, but the word 'person' is only one of several that might be used. We can also say that we are bodies and souls, or men and women, or friends and neighbours. These words all say something slightly different about us and how we think of ourselves.

The body is, perhaps, the most obvious thing about each of us. When we look at one another, the body is what we see first. But we are not just bodies; we are minds, or spirits, or souls as well. The word soul is often popularly used to refer to what is of eternal value about us, our character. The immortal soul is thought to live on after our bodies have died and returned to the dust from which they came. But there are difficulties about this way of speaking. Dividing people into body, mind, spirit, soul seems to suggest that we are made up of different components, like a motor car. But this cannot be true. Such 'components' cannot be taken apart in a workshop or a laboratory. What happens to one intimately affects the others too. It seems more true to experience, therefore, to say that I am a person: I am **me**. I am a unity, a whole, not an assembly of parts.

Although there is something in the genes in my body that is unique, there is also much about me that takes its particular form from my experiences and my relationships with others, and this changes and develops as I go through life. The word person seemed to describe this best. It comes from the word for a mask – *persona* in Latin – originally used to indicate the different characters in an ancient drama on the stage. It suggests that we find our identity in the relationships we have with other people, and that we meet others in different roles.

We know who we are as a result of our interactions with others, and with God, and they know who we are through their dealings with us.

In *Embodiment*, the American Christian ethicist James Nelson uses the term 'body-selves' to describe the unity that is a person, and to avoid any dualism, or splitting into parts. Fundamental to our body-selves is our experience of being men and women in sexual relationships with one another. Sexuality, Nelson claims, 'is a very basic dimension of our personhood'. While it is not the whole of our personhood, it nevertheless permeates and affects all our feelings, thoughts and actions (Nelson 1978: 17).

As persons, then, our closest relationships are those in which we encounter one another as lovers and as husbands and wives. These are among our deepest, our most passionate, and often our most troublesome relationships in life. In this first main chapter, therefore, I want to look at intimate relationships, at marriage and divorce, and then at homosexuality. What attitudes should Christian people have to these deeply personal matters?

MARRIAGE

What is marriage, and what is it for? One or two stories from real life can help to open up these questions for further examination. Shirley and Richard, for example, got married seven years ago and live on a new estate of luxury executive homes. She grew up in a Council house and met her husband at the local disco when she was just seventeen. It was love at first sight. They had a white wedding at church and a honeymoon at Butlin's, and started their married life in a flat on the other side of town. Richard was quickly promoted at work, and soon had a good salary and a company car. Now their expensively furnished home and foreign holidays are just what she used to dream about. Marriage has given her independence from her mum and dad, two lovely children, and a standard of living her parents had never known.

Stephen and Elaine's story is different. They are in their

thirties and both have high-powered jobs in town. They have lived together for several years in a small terraced house in the suburbs. She often feels it necessary, in a half-joking way, to excuse what they are doing, but he says it is irresponsible to get married before trying it out first. Stephen's mother Evelyn refuses to let them share a double bed when they come to stay with her. But neither of them want to be tied down, and Stephen's company has just announced a number of redundancies. The future is too uncertain for them to be willing to take on any more commitments.

How typical are these couples? The government publication *Social Trends* reveals that over 390,000 marriages take place every year in the United Kingdom. In Britain itself, in 1989, 48 per cent were civil marriages and 52 per cent religious marriages. About 60 per cent of the services took place in Anglican churches and 40 per cent in churches of other denominations. Two per cent were Jewish and other non-Christian ceremonies. *Social Trends* also shows that about half of all couples now live together before they get married, and the number has increased to this level from 16 per cent twenty years ago (Central Statistical Office 1992: 44, 192, 46).

Churches often have problems with this situation. Many couples hardly believe in God, and don't come to church. Some clergy ask those who are living together to separate to different addresses before they will marry them. Some church people think that traditional morality is sinking under the weight of modern pressures. Parents look on helplessly as their children do things, quite happily, that they would never have done themselves.

What sort of attitudes, then, should Christians have towards sex and marriage? Does chastity have any meaning today? What sort of relationship should the elements of consent, of personal commitment, of sexual intimacy, and of the marriage contract have with each other?

Property and Purity

The fundamental relationship between man and woman is put in poetic terms in the first creation story in Genesis (1:1—2:4a). '*God created man in the image of himself,*' the passage runs, '*in the image of God he created him, male and female he created them*' (1:27). The word man – *adam* in Hebrew – is better translated human beings, as it is in the REB, for no sexism is implied. There is a degree of equality in the story. Both men and women are created at the same time, and both are in the image of God.

In the second creation story (2:4b–25), however, a different relationship is described. '*Yahweh God*', the story goes, '*shaped man from the soil of the ground and blew the breath of life into his nostrils, and man became a living being*' (2.7). Later, Yahweh says, '*It is not right that the man should be alone. I shall make him a helper*' (2:18). At first animals and birds fulfilled this role, but they are not found to be suitable partners. So while he is asleep, Yahweh takes one of the man's ribs and fashions it into a woman, and brings her to him. The man says, '*This one at last is bone of my bones and flesh of my flesh! She is to be called Woman, because she was taken from Man*' (2:23). In this verse and in the next one the word translated Man – *ish* in Hebrew – means husband and the word Woman – *ishshah* – wife.

Then follow some words which have become famous: '*This is why a man leaves his father and mother and becomes attached to his wife, and they become one flesh*' (2:24). The implication seems to be that the two originally belonged together and that, in marriage, they are re-united. Husband and wife 'complement' each other. But it is clear in this second story that woman is thought to be a secondary creation, derived from man rather than equal with him. Man is the source from which woman comes, and is therefore superior to her. Man is the 'head' of woman.

These idealized pictures from a pre-scientific culture have to be set alongside the practical realities of a turbulent and passionate world in ancient times. In Genesis, for example, Tamar, a widow, pretends to be a prostitute and sleeps with

25

her father-in-law Judah in order to provide an heir for her
first husband Er (Gen. 38). According to the Gospel of
Matthew, Perez, one of the twins she then bears, is among
the ancestors of Joseph the husband of Mary, the mother of
Jesus (1:3). If a man dies childless it is his brother's duty to
produce heirs for him, and there is some shame in store if
he refuses (Dt. 25:5–10). This is what Er's brother Onan had
failed to do properly (Gen. 38:8–10). In 2 Samuel, King
David sees a beautiful woman Bathsheba having a bath on
the roof and contrives the death of her husband in order to
marry her (2 Sam. 11–12). In Ezra, Jews who had foreign
wives are told to send them back, and their children with
them (Ezra 10). A personal relationship of love and commitment, seen today as the basis of marriage, seems to have
little to do with it.

In the Ten Commandments, however, marriage is protected by the firm rule, '*You shall not commit adultery*' (Ex.
20:14). The same words appear in the other version of these
commandments in Deuteronomy (5:1–22). Also in Deuteronomy, a number of regulations are laid down governing sex
and marriage. If a husband is tired of his wife and falsely
says that she was not a virgin on their wedding night, he is
to be flogged and fined. But if he is right, and she was not
a virgin, she is to be stoned (22:13–21). If a man sleeps with
another man's wife, or with a woman who is engaged to
someone else, and this takes place in a town and she fails to
cry out, they are both to be stoned. But if it takes place in
the country, where no one could hear her cry and come to
her rescue, she can be spared (22:22–27). If a man sleeps with
a girl against her will, he must pay a fine and marry her, and
divorce is not subsequently allowed (22:28–29).

Behind all these regulations, so severe to our way of thinking, are two important ideas. First, women are regarded as
the property of their fathers and then of their husbands. The
identity of the family, and the future inheritance of all they
own, has to be protected. Women must, therefore, be submissive to the head of the family. Their primary role is to
produce heirs, and men often had many wives and concu-
bines to help with this.

Secondly, the people of Israel are to keep themselves separate from other nations, and pure or clean for the worship of Yahweh. The covenant that Yahweh has made with the people of Israel requires them to be faithful, and any practice that might compromise the relationship between them is strictly forbidden. The language of religious purity and of sexual purity occurs frequently throughout the Hebrew Scriptures. The two ideas often overlap with each other. In Jeremiah, for example, being *'faithless'*, worshipping idols, and *'playing the whore'* seem to be interchangeable: Judah is said to have *'committed adultery with stones and pieces of wood'* (3:1–10).

But in contrast to this there are also passages that show great respect for wives, as well as tenderness and love. Elkanah comforts Hannah, taunted by his other wife for being childless, with the words: *'Am I not more to you than ten sons?'* (1 Sam. 1:8). Proverbs describes a good wife active in business and charitable works, as well as caring for her family and enjoying their respect (31:10–31). The Song of Songs is full of evocative love poetry. *'How beautiful you are, my beloved . . . ,'* a passage runs, *'Your eyes are doves, behind your veil . . . Your teeth, a flock of sheep to be shorn when they come up from the washing . . . Your two breasts are two fawns, twins of a gazelle, that feed among the lilies . . . '* (4:1–5), and much more. Hosea is forgiving to an unfaithful wife, and finds a parallel with God's love for a faithless Israel.

The picture presented is as varied as actual human experience. There is the ideal of equality between husband and wife, but there is also the idea of man being superior to woman, and of woman as the property of a man. A strong emotional commitment to the partner is there, together with the practical reality in ancient times of polygamy, of multiple partners, and of sex outside marriage. Adultery is punished in horrific ways. Buried in these ancient texts are the origins of many modern views about sex and marriage, as well as of much subsequent exploitation and misery.

The Importance of Motive

In the Christian Scriptures a different spirit is to be found. Jesus seems careless of the formal family ties and responsibilities dear to the Jews. When his mother and brothers want to see him he points to his disciples and says angrily, '*Here are my mother and my brothers. Anyone who does the will of my Father in heaven is my brother and sister and mother*' (Mt. 12:46–50; Mk. 3:31–35). He is generous to the woman with the alabaster jar of ointment who washes his feet with her tears, and who has '*a bad name in the town*' (Lk. 7:36–50). When the wine runs out at the wedding at Cana, he says abruptly to his mother, '*Woman, what do you want from me?*' (Jn. 2:1–11). He refuses to condemn a woman caught committing adultery, even though the law requires her to be stoned. He merely tells her to '*sin no more*' (Jn. 8:3–11).

In the Gospels Jesus looks into people's motives. He is impatient with legalism, with hypocrisy, and with trick questions. He points to a higher loyalty than blood relationships. He opens up the kingdom of God to those who do not fit the formal requirements of family or race. In the context of his day it was a controversial stance to take.

Questions about sex and marriage are considered in some detail in 1 Corinthians (6:12–20, 7:1–40). It seems that Corinth was a place of great immorality, and that Christians there were reacting against this in different ways. Some of them were trying to deny their normal bodily sex drive altogether and were attracted, like the Stoics of their day, to a deeply ascetic life. In *Sexual Desire and Love*, the Swiss theologian Eric Fuchs notes how Seneca, a first-century Stoic in Rome, goes as far as to say, 'Too much love for one's spouse is adultery. The wise man should love his wife with his head . . . not with his heart' (Fuchs 1983: 107). Other Christians in Corinth seem to have thought that if the spirit was all that counted bodily behaviour was of no consequence, and they were using this idea as an excuse for all sorts of licence and sensuous activity.

In such a context Paul begins his discussion by affirming that '*the body is not for sexual immorality*'. The Christian is a member of Christ's body. Anyone who unites himself with a prostitute is *'one body with her'*. A Christian is united, soul and body, with Christ. The implication is that what people do with their bodies does matter. *'Keep away from sexual immorality'* Paul urges. *'Use your body for the glory of God'* (1 Cor. 6:12–20).

Paul then turns to consider specific questions asked by the Corinthian Christians. Making a link with his readers he declares, *'Yes, it is a good thing for a man not to touch a woman'*. But he goes on at once to state: *'Yet to avoid immorality, every man should have his own wife and every woman her own husband. The husband must give to his wife what she has a right to expect, and so too the wife to her husband.'* Then he adds, *'You must not deprive each other, except by mutual consent for a limited time, to leave yourselves free for prayer, and to come together again afterwards'*. Paul would really like the Corinthians to be unmarried, as he is, but *'everyone has his own gift'*, and single people and widows should marry if they do not have self-control. *'It is better to be married than to be burnt up'*, he declares (1 Cor. 7:1–9).

In the course of the next section, which is about divorce, Paul says that incompatibility of faith should not necessarily be grounds for separation because *'the unbelieving husband is sanctified through his wife and the unbelieving wife is sanctified through the brother. If this were not so, your children would be unclean, whereas in fact they are holy'* (1 Cor. 7:10–24). This strange idea harks back to Genesis 2. Marrying and having children is part of God's will in creation. It is part of the process by which men and women realize their potential, are made whole, or are saved (7:16). The same idea comes in 1 Timothy (2:15), but these references are tantalizingly brief.

Paul now turns to the general expectation in those early years that the Lord was soon to return (1 Cor. 7:25–40). He advises those who are unmarried to stay as they are, though this is only his personal view. The reason is not that celibacy is better, but that the time is short. *'This world as we know it,'* he says, *'is passing away'* (7:31). Christians can give fuller devotion to the Lord without the cares of business or marriage. This is the clue to the enigmatic words, '*He who marries his fiancée is doing well, and he who does not, better still*' (7:38).

The passage ends with a note about the freedom of widows to marry again, though within the Christian fellowship. Death does end a marriage, Paul declares, nailing a doubt in certain minds at the time. The same point is also made in Romans (7:1–3). In 1 Timothy, young widows are advised to marry again (5:14).

Although Paul does struggle with questions of sexual morality, the apparent hostility to sex and marriage in his writings is not really that at all. In its context it is positive and understanding of human nature. There is no uncompromisingly negative attitude to sex, as has often been thought, nor any real exaltation of the single state above the married. Nor should marriage be seen just as a 'remedy' against licence. Sex and marriage are gifts of God, just as being single is his gift. Different people have different gifts. But the negative note in 1 Corinthians has been the basis of the subsequent denial by Christian theologians of the goodness of sex altogether.

In a further passage in Ephesians, the sense of the imminent return of the Lord has given way to the idea that the marriage relationship, involving love and self-sacrifice, is parallel to that between Christ and the Church (5:21–33). Echoing Genesis, the metaphor is closely drawn: '*Wives should be subject to their husbands . . . as the Church is subject to Christ . . . Husbands should love their wives, just as Christ loved the Church . . .* ' They should love them '*as they love their own bodies; for a man to love his wife is for him to love himself . . .* ' The two '*become one flesh*' (5:22–25).

The analogy between the marriage bond and the fusion of Christ with the Church, the passage concludes, is a '*mystery*' with '*great significance*' (Eph. 5:32). It is from this idea that the doctrine of marriage as a sacrament was developed. The word itself – *sacramentum* in Latin – originally meant a military oath and was used to indicate the solemn, binding nature of the bond. It was but a short step from there to declare marriage permanent, just as Christ's bond with the Church is permanent. To become one flesh was not simply to become one household, or one family unit, but to become so united in being that the bond could never be broken.

To find a link between marriage itself and the saving work of Christ was to give it both high praise and profound significance. As a matter of principle, the Church could no longer think of a wife as the property of her husband, to be treated as he wished, nor of the one as inferior to the other, even though it may have taken centuries for this insight to be fully realized.

The 'Goods' of Marriage

Over the centuries the Church wrestled with these ideas and the practical realities of intimate personal relationships with increasing concern. The General Synod report *An Honourable Estate* describes something of the history of the development of marriage practice. It seems that in those early days there was little in the way of any formal marriage discipline, nor even of any set wedding ceremony. The Church simply accepted the current Roman custom whereby a marriage was a matter of consent, of bringing the bride to the husband's house, and of living together.

As time went by, however, the Church came to exercise more and more supervision over the relationship. Orders of service for weddings were developed. Fragments of the earliest ones date from the fifth century. About the same time Augustine set out the three 'goods' of marriage: 'offspring', having children and bringing them up; 'fidelity', avoiding a life of indiscipline; and 'sacrament', or permanence, the binding nature of the commitment. Later, Thomas Aquinas further developed the idea of marriage as a sacrament, as a sign of the grace that it confers. In the Reformation period, however, Martin Luther resisted this idea. For him marriage did not depend on faith. It belonged to the order of creation, not to that of redemption. The relationship that expresses itself in marriage, we might say, is something natural to human beings, which the Church helps on its way and blesses. It is not something that the Church can regulate completely by itself.

In England, it was not until the eleventh century that a priest had to be present for a marriage to be contracted between the parties, nor until the sixteenth that the ceremony had to be inside a church. And only in 1866 was marriage finally defined in law as 'the voluntary union for life of one man and one woman to the exclusion of all others' (Church of England General Synod 1988: 32).

Themes

Four themes emerge from this review of the material in the Bible, and the briefest of hints that have been given about subsequent attitudes and regulations concerning marriage. First, it is quite clear that **marriage is of great significance and is to be strongly protected**. In ancient Israel the formation of families and the procreation of children was a primary concern. It lay at the heart of community and national life. It was important for people to know who belonged to whom, who had responsibility for whom, and who stood to inherit from whom. The institution of marriage provided a framework within which to regulate these things. Sexual intercourse outside the formally recognized relationships of marriage, therefore, presented a serious threat to that institution. Adultery was to be punished in the severest way, by death.

Today, however, the bearing of children is one of many roles which women play in society. Nor is it true any more that they depend wholly on their fathers or husbands for support. Modern society makes it possible for women as well as men to live an independent life, supporting themselves. It is quite acceptable for them to stay single if that is what they wish. Legal identity is based on formal registration at birth, not on membership of a family. Inheritance is governed by legal arrangements. Property can be willed to anyone; it does not have to pass in accordance with blood relationships. Reliable methods of contraception mean that every act of intercourse no longer carries with it the possibility of pregnancy. The social factors, then, which led to the need to protect marriage in ancient times do not apply today. Marriage is still profoundly important, but for different reasons. It has more to do with personal growth and fulfilment through intimate relationships, than with financial support and inheritance.

In *Passionate and Compassionate Love*, the Roman Catholic psychiatrist Jack Dominian speaks of marriage as an intimate loving relationship that sustains and heals, and enables the partners to grow as persons. He writes, 'Sexual intercourse is now unequivocally an expression of love, combining the erotic with the personal' (Dominian 1991: 230).

Secondly, **sexual relationships between those who are not married do not seem to be explicitly forbidden in the Scriptures**. What is forbidden is sexual intercourse that breaks into an existing relationship, whether of betrothal or of marriage itself, or that is forced on others against their will, or that is bought or sold. Intercourse that follows the giving of willing consent by the two persons involved, and that expresses and deepens their commitment to each other, hardly deserves the same condemnation that was passed on adulterous, violent or exploitative sex in ancient times. As Jesus pointed out repeatedly, it is the spirit behind the act, and the nature of the relationship, that lies at the heart of the matter.

Mutual consent, freely given, is the basis of any moral human relationship. It implies that the relationship is something freely chosen and wanted. In *Marriage*, the writer on Christian ethics Helen Oppenheimer puts it like this: 'There should be no need to contrast consent and consummation. Properly understood, consent looks forward to the married life it inaugurates, in its full physical and personal reality' (Oppenheimer 1990: 35). In terms of the four elements mentioned earlier in this section, it is consent and commitment that open the door to consummation, rather than the contract itself.

Thirdly, **chastity is best understood as the maintenance of integrity in relationships rather than just as the avoidance of intercourse**. To be chaste is to love another person, to give oneself fully to him or her, to be open and honest in intimate personal relationships. To be unchaste is to exploit other people or to act violently towards them, to use them for one's own selfish purposes. On this understanding it is quite possible for husbands and wives to be unchaste in their relationships with each other within marriage. They can use each other in ways that have little to do with real love. In the same way it is possible for those who are not married to each other to have a physical relationship that is loving and committed, and that fully deserves to be called chaste.

In *Sexual Integrity*, Jack Dominian puts it in a telling phrase. 'The hallmark of chastity', he writes, 'is the conjunction of sexual activity and affection' (Dominian 1987: 54). To be chaste in one's relationships is a much tougher thing, and more difficult, than just avoiding casual sexual intercourse.

In some ways the Christian tradition has misled people in their understanding of sexual morality. Too great an emphasis on intercourse is misplaced. The ancient concern with the proofs of virginity on the nuptial sheets, and Augustine's linking of passion and pleasure with sin, are best consigned to history. The key to chastity is commitment, at first private, then public, always intending to be without term of years. Sharing life in one home, sleeping together, and having children and bringing them up, are the expressions of that commitment. They fit into place as the content, the substance, the proof of a true marriage.

Fourthly, **marriage is basically a natural human relationship; it is not in itself an institution of the Church**. It follows from this that the Church today should welcome every couple who come asking for a wedding service. Whether they have faith or not, as Oppenheimer puts it, 'To take each other as husband and wife is a humanly, indeed a legally, valid act, not a hollow show'. The Church should be 'appreciative rather than defensive' about it (Oppenheimer 1990: 77). When the elements of personal commitment based on willing consent and love, the signing of a legal contract, and consummation in sexual intercourse come together, it is a time for rejoicing. It is not necessary, today, to worry too much about the order in which these

34

elements come. The point is that they **should** all come together, and be helped to stay together until death alone breaks them apart. The Church should be glad at the human flourishing and fulfilment that flow from this commitment.

For Stephen and Elaine, as much as for Shirley and Richard, their intimate relationships can be the stuff of which dreams are made. Consent and commitment are the essential basis of marriage. The contract is there to give public witness to what already exists between them.

DIVORCE

Intimate relationships are often fraught with problems Belinda and Alan, for example, have been married for seven years. They were happy to begin with, but as time went by tensions and pressures mounted. They found themselves having regular rows. One day there was a piece of broken glass in Belinda's hand from a picture Alan had thrown at her across the room. Their little daughter Naomi was at risk, and the Social Services were called in. Weeks later Belinda walked out. But then a holiday in the Caribbean brought them together again, and a second child was on the way. Two years later she left him, this time with a solicitor's advice and a legal separation. The dream was shattered.

According to *Social Trends*, 185,000 petitions for divorce were filed in England and Wales in 1989, nearly three-quarters of them by the wife. Since 1984 couples have been able to petition for divorce after the first anniversary of their marriage (Central Statistical Office 1992: 45, 44). The only ground for divorce is the 'irretrievable breakdown of marriage' proved by one or other of five 'facts'. Adultery by the wife and unreasonable behaviour by the man are the chief of these. If a petition is uncontested, divorce can go through without an appearance in court or the services of a solicitor. People talk about 'divorce on demand' and 'divorce by post'.

But marriage is still popular. Britain has the second highest marriage rate after Portugal of all the European Community countries, and over a third are second marriages. But it also

35

has the second highest divorce rate after Denmark (Central Statistical Office 1992: 43, 44). Divorce is widespread, but is it acceptable to Christians? If so, what attitude should Christians have to second marriages? And should second marriages be solemnized in Church?

Unchastity

In the Hebrew Scriptures divorce is easily arranged. In Deuteronomy, a man can divorce his wife if *'she has not pleased him and he has found some impropriety of which to accuse her'*. He simply makes out a *'writ of divorce'*, hands it to her and dismisses her from his house. The presumption seems to be that she will then marry another man. But if the second husband *'takes a dislike to her'* she may not be taken back by her first one (24:1–4).

In the Christian Scriptures, however, there are a number of passages on divorce which indicate a quite different approach. They have troubled people ever since. Mark records an occasion when the Pharisees test Jesus with the question, *'Is it lawful for a man to divorce his wife?'* Jesus asks what the law says and they reply, *'Moses allowed us to draw up a writ of dismissal in cases of divorce'*. He then explains, *'It was because you were so hard hearted that he wrote this commandment for you'*. Quoting the activity of God in the story in Genesis 2, Jesus continues: *'But from the beginning of creation he made them male and female. This is why a man leaves his father and mother, and the two become one flesh. They are no longer two, therefore, but one flesh. So then, what God has united, human beings must not divide.'* Then he says to the disciples who question him about this, *'Whoever divorces his wife and marries another is guilty of adultery against her. And if a woman divorces her husband and marries another she is guilty of adultery too'* (10:1–12).

Luke also records these final words, but he places them on their own, immediately after a saying on the permanence of the law (16:17–18). In Luke's understanding Jesus does not mean to replace the old law with an entirely new, and very rigorous, standard in effect forbidding divorce altogether – for adultery was punishable by death – but to point to the original intention of marriage. It is to be a complete union that does not envisage any subsequent separation. Although a concession to the realities of human weakness may be necessary, the original principle itself still stands.

The same episode is recorded by Matthew, but with significant additions. '*It was not like this from the beginning*', Jesus says, putting the point about the secondary and concessional nature of divorce more clearly. Divorce is not part of God's original intention. Then he continues, '*Now I say this to you: anyone who divorces his wife – I am not speaking of an illicit marriage – and marries another, is guilty of adultery*' (19:3–9). Matthew repeats here a saying that he has already included in an earlier chapter (5:31–32).

The 'Matthaean exception', as it has been called, has been the subject of much discussion. The meaning of the word translated illicit marriage – *porneia* in Greek – is not at all clear. The NJB clearly interprets it to mean incest, marriage within the forbidden degrees of close family relationship, as set out in Leviticus (18:6–18). This was allowed by Roman law and may have been fairly common at the time. Such a 'marriage' within the Jewish and the Christian communities would have been unacceptable and separation quite proper. The REB, however, uses the translation unchastity, and the AV and other versions use the word fornication, but neither of these terms is entirely clear in its meaning. It seems that the word may refer to prostitution, or adultery, or incest, or even to sexual impurity or uncleanness in a ritual sense as described in another passage in Leviticus (15:19–32).

Matthew includes two further points. Going straight to human nature itself, Jesus says: '*You have heard how it was said, You shall not commit adultery. But I say this to you, if a man looks at a woman lustfully, he has already committed adultery with her in his heart*' (5:28). The way men think about women lies at the root of the matter. But Jesus does not seem to want to be taken literally. In the next verse he recommends tearing the offending eye out and throwing it away. He is making a point by exaggeration.

This hard line on divorce has the disciples in despair. '*If that is how things are between husband and wife,*' they say, '*it is advisable not to marry.'* Jesus replies, *'It is not everyone who can accept what I have said, but only those to whom it is granted . . . Let anyone accept this who can'* (Mt. 19:10–12). In a softening of the harshness of his earlier statement, he seems to be not only allowing divorce, as a concession to human nature, but also saying that staying single and not remarrying is also not required of everyone.

On another occasion Jesus is tested again. This time it is on the implications of the law of 'Levirate' marriage, requiring a dead man's brother to take his widow and give him an heir (Dt. 25:5–10). The Sadducees tell of a case where seven brothers all fail to do their duty in this way. *'Now at the resurrection,'* they ask, *'whose wife among the seven will she be, since she had been married to them all?'* Jesus replies, *'At the resurrection men and women do not marry; no, they are like the angels in heaven'* (Mt. 22:23–33; Mk. 12:18–27; Lk. 20:27–40). All three accounts note that the Sadducees do not believe in the resurrection, and it is clear that this is the main thrust of their attack on Jesus. The question is not really one about marriage at all. Jesus tells them that the resurrection body will be different. Angels have no sexuality. Their question, therefore, does not apply.

The underlying theme of these hard sayings on divorce seems to be the re-assertion of the importance of marriage as a relationship. It is what is in the heart that really matters. In the light of human nature and practical reality divorce may be necessary. What is quite wrong, however, is the gross inequality and the exploitation involved in a law which allows husbands to divorce their wives for almost any reason, and at their discretion alone. Jesus conceives of the possibility of a woman divorcing her husband (Mk. 10:12).

Softening the Impact

In Romans, Paul reflects the view in the Gospels that divorce followed by a second marriage is adultery (7:3), but he considers the matter more fully in 1 Corinthians. *'To the married I give this ruling,'* he writes, *'and this is not mine but the Lord's: a wife must not be separated from her husband — or if she has already left him, she must remain unmarried or else be reconciled to her husband – and a husband must not divorce his wife'* (7:10–11). The presumption against divorce is there, as it is in the Gospels, but divorce as a practical reality is clearly recognized.

Paul then gives some advice which he says is his own, *'not the Lord's'*. Divorce is not encouraged in cases where a believer is married to an unbeliever. Incompatibility of faith is not automatically to be a ground for separation. But it may be so. Paul writes: *'If the unbeliever chooses to leave, then let the separation take place: in these circumstances the brother or sister is no longer tied.'* The passage concludes with the very human advice, *'God has called you to live in peace'* (1 Cor. 7:12–16).

Paul continues with further advice of his own. *'It is good for people to stay as they are'*, he says. *'If you are joined to a wife, do not seek to be released; if you are freed of a wife, do not look for a wife. However, if you do get married, that is not a sin, and it is not sinful for a virgin to enter upon marriage'* (1 Cor. 7:25–28). The sequence of thought in this passage suggests that getting married again after being 'freed' is acceptable, just as getting married for the first time is acceptable.

Given Jesus' hard words, the questions about mixed marriages, divorce, and second marriages seem to have presented considerable problems for the first Christians. The 'Pauline privilege', as it has been called, allowing them to separate and try again in certain circumstances, needs to be understood against the background of the pressure of human nature, and the pressure on the Church at the time to cut itself off from society. We can, perhaps, hear Paul saying that marriage is a human institution. There is no special 'Christian' marriage with a different character from other marriage. There is only marriage, part of God's intention for everyone in creation. Unbelievers may find something of their own salvation through the healing relationship of marriage (1 Cor. 7:14). But if this is hindered by discord at home, it is better for people to go their separate ways.

The tentativeness of Paul's advice suggests that the whole matter was not easily resolved in the early Church. In

Hebrews, the emerging rules are put a little more firmly: *'Marriage must be honoured by all, and marriages must be kept undefiled, because the sexually immoral and adulterers will come under God's judgement'* (13:4). The word translated sexually immoral – *pornous* – is from the same root as *porneia*.

Themes

The themes that emerge from this review of the passages on divorce and remarriage in the Bible are these: First, it is clear that **divorce is no easy option**. In ancient Israel it was a simple matter; it could be arranged on demand, though only by the man. By contrast the standard that Jesus introduces is extremely rigorous. If the harder text of the passage in Mark and Luke is to be preferred to the softer one in Matthew, Jesus appears to forbid divorce and remarriage altogether. This saying is much like other hard sayings about the family, or about wealth. Jesus makes his points by stating principles which few if any can meet. Actual experience, however, demands a more compassionate response to the realities of daily life. And Jesus recognizes this. Human beings are hard-hearted. The first Christians, too, found ways of trying to preserve the principle, while allowing exceptions so that men and women would not be completely torn apart. If there was unchastity, sometimes it could not be borne; if there was disparity of faith, sometimes it could not be endured. Reconciliation is urged if at all possible, but sometimes there is no alternative. Divorce is an accommodation to the reality of human relationships.

Secondly, in his sayings on this matter, **Jesus points beyond the outward form of the marriage contract to the underlying spirit, the motive, behind it**. Marriage is part of God's intention in creation. Men and women find each other, and themselves, in intimate relationships and this belongs to their ultimate fulfilment as persons. Adultery, or incest, or sex that is forced on another or bought and sold, breaks this healing, saving, process. It is the relationship that is central, and where this is good, divorce does not come into consideration. This is the key to understanding the matter, and other aspects need to be assessed in relation to it.

Thirdly, **Paul softens the impact of the view in the Gospels that a second marriage following divorce is forbidden**. In the ancient world it was assumed that women would marry again. There was no other way in which they could be honestly supported. In the Christian Scriptures it is clear that the question of an appropriate marriage discipline is still in the process of being worked out. There are not yet any firm rules to cover every eventuality. So far Paul is simply able to give his own opinion about what it is best to do. Incompatibility of faith, he suggests, may be a ground for separation, and if this happens the Christian man or woman is *'no longer tied'* (1 Cor. 7:15). Because of the shortness of the time people should stay as they are, but getting married again is not a sin (1 Cor. 7:26–31). Paul does seem to foresee the possibility of second marriages. It may not be wrong to imagine that, in the course of time, he would have extended this permission to those who had been divorced in more explicit terms.

Fourthly, **a second chance after a divorce is the most sustaining and healing course of action**. Marriage is something natural and human. It is there to enable men and women to become what they have it in them to be. Where such a positive, creative relationship has broken down, or has faded away, or is destroying people rather than building them up, divorce and a second marriage should be accepted.

From this perspective it seems right that the divorce law in Britain should no longer be based on the concept of a 'matrimonial offence' but on that of the irretrievable breakdown of the relationship. Where a petition for divorce is not contested and there is genuinely no loving relationship left, there is no real reason for resisting it. But with this attitude of understanding and compassion should go strong support for couples in their intimate relationships, and for family life, at every stage. Efforts need to be made to restore strained relationships before they can be judged to be irretrievably broken. Marriages need nurturing, and those that are in trouble need help long before the point of no return has been

41

reached. The Church should put considerable professional resources into marriage support and counselling to match the high view it has of the importance of this relationship.

Where there is no longer any free consent, and no commitment, there is no marriage, humanly speaking. There should be a clean break and as much care for the couple and for the welfare of any children involved as possible, and the contract brought to an end.

In *Living in Sin?*, John Spong, Anglican Bishop of Newark in America, suggests that a 'Service for the Recognition of the End of a Marriage' to offer to God the pain of a divorce would be pastorally helpful for some people (Spong 1990: 189). Second marriages in church should also be available to those who, with due penitence and preparation, want to try again. This is not a weakening of the Christian witness to the permanence of marriage, but rather a way of demonstrating more effectively what marriage really is. The Church does not make the marriage; its role has always been to witness to it and to bless it, and to point to its significance as a human institution in the providence of God.

If things do not work out for Belinda and Alan, the Church should be there to support them fully through the crisis and the pain, and to help them try again.

HOMOSEXUALITY

Intimate relationships do not only take place between men and women. Some people are attracted wholly or mainly to those of their own sex. For most of them it is not a matter of choice; it is the way they are. Nor are they able to make any real distinction between the feelings they have and the physical expression of them. They are body-selves like everyone else. The word sexual 'identity' seems to express this truth more fully than the words sexual preference or orientation. Identity is about one's innermost being and one's relationships with others as a whole person.

Charles is unmarried. He met Maurice at a management training conference run by the company they both work for, and they found themselves in the same discussion group. When the others had gone off to the bar for a drink they were left together in the room. Maurice began in a round about way to talk about how some people are different from others. Suddenly Charles realized what he was talking about and they become close friends. A shadow fell off his shoulders as he came to realize the truth about himself, and to admit it to another person. It was an important moment of insight in his life. Years later he heard that Maurice had been arrested for an act of indecency in a public lavatory in London, and had ended up in court. He understood something of the pain that lay behind what Maurice had done. Gay people long for warmth and affection like everyone else.

Why are some people attracted to those of the same sex as themselves? In *Gay Christians*, Peter Coleman, Anglican Bishop of Crediton, gives some background details. It is thought that between five and ten per cent of people in the developed world are this way, and that it has always been so. The agreed facts about homosexuality, however, are few. Gender is determined by chromosomes, some X and others Y, but there is no proof that they cause homosexuality. As children grow up they learn patterns of behaviour associated with being boys or girls, but sexual identity is not just something acquired from outside influences. At puberty hormones are secreted to reinforce genetic orientation, but homosexuality is not merely a stage in teenage development. Social factors, such as being in a single-sex organization – some parts of the armed forces or a school, for example – may push or pull people one way or the other. Psychological factors, such as fear of emerging sexual awareness, may influence people, too. It has been said that homosexuality may find its origin in a deficiency of love from the same-sex parent during childhood. But these are all theories, and there is no general agreement about any of these suggested causes. Research done in America by Albert Kinsey and colleagues, and published in 1978, indicated that there is a spectrum of orientation from exclusively heterosexual at one end to exclusively homosexual at the other. Most people find them-

43

selves somewhere between these two extremes (Coleman 1989: 17–24).

It seems most true to say, therefore, that there is something heterosexual and something homosexual in all of us. It is part of our nature as human beings. Although some 'cures' have been claimed, and some people do move from one orientation to the other, there are gay and lesbian people for whom there is no choice and no sense of being handicapped or damaged. It is the way they believe God has made them. Homosexuality is their gift from God.

It is thought that the word 'gay' may be derived from the name Ganymede, a Greek youth loved by Zeus the king of the Gods. The word lesbian comes from the Greek island of Lesbos, where a community of women lived in Classical times. Homosexuality was accepted in ancient Greece and Rome. But gay men and lesbian women today often find themselves being discriminated against socially, and at work, even persecuted for simply being as they are. Some people fear homosexuals, without having any real understanding of why they feel afraid. An eighteenth-century lawyer described homosexual practice as 'the infamous crime against nature not fit to be named among Christians' (Coleman 1989: 5).

Although there is pain for those who have not felt able to 'come out', many gay and lesbian people are proud to be open about their identity. In his trial a hundred years ago, the playwright Oscar Wilde spoke movingly about same-sex love. 'It is beautiful,' he said, 'it is fine, it is the noblest form of affection. There is nothing unnatural about it' (Coleman 1989: 28).

Christians are faced with particular uncertainties about what to think about homosexuality, and how to act towards gay and lesbian people. On the one hand, the Bible seems to condemn homosexuality outright, and public opinion is generally hostile. But on the other, Christians are to love their neighbours as they love themselves.

What attitudes should Christians have, then, towards homosexuality as a condition, and homosexual practice as the physical expression of it? And what is it exactly that the

Bible condemns in the passages which mention same-sex relationships?

Sexual Violence

In the Hebrew Scriptures there is one episode in which homosexual practice plays a part. In Genesis, two angels come to the town of Sodom and Lot invites them in for a meal. The men of Sodom *'both young and old, all the people without exception'* then surround the house and demand to see the visitors. Calling out to Lot they say, *'Where are the men who came to you tonight? Send them out to us so that we can have intercourse with them'*. Lot tries to dissuade them from this wickedness and says: *'Look, I have two daughters who are virgins. I am ready to send them out to you, for you to treat as you please, but do nothing to these men since they are now under the protection of my roof.'* But the crowd turns nasty and threatens Lot as well. The angels then pull Lot back inside the house and dazzle their attackers so that they cannot find the door. Later Lot escapes with his wife and his daughters, and Sodom is destroyed together with the whole region around it (19:1–28).

This story follows directly after a chapter in which Abraham offers hospitality to three travellers on their way to Sodom to see if it is really as wicked as its reputation, and his unsuccessful attempt to get the city spared (Gen. 18). The failure of the people of Sodom to offer proper hospitality to strangers, and their violent behaviour, demonstrates their wickedness. The story gives a general reason for the destruction of the city. It is worth noticing, too, that angels traditionally had no sexuality, one way or the other. This, together with the fact that Lot offers his daughters as an alternative, indicates that homosexual practice was not the main point. Later in the story the future sons-in-law of Lot's daughters are mentioned (19:14), and this heightens the sense of outrage about this violation of the hospitality rules. To sleep with a woman who was betrothed to be married would merit the death penalty. Even this, the story seems to

45

suggest, would have been better than failing to treat strangers properly.

Another story, rather similar in form, appears in Judges. A Levite is travelling from Jerusalem to the highlands of Ephraim with his servant, his concubine and two donkeys, and they turn aside into the Benjaminite town of Gibeah for the night. At first no one offers them hospitality, but eventually an old man takes them in. Then *'some townsmen, scoundrels'* batter on his door and demand that the man is sent out. *'We should like to have intercourse with him'*, they say. They refuse the alternative offer of the old man's daughter, and the Levite sends out his concubine to them instead and they ill-treat her all night. In the morning she is found dead on the doorstep. The Levite then cuts her up and sends one piece to each of the twelve tribes throughout Israel. Later the inhospitable and violent behaviour of the people of Benjamin is avenged with much bloodshed (19:1—20:48). The dismembering of the concubine does not seem to merit any punishment.

This story is about heterosexual rape and murder, but the parallel with the episode in Genesis 19 suggests that both stories are making the same point. Violence and inhospitality to visitors are totally unacceptable.

A verse in Leviticus refers more explicitly to homosexual practice: *'You will not have intercourse with a man as you would with a woman. This is a hateful thing'* (18:22). Similar words appear in a later chapter, concluding, *'They have done a hateful thing together; they will be put to death'* (20:13). The word translated hateful thing, or abomination in the AV and the REB, – *toebah* in Hebrew – is used of a number of activities. Its main meaning seems to be religious: it is frequently used of Canaanite idolatry. It also has social and economic meanings and is used of eating with foreigners (Gen. 43:32), and using false scales in business (Prov. 11:1). The word does not just have a moral meaning. It does not only refer to sexual behaviour, nor does it necessarily express any emotional disgust. The complex codes of practice that keep Israel pure for the worship of Yahweh, and separate from other nations, lie behind its use (Lev. 20:26).

46

In Ezekiel, the sin of Sodom is described as *'pride, gluttony, calm complacency'* and never helping *'the poor and needy'* (16:49). Throughout subsequent history the identification of Sodom with homosexual intercourse has been somewhat unfair.

Changing Partners and Lust

There are no references to homosexuality in the Gospels, though Sodom is mentioned a number of times, mostly in connection with lack of hospitality and without any sexual meaning (Mt. 10:15, 11:23–24; Lk. 10:12, 17:29).

Paul, however, does have something to say about the matter. In a strongly worded passage in Romans, he attacks those who worship idols and describes homosexual practice as the outcome of such idolatry. He writes: *'That is why God abandoned them to degrading passions: why their women have exchanged natural intercourse for unnatural practices; and the men, in a similar fashion, too, giving up normal relations with women, are consumed with passion for each other, men doing shameful things with men and receiving in themselves due reward for their perversion'* (1:26–27). He goes on to list other consequences of the failure to discern God's intentions in creation, namely *'all sorts of injustice, rottenness, greed and malice'*. Such godless people are *'full of envy, murder, wrangling, treachery and spite'*. They are *'without brains, honour, love or pity'* (1:28–32).

In this passage Paul is thinking only of the exchange of one partner for another. It is a matter of choice, or preference. It is an action done under the influence of lust, and it is this that is condemned. There is no sense of any exclusive orientation to those of the same sex, nor of any faithful homosexual love for one partner alone.

The words natural and unnatural also need careful interpretation. Their use here may reflect a view of the purpose for which things were intended, as this was understood at the time, rather than implying any moral judgement. If sexual intercourse, for example, was intended to produce children, then its use for any other purpose was thought to be 'unnatural'. On this understanding some medical intervention in the

47

workings of the human body would be unnatural. To use artificial means of contraception, for example, would be against nature, and this is still one of the official Roman Catholic reasons for opposing this practice.

A reference in 1 Corinthians adds a further insight into Paul's understanding of this matter. He writes, *'Make no mistake – the sexually immoral, idolaters, adulterers, the self-indul-gent, sodomites, thieves, misers, drunkards, slanderers, and swin-dlers, none of these will inherit the kingdom of God'.* Paul continues pointedly, *'Some of you used to be of that kind . . .'* (6:9–11). The word sodomite translates two words in the original Greek – *malakoi* and *arsenokoitai*. These words may refer respectively to the passive or, as it was considered, the softer female role and the active or male role in intercourse. But it is more likely that there is a reference here to pederasty, involving a young boy, the softer one, and an older man. This practice was common in Greek society at the time. The other vices listed are well-known pagan ones, and these verses follow immediately after a passage in which Paul complains about the practice of seeking judgement from sinners in Gentile courts instead of sorting out quarrels within the Christian community itself (6:1–8). The contrast between Christian and Gentile behaviour is in Paul's mind at this point. If this is a reference to pederasty, then, it is this rather than homosexual practice between consenting, faithful adults that is being condemned.

Finally, in 1 Timothy, homosexuals – *arsenokoitai* – are mentioned in a list which echoes the Ten Commandments, moving from godlessness to the killing of parents, murder, sexual sins, and perjury, for which the law was framed (1:8–11). There is also a reference in Jude to the sexual immorality of the people of Sodom and their *'unnatural lusts'* (verse 7).

A Growing Acceptance

There is no doubt, however, that moral condemnation of homosexuality has been the general attitude from the days of the Bible until now, though with some exceptions and with some tolerance in some places. In England the death penalty for sodomy was in force until 1861, when it was replaced with imprisonment. In 1885 the offence of gross indecency was established, and led to prosecutions for procuring as well as for practice, though it did not apply to women. Oscar Wilde was a celebrated victim of this change in the law.

More recently there has been a growing acceptance. In 1967 homosexual acts done in private between consenting males over 21 were removed from the concern of the law. The Wolfenden committee, and the Church of England, had claimed that homosexuality might be a sin, but it should not be a crime. The Churches have continued to discuss this matter, though with no clear outcome.

In 1979, in the report *Homosexual Relationships*, the members of a General Synod Board for Social Responsibility working party came to the conclusion that: 'In the light of some of the evidence we have received we do not think it possible to deny that there are circumstances in which individuals may justifiably choose to enter into a homosexual relationship with the hope of enjoying a companionship and physical expression of sexual love similar to that which is to be found in marriage' (Church of England General Synod BSR 1979:52).

This conclusion never received wide acceptance, however, and continuing unease has been expressed in the Churches in recent years. A General Synod debate in 1987, for example, regarded homosexual relationships as falling short of the ideal that intercourse belongs properly within marriage, and declared that they should be met with repentance, as well as with compassion. A general hardening of public attitudes was reflected in clause 28 of the 1987 Local Government Act prohibiting the promotion of the gay lifestyle in any sex education in schools. At the end of 1991, the Church of England bishops sought to hold together traditional attitudes and modern understandings in their booklet, *Issues in Human Sexuality*.

Themes

Three themes emerge from this examination of the references to homosexuality in the Bible. First, **the homosexual acts which are condemned in the Bible are those which involve violence and lust**. Rape and gang-rape are condemned. Swapping from one partner to another, male or female, under the influence of lust is also condemned, together with sexual relationships involving an adult and a youth. There is simply no mention of the possibility of a relationship between two adults of the same sex, which is loving and faithful, committed and exclusive, and sexual. Yet such relationships exist today. They cannot properly be forbidden by reference to the Bible.

Secondly, **the distinction between what is natural and what is unnatural cannot form the basis on which any firm judgement about this matter can be built**. There is no single 'purpose' for which each part of the body is designed. Human beings are complex living organisms; each 'part' is interwoven with all the rest into one whole. We are persons, continually developing, discovering our potential and our nature in relationship with others and with God. What is natural is best defined, therefore, as what belongs to me as a person, to me as I discover myself to be. Many gay and lesbian people just are the way they are. It is in their nature to be like that. They have not chosen their condition, and where no choice is made there can be no blame.

Thirdly, **the distinction between orientation and practice, between condition and behaviour, cannot easily be sustained**. This distinction was unknown in ancient times and is not made in the Bible. But in our own day it is regularly made. The Church, for example, is often willing to accept that some Christian men and women are gay or lesbian, including a number of clergy, and some pressure is put on them to remain celibate. This rule, however, accepting orientation and prohibiting practice, is based on a distinction that is not to be found in the Bible. Indeed, for Paul, celibacy is a gift, or a vocation, and it cannot be required of anyone (1 Cor. 7:7,9,17). Natural justice dictates that it is wrong to condemn people for things that do not involve any element of choice; because they are, for example, black or physically handicapped. A modern understanding of the integrated nature of body, mind and spirit, of the person as a unity, a body-self, suggests, too, that we cannot have it both ways: either orientation and practice are both to be condemned, and that is clearly unjust, or they must both be accepted. A homosexual is a person like everyone else.

It seems better to say, therefore, that what is required is that, as the marriage service in the 1928 Anglican prayer book so graciously puts it, 'the natural instincts and affections, implanted by God, should be hallowed and directed aright'. Discipline in sexual behaviour should apply equally to everyone. The faithful, committed, exclusive love that is best for the heterosexual is best for the homosexual too.

In *Living in Sin?*, Bishop John Spong supports the idea of services in church in which gay and lesbian couples can make 'a solemn covenant of love' with each other similar to that in the marriage service (Spong 1990: 205–206). It may be that, if it is discreetly and sensitively done, there will be an increasing demand for this form of pastoral ministry in the Church.

In the meantime Charles and Maurice, and many others like them, want equal treatment. They long for the loving, affirming intimate relationships that society publicly offers to those who are heterosexual. The 'homophobia', the fear and hostility, and the prejudice that serves to keep them in the 'closet' offers them little more than personal shipwreck and disintegration. For some it leads to a falling away from Christian faith. Others, struggling to discover the will of God for themselves with little help from the Church, continue to wait for their convictions to be valued and their committed partnerships to be recognized.

3.

FAMILY AND COMMUNITY

Former Prime Minister Margaret Thatcher once said that there is no such thing as society, there are only individuals and families. This was widely thought at the time to deny the bonds that tie people together into wider groups, which together make up society as a whole, and to be a licence for selfish individualism. But there is no serious doubt that human beings are all bound up in the communities they belong to and that their interests, as well as their attitudes and opinions, are strongly influenced by those communities.

The family is certainly one of the most significant of these groups. It is often said to be the basis of society itself. Intimate relationships lead to the birth of children and new families are formed every day. Many people think that if the institution of the family is threatened, the whole of society is threatened, too.

But the nature of British society is changing. Fewer families seem to conform to the traditional pattern. The communities of the places where people work, or of the leisure and sporting organizations they belong to, are often more significant to them than the community of the home. Many people stay single, or are on their own for a large part of their lives. More women go out to work, and often find it hard to make their way in their own right in business or in public life. Britain is also now a plural society, made up of many different ethnic groups and cultures. Black and Asian people meet discrimination as well in subtle and not so subtle ways. In this chapter, therefore, I want to look at people in the wider context of their family relationships, at

52

the place of women in society, and then at some questions about race and nationality.

PARENTS AND CHILDREN

The government report *Social Trends* reveals that just over half of all households in Britain consist of married couples with children, and almost a quarter consist of married couples on their own. Nearly 11 per cent of households consist of single people, and nearly 7 per cent are lone parent households with dependent children. At the other end of the age range, just over nine million people are over 65, nearly 16 per cent of the population, and the numbers of the very elderly, those over 80, are growing as people live longer (Central Statistical Office 1992: 42, 27). Family life is a source of great joy, but it is not the pattern for everyone, and it is often fraught with problems.

Louise and Andrew, for example, have three children and a fourth is on the way. They live in a small house on the edge of town, and much of the time it's chaos. Craig the eldest was behaving in a peculiar way at school and being impossible at home: he knew that something was going on that wasn't quite nice. Evie his sister used to visit her uncle on the other side of town and often came back sullen and withdrawn. Eventually Louise blurted out her suspicions to her friend Anne and help was called in. Now Evie doesn't go to see her uncle so much, but relationships in the family are strained and no one knows quite who to trust any more.

It seems that as many as one person in ten has been sexually abused in childhood and that most of this takes place within the family. The emotional scars of family life sometimes never heal.

Families are a major industry in Britain, and not just for Mothercare and Boots. The government spends large sums on social security. Hospitals and doctors spend hours on family health. Social workers and lawyers get involved when things go wrong. Children and old people are among the poorest in society. In the Church there is a persistent emphasis on the family, sometimes to the embarrassment of those who do not live in traditional relationships, or who are single anyway. What are we to think, then, about family life?

An Ordered Society

The origins of the family are described in the creation stories in Genesis. God creates men and women and says, *'Be fruitful, multiply, fill the earth and subdue it'* (1:28). Human fruitfulness, the procreation of children and their upbringing, is part of the purpose of creation. This is the basic mandate for sexual relationships and for family life. The creativity involved reflects something of the nature of God himself, for humans are made in his image.

The Hebrew Scriptures reveal an ordered pattern of family and community life, with authority flowing downwards. It is a 'patriarchal' society. God is pictured as a parent. In Exodus, as Moses tries to secure the release of the Israelites from slavery in Egypt, God says, *'Israel is my first-born son'* (4:22). In the Ten Commandments an attitude of respect is indicated: *'Honour your father and your mother so that you may live long in the land'* (20:12). When the Israelites enter Canaan and worship Yahweh, he says to them, *'I shall bless your food and water, and keep you free of sickness. In your country no woman will miscarry, none be sterile, and I shall give you your full term of life'* (23:25–26). Prosperity and social stability seem to depend on this attitude of respect for authority, both that of God and that of parents within the family.

A psalm declares that sons are *'a birthright from Yahweh . . . How blessed is the man who has filled his quiver with them'* (127:3–5). In Proverbs, it is within the family that wisdom is passed on from one generation to the next: *'Listen, my child, to your father's instruction, do not reject your mother's teaching'* (1:8). *'Only a fool spurns a father's discipline'* (15:5). In Isaiah, the aged are among the resources of the community and are to be respected (3:1–5). There is a vision of a time when there will never again be *'an infant there who lives only a few days, nor an old man who does not run his full course'* (65:20).

But this ideal picture is balanced by a down-to-earth reflection of the realities of family life. Conflict is there right from the start. Cain kills his brother because his offering is rejected and Abel's is accepted by the Lord. When he is questioned about it, he tries to deny all knowledge of what has happened. *'Am I my brother's guardian?'* he asks (Gen. 4:9). In the Psalms, something of the apprehension about the future that comes with increasing age is pictured. *'Now that I am old and grey-haired,'* says the Psalmist, *'God, do not desert me'* (71:18). The transitory nature of life is well expressed in another psalm: *'The span of life is seventy years – eighty for those who are strong – but their whole extent is anxiety and trouble, they are over in a moment and we are gone'* (90:10).

Special provision is to be made for certain family members. Widows and orphans are not to be ill-treated (Ex. 22:21). They are to be supported by food from tithes; they are to have a place in religious celebrations; their rights are not to be infringed (Dt. 14:28–29, 16:11,14, 24:17). A childless widow is to be taken on by the dead husband's brother so that she may give him an heir (Dt. 25:5–10). Orphans and widows are to be treated fairly and not exploited (Jer. 7:5–6). Those who oppress them will be met with divine judgement (Mal. 3:5).

There seems to be a background of family tension, even of oppression and bad treatment, behind these references, but the general picture is of an ordered, hierarchical society in which children respect parents, the young respect the old, and families accept responsibility for all their members. On this family basis society is built, under the ultimate authority of God himself.

A Higher Allegiance

In the Christian Scriptures, however, quite a different view begins to emerge. Matthew records an occasion when the disciples ask about authority and status in heaven. Jesus calls a child to him and says, *'In truth I tell you, unless you change and become like little children you will never enter the kingdom of heaven. And so, the one who makes himself as little as this little*

55

child is the greatest in the kingdom of heaven' (18:1–4). The penalty for anyone who causes the downfall of *'one of these little ones who have faith in me'* is strongly put: it would be better for him to be *'drowned in the depths of the sea with a great millstone round his neck'* (Mt. 18:5–6). To exalt children over their parents in this way was to strike a blow at the basic structure of society at the time. The fact that Jesus was unmarried may also have been of some concern to people. That too struck at the roots of a society built up out of family units.

Jesus constantly refers to God as his Father: in the Temple as a twelve-year-old talking with the teachers there (Lk. 2:49), in the Lord's Prayer (11:2), in the farewell discourses before his trial and passion (Jn. 14–17). He even speaks of him in the Aramaic form *Abba*, Daddy (Mk. 14:36). Such familiarity was shocking to the religious establishment at the time. It is characteristic of Jesus that he constantly overturns the conventional attitudes of his day and points to something deeper.

The conflict between blood relationships and the community of faith is starkly put in several passages. Jesus speaks uncompromisingly to a potential disciple who wants to go and bury his father before following him. *'Leave the dead to bury their dead,'* he says; *'your duty is to go and spread the news of the kingdom of God.'* Someone who simply wants to go and say goodbye at home first is told, *'Once the hand is laid on the plough, no one who looks back is fit for the kingdom of God'* (Lk. 9:59–62).

Jesus seems to offer families division rather than peace. *'From now on,'* he says, *'a household of five will be divided: three against two and two against three; father opposed to son, son to father, mother to daughter, daughter to mother, mother-in-law to daughter-in-law, daughter-in-law to mother-in-law'* (Lk. 12:51–53). It is a fierce position to take. It is fiercer still in these words: *'Anyone who comes to me without hating father, mother, wife, children, brothers, sisters, yes and his own life too, cannot be my disciple'* (Lk. 14:26). Matthew makes the same point, though in more muted language (10:37). Jesus' disciples are his true family. *'Anyone who does the will of my*

Father in heaven,' he says, *'is my brother and sister and mother'* (Mt. 12: 46–50). Those who follow Jesus have a higher allegiance than that of their natural families.

But there is a tenderness, too, and an understanding that the family is the main means of support for people. In John, Jesus sees his mother from the cross and the disciple whom he loved, and says, *'Woman, this is your son'.* He says to the disciple, *'This is your mother'.* From that moment, the passage continues, *'The disciple took her into his house'* (19:25–27). It is the function of sharing experience and outlook, and of caring for one another, rather than of blood relationship, that is at the heart of the true family.

In Acts, the Church itself begins to take on the character of a family. In those early days, *'all who shared the faith owned everything in common'.* They met *'in their houses'*, and *'shared their food gladly and generously'* (2:44–46). Whole households adopted the faith (16:31–34).

The Household Codes

In the writings of Paul and in the other letters, there are a number of passages that seem to be formal codes of practice for regulating relationships within the household. The earliest of these is probably the version in Colossians (3:18–4:1). Here Paul begins with marriage: wives are to be subject to their husbands and husbands should love their wives and *'not be sharp with them'.* Then he turns to other family relationships. *'Children,'* he writes, *'be obedient to your parents always, because that is what will please the Lord. Parents, do not irritate your children or they will lose heart.'* Then comes advice to slaves, who would also have been part of the household, and to their masters: *'Slaves, be obedient in every way . . . Masters, make sure that your slaves are given what is upright and fair, knowing that you too have a Master in heaven.'*

A second household code appears in Ephesians, following the same pattern of thought, though at greater length (5:21–6:9). At each point a theological justification is given: Wives should be subject to their husbands . . . *'as Christ is head of the Church . . . so is a husband the head of his wife'.*

57

Husbands should love their wives . . . *'just as Christ loved the Church . . .'* They should love them as they love their own bodies . . . *'that is the way Christ treats the Church'*. Every wife should respect her husband. Children should be obedient, as the commandment to honour father and mother requires . . . and parents are never to drive them to resentment, but to bring them up with *'correction and advice inspired by the Lord'*. Slaves are to be obedient . . . *'as you are obedient to Christ'*. And employers are to reward them properly, never forgetting that they *'have the same Master in heaven'*. Respect within the family, and within society, the code seems to be saying, has its roots in the divine order of things.

In 1 Timothy, advice is given on some other matters (5:1–16, 6:1–2): *'Never speak sharply to a man older than yourself, but appeal to him as you would to your own father; treat younger men as brothers, older women as mothers and young women as sisters with all propriety.'*

Detailed instructions follow about the care of widows: *'Be considerate to widows – if they really are widowed.'* If there are children or grandchildren, they are to *'do their duty to their own families and repay their debt to their parents'*. The importance of this is firmly put: *'Anyone who does not look after his own relations, especially if they are living with him, has rejected the faith and is worse than an unbeliever.'* The sense of family responsibility is strong. It is interesting to note that the true widow is someone who has no relatives to support her, not simply someone whose partner has died (1 Tim. 5:3–8).

Those over 60 can join an official roll of widows, supported by the Church, provided they are of good reputation and are known for their *'good works'*. They devote themselves to prayer. We can sense here, perhaps, the beginning of a religious order of single women. Younger widows are advised to marry again. The support of widows seems to have been something of an expense to the Church (1 Tim. 5:9–16). In Acts it is indicated that neglecting to support them on a daily basis is not acceptable, and a number of people are set aside to look after the matter (6:1–6)

Perhaps reflecting a later stage in the development of the Church, 1 Timothy recommends slaves to have *'unqualified respect'* for their masters. They are not to respect them any the less if they are also believers (6:1–2).

There is more in Titus (2:1–10): *'Older men should be reserved, dignified, moderate, sound in faith and love and perseverance.'* Older women should *'behave as befits religious people, with no scandal-mongering and no addiction to wine'*. They should teach right behaviour, and show younger wives how to love their husbands and children, how to be sensible and chaste, and how to work in their homes. They should be gentle and obedient to their husbands.

The letter continues with other advice. Younger men should be *'moderate in everything'*, and slaves are to be *'obedient to their masters in everything, and do what is wanted without argument; and there must be no pilfering . . .'*. We can only guess at the excesses and the disputes that lay behind this catalogue of correction. Clearly Christian faith did not immediately lead to good behaviour.

The same ideas are repeated in 1 Peter (2:18 — 3:7, 5:5). Slaves should be obedient and respectful to their masters, including *'those who are difficult to please'*. Wives should be obedient to their husbands, and modestly dressed. Husbands must *'always treat their wives with consideration'* in their life together, a clear sexual reference. Younger people should be subject to the elders. Indeed, *'humility towards one another must be the garment you all wear constantly'*. Finally, James adds that *'coming to the help of orphans and widows in their hardships'* is a work of *'pure, unspoilt religion'* (1:27).

The image of Christians as the family of God is repeatedly used. It is found particularly in 1 John (2:1,12–14, 3:1–10, 18, 4:4,7, 5:1–4) and in 2 and 3 John. It is a source of joy to the writer to find that children are *'living the life of truth'* (2:4, 3:4).

There is a clear indication in the household codes and the other related material that Christian faith has implications for the life of the family. Theological reasons are given for certain ways of behaving. God's relationship with human beings is pictured as that of parent to child. The relationships that are appropriate within the community of faith often stand in contrast to those of the natural family of the day.

Themes

Three themes stand out in these passages about relationships in the family and the immediate community. First, **the responsibility to support and care for others stretches beyond the nuclear family – husband, wife and children – and blood relatives**. The extended family stretching across the generations is just as important. For Jesus the community of interest is more important than the blood relationship. The family is where the faith is handed on to others. It is this insight that eventually made it possible for the Church to think of itself as a family, with obligations and responsibilities to its members. In the same way, today, the social family – involving adults and step-children or adopted or fostered children, or simply those who live in the same household and feel a sense of community with each other – deserves the same degree of support. It is common experience and outlook rather than common ancestry and genetic relationship that makes the real family unit.

Secondly, **there is a constant emphasis on the need for mutual respect and for submission to one another in this extended family**. Ordering people about and dominating them is clearly ruled out. In its time this emphasis on liberation from the normal restraints of class and hierarchy within the family, and from a male-dominated social structure, must have seemed revolutionary. Hence the need to set down the nature of this new relationship in the household codes. But the early Church was not able to escape completely from these constraints in the society of its time: women were still subordinate and employers did still own slaves. But the seeds of an emancipation that took centuries to come are clearly there. Our society today has still to throw off some of the shackles that hinder mutual respect and equal regard. There are dimensions of love that still have to be realized.

Thirdly, **mutual respect and support are to be characteristic of society as a whole**. Much of the advice given may have been specific to particular congregations and situations in the early Church, and to the Christian community itself, but the relationships that are commended between men and women, young and old, employer and employee are not an alternative to those of society as a whole. They are an example to that society, and not an eccentric option for the religious alone. This wide vision could hardly be worked out fully in those early days, but it is implied within the codes of behaviour that did emerge. The Church demonstrates to the world what is in its own best interests, and what belongs to its deepest fulfilment. The implications of this insight were dynamite – still not fully set alight.

Some of the tensions that Louise and Andrew's family went through are at one level quite normal and natural. Everyone's rough edges are knocked off by them. But at another level the abuse of children or of adults is quite at variance with the mutual respect and support indicated in the Bible. That the advice given was repeated so often in those early days may suggest that abuse in one form or another was common. To counter it the early Church developed an ethic of mutual respect. It is as badly needed today as it was then.

WOMEN

Oppression and lack of respect is not only found within the family; they are deeply rooted in our wider relationships, too. Sarah, for example, had a demanding professional job before she left to have a family. Now she is stuck at home with two little ones, and Duncan is out at work all the hours of daylight. Sometimes he is away for days at a time. Harriet and Simon are growing up with a weekend dad, and Sarah is desperate for something to stretch her mind again.

She is typical of many. In *Women and Men in Britain 1991*, the Equal Opportunities Commission has painted a grim picture. Men consistently receive higher hourly earnings than women. Women's hourly rates of pay are on average only three-quarters of those of men. Most occupations remain heavily segregated. Men continue to dominate the ranks of management. A higher proportion of men receive training

(Equal Opportunities Commission 1991: 3, 13, 15, 17). Lack of adequate child care makes it impossible for many women to go out to work even if they find a job.

Sarah's situation, however, hides a deeper problem in society, that of discrimination against people on grounds of their gender alone. Assumptions are made about people simply because they are women, or because they are men. In *Distorted Images*, the Christian feminist writer Anne Borrowdale describes the falseness of this stereotyping. Men, on the one hand, she says, are thought to be 'rational, logical, intelligent, creative, strong, technically competent, and born leaders'. It is natural, therefore, the argument continues, that they should have the most significant jobs. But they also have 'animal natures'. They are considered to be 'incapable of forming tender relationships. They are naturally promiscuous. They cannot cope with small children, washing machines or women.' She concludes that these stereotypes cannot both be true: 'How can men look after women's interests if they cannot understand them? How can they make rational decisions in meetings whilst suffering from uncontrollable lust? How can they be responsible for mending cars when they are confused by the controls of a washing machine?' (Borrowdale 1991: 31–32).

Borrowdale then goes on to describe vividly the way in which women have been oppressed by the assumption that their purpose is to be found in the nurture of children and in service in the home. The image that men have of women reinforces this oppression. She quotes a popular comparison of attitudes: 'He's ambitious. She's pushy. He's having lunch with the boss – he must be doing well. She's having lunch with the boss – they must be having an affair. He gets on well with people at work. She's always gossiping. He's moving on – he must be a good worker. She's moving on – women are so unreliable' (Borrowdale 1991: 53). There is more truth in these pictures than is comfortable. These attitudes are present in the Church as much as in the community at large.

The Subordination of Women

The falseness of sexual stereotyping is clear. But male domination in society, the system of patriarchy, as feminist writers have shown, is deeply entrenched in our culture, just as it was in the days of the Bible.

The subordination of women is there from the beginning. In the second creation story in Genesis, man is created by God himself but woman is a secondary creation, fashioned from his rib (2:21–22). It is the woman who gives the man some of the forbidden fruit from the tree in the middle of the garden, and he blames her for it (3:6,12). As a result of her act of disobedience, God says to the woman, '*I shall give you intense pain in childbearing, you will give birth to your children in pain. Your yearning will be for your husband, and he will dominate you*' (3:16). In these passages the subordination of women is both part of the creation itself and also a result of sin. The pain of childbirth and woman's domination by man are a punishment for disobedience.

Women are also exploited and treated with violence in a number of passages in the early books of the Hebrew Scriptures. In Genesis, Lot's daughters are offered to the angry crowd in place of the male visitors (19:8). Hagar the Egyptian slave-girl is sent by Abraham into the desert with Ishmael to die. Her son is not to share the same inheritance as Isaac (21:9–21). In Judges, Jephthah sacrifices his daughter as a result of a vow made to secure victory in battle and she submits to it (11:30–40). The Levite's concubine is gang-raped and cut to pieces (19:25,29). In 2 Samuel, Tamar is tricked, overpowered and raped by her brother Amnon and then thrown out. David their father is angry, but he doesn't wish to harm Amnon (13:1–21).

In ancient Israel women belonged to their fathers or their husbands as their property. They were entirely in their power. Their role was to produce heirs. They could be divorced at will. They were required to obey and to submit to the head of the family, a man. A patriarchal society often treated women roughly, and they had little or no means of redress.

63

But the picture is not all so grim. Miriam the sister of Moses and Aaron takes an active role in celebrating the crossing of the Red Sea (Ex. 15:20–21). Mothers are to be honoured (Ex. 20:12), respected (Lev. 19:3), and obeyed (Dt. 21:18). Women can take 'nazirite' vows of devotion to God alongside men, either on a temporary basis or for life. This involved detailed ritual purity requirements, including leaving the hair uncut (Num. 6:1–21). Deborah is a judge and helps to secure the defeat of Sisera, and Jael murders him with a tent peg (Jgs. 4:4–16,17–22). Ruth is held up as a model of faithfulness, though her future is determined by the men alone in the town gate (4:1–12). Jezebel is a formidable influence, though she comes to a sticky end (2 Kgs. 9:30–37). Huldah is a prophetess, and not afraid to give a hard message to the priests who come to her from the king (2 Kgs. 22:14–16; 2 Chron. 34:22–24). Esther manages to become queen and exercise political power even though male authority in the household is affirmed by royal decree (Esth. 1:20). Judith, too, in the Apocrypha, secures the deliverance of her people by political and sexual astuteness (Jud. 13:14–16). Women can be involved in the community and in business in their own right (Prov. 31:16,20,24).

There is little doubt, however, that these were exceptional cases. If some of the things these women did had been done by men they would have seemed quite normal. The very fact that their stories were recalled indicates how unusual they were.

Towards Equality

A fundamentally different picture begins to emerge, however, in the Christian Scriptures. Although women are still subordinate to men in domestic and public life, there are important signs of a new understanding. Time after time Luke gives women a prominent place, telling the stories in which they appear with vivid detail and a gentle touch. At the announcement of Jesus' conception he includes the reassuring words, *'Mary, do not be afraid; you have won God's favour'*. The baby in Elizabeth's womb leaps for joy when she visits her with the news. Mary plays a role in the story of salvation and the renewal of society, and she says in what has become the Magnificat: *'From now onwards all generations will call me blessed'* (1:30,44,48). At the birth of Jesus Luke mentions the swaddling clothes and the manger (2:7). He also records Anna's greeting to the child in the Temple (2:36–38).

Luke often mentions women in the course of Jesus' ministry. The woman who was a sinner is accepted. Jesus says, *'I tell you that her sins, many as they are, have been forgiven her, because she has shown such great love'* (7:36–50). Mary the sister of Martha is commended for sitting at Jesus' feet and listening to his teaching, something normally done only by men. Martha is busy with housework, but Jesus says, *'It is Mary who has chosen the better part'* (10:42). A widow won't give a judge any peace, saying, *'I want justice from you against my enemy!'* and her persistence is commended (18:3). Women are present at the crucifixion (23:49). They play a vital role as witnesses to the resurrection: Mary of Magdala, Joanna and Mary the mother of James, who go to the tomb and discover it empty, are remembered by name (24:10).

Mark has less to say about women, though he does stress their presence at the foot of the cross, mentioning their names and the fact that they used to look after Jesus when he was in Galilee (15:40–41). Matthew adds an appearance of Jesus to the three women at the empty tomb (28:9), that is not in Luke's account.

John also gives important roles to women in his presentation of the story. Mary the mother of Jesus is busy at the wedding at Cana, the first of the series of 'signs' of the kingdom in this Gospel (2:1–11). The story of the Samaritan woman at the well shows that the gospel is not just for the Jews (4:1–30). Martha and Mary are given a special place in Jesus' affection (11:5). Mary anoints Jesus' feet with expensive ointment to the dismay of Judas, who would have preferred the money to be given to the poor (12:1–8). Jesus appears to Mary of Magdala after his resurrection, and she supposes him to be the gardener. *'Mary!'* he says simply to her. She replies, *'Rabbuni!'*, the Hebrew for Master (20:16).

The impact of all this must have been profound in its time.

Women were not among those who studied the law, but they followed Jesus. Women's testimony was not necessarily believed, but they were the first witnesses to the resurrection and tell the others about it. The faith was primarily a man's concern, but women are put forward as examples of faith.

Too much should not be claimed, perhaps, for this new attitude. Much of Jesus' ministry was conducted among men, and he still chose men to be his twelve disciples. In *Women and the Genesis of Christianity*, the American biblical scholar Ben Witherington assesses the situation by saying that Jesus 'was attempting to reform, not reject, the patriarchal framework under which He operated' (Witherington 1990: 238). But the seeds of a greater emancipation are there.

In Acts, women are among prominent converts to the Christian faith and take positions of leadership in the Churches. Ananias and his wife Sapphira owned property, though they pay with their lives when they try to cheat the Church (5:1–11). Tabitha, or Dorcas as she was called in Greek, a disciple full of good works and apparently a former member of an order of Christian widows, is raised from the dead (9:36–42). A congregation meets in the home of Mary the mother of John Mark. She is rich enough to be able to entertain *'a number of people'* and to have a servant Rhoda (12:12–13). Lydia, a business-woman in the *'purple-dye trade'* in Philippi can invite Paul to stay, and also has a church in her house (16:11–15,40). Priscilla and her husband Aquila teach Apollos about Christian baptism (18:24–26). Philip in Caesarea has four unmarried daughters who are prophets (21:8–9). Agrippa the Roman governor and Drusilla his wife are interested in hearing Paul talk about faith in Christ (24:24). King Agrippa and his wife Bernice also listen to Paul favourably. Agrippa says, *'A little more and your arguments would make a Christian of me'* (25:22–23, 26:28).

These stories must have been important for the early Church. They showed that women, ordinary as well as prominent and wealthy women, even – almost – women at the palace, could belong to the Christian community and have a role within it. At first Christians were mostly working people and slaves; but Luke seems to be saying: Look what is possible now! In commenting on the significance of this Witherington says that the gospel 'liberates and creates new possibilities for women'. In place after place, 'we find women being converted or serving the Christian community in roles that normally would not have been available to them apart from that community' (Witherington 1990: 224).

One of the most significant references to this new under-standing of the role of women comes in Galatians. It has been much quoted and discussed. In the community of the baptized, Paul writes, *'There can be neither Jew nor Greek, there can be neither slave nor freeman, there can be neither male nor female – for you are all one in Christ Jesus'* (3:28). The RV uses the translation 'no male and female', representing more accurately the slightly different phrasing in the Greek at this point. Similar expressions appear in 1 Corinthians (12:13) and Colossians (3:11), though the reference to male and female is omitted.

It is thought that these words were a formula for use at baptism. They indicate that treating people differently because of their race, or their class, or their gender is funda-mentally set aside in the Christian community. Although the distinction between men and women continues, women do not gain their identity solely from their role in child-bearing, nor are they to be subordinate and inferior any longer. In *In Memory of Her*, the American Roman Catholic feminist theologian Elisabeth Schuessler Fiorenza puts it like this: 'Women and men in the Christian community are not defined by their sexual procreative capacities or by their religious, cultural or social gender roles, but by their discipleship and empowering with the Spirit' (Fiorenza 1983: 212–213).

Order and Dignity in Worship

Two passages in 1 Corinthians, however, appear at first sight to indicate a different view. In the first of these (11:2–16), Paul gives instructions about the conduct of public worship. He begins by saying, *'I should like you to understand that the head of every man is Christ, the head of woman is man, and the head of Christ is God'*. He goes on to say that when a woman

67

prays or prophesies she should wear a veil out of respect to her head, or source, man, whereas a man should not do this, for that would be to show disrespect to his head, Christ. The argument seems to be based on the creation story in Genesis 2. It is not right for a man, Paul declares, *'to have his head covered, since he is the image of God and reflects God's glory; but woman is the reflection of man's glory'*.

Paul continues, however, to qualify this in significant ways. *'In the Lord,'* he writes, *'though woman is nothing without man, man is nothing without woman; and though woman came from man, so does every man come from a woman.'* Nevertheless, this equality does not mean that women should be allowed to lead in worship unless they are authorized to do so. *'We have no such custom,'* he concludes, *'nor do any of the churches of God.'*

In this involved and complicated passage Paul is recognizing that women can have authority to take part in public worship, and this was a radical step in its context. But he is not being so radical as to set aside completely the traditional understanding of the way authority was derived. The covering, which may not have been a veil but some form of cloak or shawl, is the sign of that authority. We can feel for Paul, perhaps, as he struggles with the conflicting pressures of tradition and social custom on the one hand, and the liberation of the gospel on the other. The passage cannot properly be used to indicate that women should not take any leadership role over men in the Church. In reality it indicates that women can be authorized to do just this.

In the second passage from 1 Corinthians which appears to reverse the new understanding of the liberation brought by the gospel, Paul considers the matter of women speaking in the assembly for worship (14:33–35). *'As in all the churches of God's holy people,'* he writes, *'women are to remain quiet in the assemblies, since they have no permission to speak: theirs is a subordinate part, as the Law itself says. If there is anything they want to know, they should ask their husbands at home: it is shameful for a woman to speak in the assembly.'*

These words seem to contradict the permission to take part in worship given previously. They also fit awkwardly in their context, and they may be a later addition to the text. Perhaps some enthusiastic women in Corinth had been interrupting others, or publicly arguing with the interpretation of what was being said, and these words were inserted here to try to stop this unruly behaviour? It is worth noticing that the passage comes immediately after the words: *'God is a God not of disorder but of peace'* (14:33), and that the discussion continues two verses later as if this small section had not been there at all (14:36). The whole passage concludes, *'Make sure that everything is done in a proper and orderly fashion'* (14:40).

Again, therefore, it is a question of order and dignity in worship. The emancipation given to women elsewhere, and their authority to lead in worship when authorized to do so, should not be over-ridden by apparent excesses at one particular time and in one particular congregation.

A similar passage appears in 1 Timothy (2:9–15). Here women are to dress modestly, *'without braided hair or gold and jewellery or expensive clothes'*. Their adornment is to be good works. The passage then goes on, *'I give no permission for a woman to teach or to have authority over a man'*. This is justified, as in 1 Corinthians, by a reference to Genesis 2. It seems that differences of wealth or class were leading to jealousy or argument in the churches of Ephesus, to which this letter may have been addressed, and it is this that is unacceptable. The passage is not a general prohibition of dressing well.

The second part of the passage is more difficult to interpret. This is the only place where the word translated 'have authority over' – *authentein* in Greek – is used in the Christian Scriptures, and its implication is not entirely clear. Witherington understands it to mean that 'women are not permitted to "rule over," "master," or "play the despot" over men'. It is about domineering, and perhaps also about the unauthorized teaching of false doctrines in the Church. It does not forbid all teaching done by women. Indeed no one in the Christian community should dominate others: mutual respect and submission are the appropriate attitudes. 'Once again . . . ' Witherington continues, 'the dictum applies: "abuse does not rule out the proper use of privilege" '

69

(Witherington 1990: 194). In the verses that follow other leaders in the Church are told to be temperate, respectable, moderate. This is what will earn them *an authoritative voice in matters concerning faith in Christ Jesus* (1 Tim. 3:13).

Finally, it is interesting to note how many women there are in positions of leadership in the churches. Phoebe a deaconess and Prisca, Mary, Junias, Tryphaena and Tryphosa, Persis, the mother of Rufus, Julia, and the sister of Nereus are mentioned in Romans in a list of 29 *fellow-workers* and others who *work hard in the Lord* (16:1–16). Euodia and Syntyche are also mentioned as fellow-workers in Philippians (4:2–3).

Defective Males

Later attitudes to women and the roles they played in the family and the community were not always in line with this interpretation of the emerging tradition in the Christian Scriptures. Some details are given in *Feminist Theology: A Reader*, edited by the feminist theologian Ann Loades. Augustine, for example, speaks of part of woman's reason 'turned aside to regulate temporal things'. For Aquinas it is woman's role in generation that makes her man's helpmate; in other areas of life 'man can be more efficiently helped by another man'. Luther seems to have had a range of opinions about women. On the one hand he idealizes the godly wife and mother, but on the other he can still write offensively: 'God has created men with broad chests and broad shoulders, not broad hips, so than men can understand wisdom. But the place where the filth flows out is small. With women it's the other way around. That's why they have lots of filth and little wisdom' (Loades 1990: 92, 96, 123).

Most extraordinary of all, to our way of thinking today, is the widespread view among theologians from the early Fathers onwards that only the male was the 'perfect' expression of the human species. This view was based on the biology of Aristotle. The American theologian Rosemary Radford Reuther has summarized the argument like this: 'The male alone provided the seed or genetic form of the child, while the female provided only the material substratum which was formed. Since the seed from the father is male, a fully formed offspring would also be male. Females are the result of a defect in gestation by which the maternal matter is not fully formed, and so a female, or "defective" male, is produced who is inferior in body, intelligence and in moral self-control' (Loades 1990: 140). One result of this false biology, as it is now known to be, was that Christ had to be male for only the male had the fullness of human nature.

The subordination of women, which is reflected in the Bible and which was adopted by Christian theologians, has deeply affected thinking in the Church ever since. It still hangs on today. Brides, for example, wear wedding veils, without realizing that they symbolize their subordination to men. It is often said that men are more logical than women, or that a woman's place is in the home, though there is no rational evidence to support these views. There is a double standard that calls a man with several sexual partners a 'lucky dog', but a woman a 'tart'. Sexist language in society, as well as in the Church, is still widespread. God is spoken of as Father, or Lord, even though 'he' must be above gender and some of the images of 'his' activity in the world are female (Isa. 49:14–15, 66:10–13; Mt. 23:37). The assumption, the prejudice as it really is, that women are in one sense or another inferior to men is deeply rooted still.

Themes

Two points emerge strongly from this review of the attitudes to women reflected in the Bible and in subsequent Christian history. First, **the subordination of women, and the use of violence against women, are fundamentally undermined by the actions of Jesus**. In the Gospels the beginnings of a revolutionary new relationship of equality between men and women can be clearly seen. Although this new attitude could not have been expected to make its way very far into the male-dominated, patriarchal society of its time, a process of liberation has begun. In the early Church women

71

are able to find opportunities of leadership denied to them elsewhere.

In our own day, however, the liberation of women from oppression in all its forms has still some way to go. The struggle against sexism is an expression of the love that offers equal regard to others. A process that has its roots in the actions of Jesus has still to reach its full realization.

Secondly, **the idea that women have a 'role', whether it is in the home or in child-bearing or elsewhere, and that they 'complement' men in fulfilling it, is false**. A man is a man and a woman is a woman. According to the first creation story in Genesis (1:27), both are made in the image of God. They are equals, and each has as much right to reason, to act and to decide as the other within the community as a whole. Mutual respect and submission alone qualifies this right.

In practice social conditioning shapes and moulds us, whoever we are, into patterns of being in the world that are, in the end, not always of our own choosing. They are often the result of the exercise of power by those who have power, by men. In *The Second Sex*, the French philosopher Simone de Beauvoir puts this in a phrase that has become famous: 'One is not born, but rather becomes, a woman' (de Beauvoir 1972: 295). There is more truth in this than may at first appear. Being part of a community, and accepting its values and customs, can be a creative and life-enhancing thing, but it can also dominate and enslave people. It can corrupt attitudes of mutual respect and toleration. But prejudice against women and discrimination against them solely on the grounds of gender are unacceptable. The Christian gospel stands in opposition to such attitudes and behaviour wherever they may be found.

From one point of view Sarah is trapped by the conventions of our day which give priority to men in the field of employment. It may be some years before she can go out to work again, and her career may not recover from the years taken out of it by the birth and the early nurture of her children. But from another point of view there is hope in the growing public awareness of discrimination against women and the need to take effective steps to overcome it. The Church has every reason to be in the forefront of this movement. It is one way in which the command to love the neighbour can be given practical effect in society today.

RACE

Prejudice knows no boundaries. People who belong to ethnic minority groups in Britain often find it as hard to make their way in their own right as women do. Racism is as widespread as sexism.

Winston, for example, belongs to a group of Christians who meet to look at race and community relations problems. In the local paper he read about a demonstration by the Muslim community against the Council's failure to provide them with a proper burial ground. They put an empty coffin on the town hall steps in protest. At a meeting of the group Ralph, who had grown up in India, said that Islam was a false religion and that Asian people who come to Britain should adopt our customs or go back home. Winston felt that, on the contrary, it was part of the British way of life to be accepting and tolerant of others. He wanted the Church to show its love for people by actively supporting the Muslim demand. So a representative of the Muslim community was invited to talk to the next meeting, and then a letter was written to the leader of the Council to support their case.

Discrimination against people of different ethnic origin is deeply rooted. Racist attitudes are to be found just under the surface in every part of the country, and not just where black faces are to be seen. It was not long ago, for example, that Jewish people were subject to open anti-semitism. But Britain has traditionally provided a home for people from many other parts of the world. The Romans were here for four hundred years; the Normans invaded; many Huguenots, refugees from religious persecution in Europe, settled here; Commonwealth members had a right to come here as British subjects, until Acts of Parliament in 1948, 1971 and 1981 amended this right in progressively restrictive ways.

The government now keeps records of ethnic groups under ten headings: White, West Indian or Guyanese, Indian, Pakistani, Bangladeshi, Chinese, African, Arab, Mixed, and Other. The government publication *Social Trends* shows that something over 2.5 million people in Britain belong to the nine non-white ethnic minority groups, just over 4.5 per cent of the population (Central Statistical Office 1992:28). They are mostly young, and also mostly born in this country. Gypsies have recently been recognized as an ethnic group, too. Like everyone else, they are protected by the 1976 Race Relations Act and the work of the Commission for Racial Equality. It is widely thought that the ethnic minority population is larger than the official figures suggest.

Attitudes, however, bear little relationship to numbers. Prejudice is felt to be widespread. An opinion survey conducted for the Runnymede Trust and *The Independent on Sunday* and published in the Trust's Bulletin *Race and Immigration*, shows that two-thirds of black people believe that ethnic minorities are treated worse than white people by employers, and three-quarters that they are treated worse by the police. Significantly fewer white people in the survey felt the same way about these things (Runnymede Trust July/ August 1991: 4). A handful of African-Caribbean and Asian MPs and trade union officials do not make Britain a non-racist country. Discrimination against people on racial grounds is not just a matter of private attitude; it has got caught up in the structure of society. Assumptions are made about people purely because of the colour of their skin. Racism has become institutionalized in our society.

There is a strong link, too, between racial origin and religion and culture, and they are often confused with each other. In a paper in *A Time to Speak: Perspectives of Black Christians in Britain*, the former Hindu Raj Patel writes pointedly, 'Is the tie a sign of the cross?' This question, he continues, 'was asked by a Hindu of a missionary as the uppermost difference he could see in the lives of those Hindus who have converted to Christianity, was that they now wore ties' (Grant and Patel 1990: 87). Race, culture, religion and nationality are complex matters which merge into each other in the human mind.

Racial Divisions

An awareness of racial difference also permeates the Bible. In Genesis, the origins of the separate clans and languages, countries and nations are traced to Noah's sons Shem, Ham and Japheth, and from them *'the whole earth was peopled'*. Ham is the father of Canaan, who is cursed because he saw Noah naked (Gen. 9:18–27). In the Psalms, Egypt is described as *'the country of Ham'* (105:23), and the curse of Canaan has been thought to have fallen on black people ever since. The descendants of Noah's sons are carefully listed, and from them *'other nations branched out on the earth after the flood'* (Gen. 10, 11:10–32).

The story of the tower of Babel explains the divisions that exist between different people (Gen. 11:1–9). The story begins, *'The whole world spoke the same language, with the same vocabulary'*. Travelling eastwards the people determine to build a city and a tower reaching to heaven *'so that we do not get scattered all over the world'*. Yahweh goes to see what they are up to and observes the power that they have as *'a single people with a single language'*. He then confuses their language *'so that they cannot understand one another'*, and scatters them all over the world. There is no suggestion here of any inferiority, but distinctions of language, and dispersal, are presented as a punishment and as a way of keeping people weak and in their place.

With the call of Abram, later in Genesis, comes the promise that Yahweh will make him a great nation and a blessing on others. Yahweh says to Abram, *'All clans on earth will bless themselves by you'* (12:3). The choice of a people to become a nation is linked with a sense of purpose beyond itself. Nationality is not to be an exclusive arrangement, but one that brings benefit to others.

Something of the common humanity that everyone shares is reflected in the hospitality regulations in Leviticus: *'If you have resident aliens in your country, you will not molest them. You*

75

will treat resident aliens as though they were native-born and love them as yourself – for you yourselves were once aliens in Egypt' (19:33–34). The same punishment for murder – a life for a life – is to apply to alien as to native-born (24:22)

In Deuteronomy, the people of Israel are to *'love the stranger'* for they were once strangers in Egypt (10:19). A foreigner resident in the community is not to be exploited. He should be treated the same as one of the brothers. A further passage declares: *'You must pay him his wages each day . . . You must not infringe the rights of the foreigner.'* A sheaf overlooked in the field at harvest time, olives left on the tree and grapes on the vine are *'for the foreigner'* as much as for the orphan and the widow (24:14–15,17–22).

Later in Deuteronomy, there is a sense that God has caused national divisions, and that positive benefits are attached to nationhood, or to one particular nation: *'When the Most High gave the nations each their heritage, when he partitioned out the human race, he assigned the boundaries of nations according to the number of the children of God, but Yahweh's portion was his people, Jacob was to be the measure of his inheritance'* (32:8–9). Israel may have a special place, the passage seems to say, but everyone is a child of God.

In Isaiah's vision, the divine banquet which God is preparing, is for *'all peoples'* (25:6–8). Israel is to be *'a light to the nations'* (49:6). Yahweh is coming *'to gather every nation and every language . . . All humanity will come and bow in my presence, Yahweh says'* (66:18,23). In Amos, Yahweh is seen to be behind the migration of peoples, Philistines and Aramaeans as well as the children of Israel (9:7). The sense of God's concern for every nation, and the vision of eventual unity, is clear.

The idea that Israel has a mission that stretches beyond itself comes out in Zechariah. *'In those days,'* says Yahweh, *'ten men from nations of every language will take a Jew by the sleeve and say: We want to go with you, since we have learnt that God is with you'* (8:23). In Malachi, Yahweh says, *'From farthest east to farthest west my name is great among the nations'* (1:11). It would be wrong to see this theme of universal salvation in the Hebrew Scriptures as any sort of tolerance of the religion of others. There is no doubt in these passages where right lies: it is with faithfulness to Yahweh, and others are to fall in with this.

The Unity of All People

The sense that the ancient divisions into clan, language, country and nation are to be done away with is stressed in ever more insistent ways in the Christian Scriptures. Special attention is paid to the Samaritans, a people of mixed race and religion traditionally despised by the Jews. In Luke, Jesus rebukes his disciples when they are angry with their rejection by the Samaritans (9:54–55). He chooses a Samaritan as his example of a neighbour who fulfils the Law (10:25–37). In John, it is a Samaritan woman at the well who gives Jesus water and discusses theology with him. He tells her that the Messiah is for all, not just for the Jews. This makes a considerable impact on her and on the people of Sychar when she tells them (4:4–30).

In Matthew, a different note is struck when Jesus forbids the twelve disciples to go to gentile and Samaritan territory; they are to go instead to *'the lost sheep of the House of Israel'* (10:5–6). Later, however, Jesus meets his disciples in Galilee and tells them to *'make disciples of all nations'* (28:19). Luke includes the same point when Jesus appears to the disciples in Jerusalem just before the ascension. The gospel is to be *'preached to all nations, beginning from Jerusalem'* (24:47).

In Acts, this theme is expanded in a particularly powerful way. Jesus tells the apostles that they are to be his witnesses *'not only in Jerusalem but throughout Judea and Samaria, and indeed to earth's remotest end'* (1:8). At Pentecost the apostles were all filled with the Holy Spirit and *'began to speak different languages as the Spirit gave them power to express themselves'*. Devout men *'from every nation under heaven'* assemble and to their amazement each one hears the apostles *'speaking his own language'* (2:1–13). The division and the confusion of language of the tower of Babel is symbolically overcome by the power of the Holy Spirit. The gospel heals the separation into racial

77

and national groups that keeps people from each other and from God.

Later in Acts, Stephen engages in powerful debates with people from Cyrene and Alexandria in Africa, and with others from Cilicia and Asia, and then gives the members of the Sanhedrin a long account of the history of Israel, and of Israel's unfaithfulness to God. The ancient promise to Abraham, he argues, is fulfilled in Jesus. It is little surprise that this leads to his death by stoning (6:8—7:60). In *Struggle in Babylon*, the urban theologian Kenneth Leech calls this 'a major attack on any ethnocentric understanding of revelation' (Leech 1988:199).

Peter learns the same lesson. The story is told in Acts of his visit to Cornelius' house, where he declares, '*You know it is forbidden for Jews to mix with people of another race and visit them; but God has made it clear to me that I must not call anyone profane or unclean . . .*' He continues, '*I now really understand that God has no favourites, but that anybody of any nationality who fears him and does what is right is acceptable to him*' (10:28, 34–35). The Jews were astonished that the Holy Spirit '*should be poured out on gentiles too*', but the evidence is plain for all to see (10:45).

Acts reveal that it is in Antioch, when the gospel is preached to Greeks and north Africans as well as to Jews, that the name '*Christians*' is first used (11:20, 26). The multi-racial character of the Church marks its members out for this distinctive name. The point is made again when Christians who had formerly been Pharisees demand circumcision of gentile converts. Paul rejects this and says, '*God made no distinction between them and us, since he purified their hearts by faith*' (15:5–11).

Again in Acts, in his speech to the Areopagus council in Athens, Paul declares that the God he proclaims has '*made the world and everything in it*', and is himself '*Lord of heaven and earth . . . It is he who gives everything – including life and breath – to everyone*'. He goes on: '*From one single principle he not only created the whole human race so that they could occupy the entire earth, but he decreed the times and limits of their habitation. And he did this so that they might seek the deity and, by feeling their way towards him, succeed in finding him; and indeed he is not far from any of us . . . We are all his children'* (17:22–28). Paul is claiming that there is something in everyone that is able to reach out to God, and something of the true God in every form of worship. Human beings all share a common origin and a common humanity. Even differences of religious faith are not clear-cut, for God is close to us all. Paul's natural theology is profoundly significant. It undermines all racial distinctions, as well as any alleged exclusiveness on the part of any one faith. Christ may reveal the fullness of God, but that does not mean that all else is of no value.

The frequent repetition of the point that the gospel reaches across the boundaries of race and nationality may indicate that there were frequent attempts to deny it. This racial unity brought by the gospel was, in any case, very significant to the early Church. In Romans, Paul speaks of gentile branches being grafted into the one vine (11:11–24). In Galatians, he reprimands Cephas and others for continuing to keep the Jewish purity rules and eating separately from gentile Christians (2:11–14). Now that faith has come and people have been baptized, he is able to pronounce, *'There can be neither Jew nor Greek . . . for you are all one in Christ Jesus. And simply by being Christ's, you are that progeny of Abraham, the heirs named in the promise'* (3:23–29).

In Ephesians, the barriers between gentile and Jew have been broken down: *'He has made the two into one entity.'* Through the cross the hostility is overcome; peace has been restored; both have access to the Father, so they are no longer aliens or foreign visitors, but *'fellow-citizens with the holy people of God and part of God's household'* (2:11–22). There are many other references to this overcoming of racial barriers (e.g. Rom. 1:16; Gal. 6:15; Col. 3:11). In the Christian community such distinctions have been done away with altogether.

Finally the separation of race and nationality described in Genesis and broken apart at Pentecost, and which seems to have caused so much concern to the early Church, is overcome in the grand vision in Revelation. *'I saw that there was a huge number,'* the passage declares, *'impossible for anyone to*

79

count, of people from every nation, race, tribe and language . . .
They shouted in a loud voice, "Salvation to our God . . . " '
(7:9–10).

Themes

The themes that emerge from this powerful thread within
the pages of the Bible are these: first, **the sense of identity
that is provided by race and nationality can be something positive and creative**. It can reflect the basic human
need to belong, to know where one has a right to be. There
is no doubt that identifiable groupings are important to
people. We cannot easily feel we belong to 'world
humanity'. An awareness of community enables common
experience and culture, and common purpose. Without this
people feel powerless, life is too impersonal and identity too
vague.

Secondly, however, **the tendency to claim superiority
over others and special privilege, which slips in all too
easily, is unacceptable**. This tendency had constantly to be
restricted in ancient Israel. In its origins in Genesis, the sense
of being a nation – a chosen race – was not a basis for
superiority, but for mission. It was in order to bring a blessing to the world as a whole. Jesus approached the matter in
his characteristically robust way by simply extending the
promise of salvation directly to the Samaritans. In the early
Church the tendency to exclusiveness kept re-emerging, and
the wider vision of the purpose of the faith was constantly
proclaimed in order to correct it. Where national identity,
today, or religious identity for that matter, loses this sense
of purpose beyond itself, it has lost touch with its very reason
for existence.

Thirdly, it is clear that **discrimination based on race
and, following Galatians, discrimination based on class,
or wealth, or gender, has no place in the Christian community and should have no place in the world as a
whole**. Human beings share a common humanity which is
more significant than any other feature only some of them
share. The vision of unity is a global one. It is not that

differences are to be ignored. Circumcision cannot be undone; men and women are still male and female. Differences can enrich and allow variety and individuality. But where they are used to exclude people, or to discriminate unfavourably against them, or where they lead to hatred and violence, they deny the unifying thrust of the Christian vision. The prejudice that lurks in people's hearts, as well as in the institutions and structures of society, and the deprivation and conflict that so often go with it, is fundamentally challenged by the gospel.

Fourthly, **the hostility that some Christians show, today, to other faiths is also unacceptable**. Faith and culture, faith and country, faith and nationality all merge with one another and cannot easily be distinguished. For Paul varieties of religious experience, and expression in worship, all have their origin in the one God. There is only one God. Human reason and human religious strivings all tend in the same ultimate direction. There is much that one faith can learn from another, without compromising on deeply-held convictions vital to both. In our own day, this lesson has still to be learned in Britain as much as anywhere. Kenneth Leech writes, 'Our society is plural, a society containing a variety of ethnic and religious groupings. But it is not yet *pluralist,* that is, it is not yet a society which has accepted its new character' (Leech 1988: 126). We are not yet a tolerant and loving society.

The impulse that led Winston to support the Muslim claim to adequate burial grounds is one that finds its roots in the pages of the Bible. The action taken by the group he belonged to speaks of our common humanity, and of the love for the neighbour, for the stranger, even for the foreigner, the Samaritan, that should lie behind all that Christians try to do.

4.

WEALTH AND POVERTY

In *Three Men in a Boat*, the story of his journey down the Thames with two companions and a dog, Jerome K. Jerome says, 'I like work; it fascinates me. I can sit and look at it for hours' (Jerome 1957: 144). It is true; most people feel a deep sense of ambivalence about work, and about wealth and poverty as well. On the one hand, they are desperate to have a job, and not just for the money, but on the other, their work is often the source of great frustration and anger. They long for riches and the 'good' life, but they pour scorn on the 'idle' rich. Their hearts are moved to compassion by the sight of starving children on television, flies crawling unchecked over expressionless faces, but they hurry past a beggar in the street with an embarrassed glance.

Questions about economics, about work and wealth, and how they are distributed in society, are basically questions about human relationships. They are also moral questions, about what is good and right, and how we can love our neighbours in the wider context. I want to look, therefore, at these economic issues in this chapter.

WORK

Robert had a well-paid job in a bank. But the work was monotonous, and relationships with his boss were strained. When the chance came to be declared redundant, he jumped at it. A year's salary as compensation and twelve months to find another post looked good. 'I can always get another job!' he declared bravely. But Jane, thinking of their three

82

children and the mortgage, felt differently. 'It's kind of scary', she said to Tessa one afternoon as they waited for the children at the school gate.

Robert is just one of many who face an uncertain future as far as work and income are concerned. The government report *Social Trends* gives the details about the country's economic life. Out of a population of 55.5 million in the United Kingdom some 28 million are in the civilian labour force. By October 1991, around 2.5 million of these were registered as unemployed and claiming benefit, the numbers having risen by around a million in the previous eighteen months. Since 1971 just over 3 million more people have joined the labour force, most of them women. About half the men and two-thirds of the women in employment are in clerical, managerial, professional and other non-manual jobs, and the rest are in craft, labouring and other manual jobs (Central Statistical Office 1992: 26, 70, 80, 70, 74).

Questions about employment and unemployment are of major concern to every family. But is work a means by which people contribute to society, find fulfilment, even work out a vocation to serve others? Or is it simply instrumental, a means of earning enough money to be able to go out and do what we really want?

Blessing and Curse

In the Bible there is also a sense of uncertainty about the significance of work. It is both a blessing and a curse. On the one hand, in the first creation story in Genesis, work is pictured as the activity of God himself. In many of the stages of creation it is an act of God's will alone: '*God said, "Let there be light," and there was light.*' But a variety of other words are also used: the earth produced vegetation and living creatures. God made the sun and moon and set them in the vault of heaven. He created marine life, and made animals and humankind. In every case the product of this work is said to be good (1:1—2:4a).

In the second story (2:4b–25), God shaped man from the ground, planted a garden, and took him and '*settled him in the garden of Eden to cultivate and take care of it'* (2:15). Finally he fashioned woman out of the man's rib. God's work is pictured as creative activity, involving the will as well as various forms of direct and indirect labour. Human beings share in work. They are in the garden *'to till it and care for it'*, as the REB translates it. From these ancient stories comes a basic affirmation of the dignity of work. God is the creator and men and women are made in his image. They are creators, too.

The story of the fall, on the other hand, is the source of the idea that work is also cursed. After he had eaten from the fruit of the forbidden tree in Genesis, the man is told, *'Accursed be the soil because of you! Painfully will you get your food from it as long as you live . . . By the sweat of your face will you earn your food . . . '* (3:17–19). It is worth noticing that it is the ground, not the work, that is cursed. The result is that work, once enjoyable in the garden with God, has become labour, painful and hard, outside the garden, and winged creatures and a sword guard the way back (3:23–24). But the work itself continues to be creative and good, as it was before. The woman, too, shares in this curse. God says to her, *'I shall give you intense pain in childbearing, you will give birth to your children in pain'* (3:16). Having children, though, is still a good and essentially creative activity. It is the conditions of work that are affected, not the work itself.

God's Work and Human Work

The parallel between divine and human work is reflected elsewhere in the Hebrew Scriptures. In the Ten Commandments, no work is to be done on the sabbath for *'in six days Yahweh made the heavens, earth and sea and all that these contain, but on the seventh day he rested'* (Ex. 20:8–11). The language of human work is used to describe that of God's creation. In the Psalms, the heavens are shaped by his *'fingers'*; the vault of heaven proclaims his *'handiwork'*; he stretched out the heavens *'like a tent'* and fixed the earth on its *'foundations'* (8:3, 19:1, 104:2–5), and similar points are made in other Psalms (24:1–2, 121:2). God is involved in his creation, and just as he is active in it still, so *'man goes out to work, to labour till evening falls'* (Ps. 107:25–38, 104:23). In Isaiah, Yahweh's creative work is compared to that of a potter, and to parents having children (45:9–12).

It is in the context of their work that men and women *'hear the sound of Yahweh God walking in the garden in the cool of the day'*, though they hide from intimate contact with him (Gen. 3:8). Creative work which is good in its intention, its processes and its outcome, is easily degraded. Creativity carries with it great potential for good or ill.

The idea that men and women share with God in work in the world, is reflected in a number of passages. In Exodus, the work of craftsmen and artists is pictured as inspired by God. As the Temple sanctuary is built, Yahweh says to Moses, *'I have singled out Bezalel . . . and have filled him with the spirit of God in wisdom, knowledge and skill in every kind of craft'*. He has Oholiab to help him. God has *'endowed the hearts of all the skilled men with the skill'* to make everything that is required, and a detailed description of their work is given (31:1–6, 35:30—36:1, 36:8—39:43).

Manual labour is appropriate even for the highest in the land. King Saul works in the fields *'behind his oxen'* (1 Sam. 11:5). David, his successor, is taken from shepherd's work, tending ewes, *'to pasture his servant Jacob'* (Ps. 78:70–72).

Later, after the exile, Nehemiah encourages the people to rebuild the walls of ruined Jerusalem. They say, *'Let us start building at once!'* and they set their hands to *'the good work'*. They put *'their hearts into the work'* and their enemies eventually realize that it has been accomplished by the power of God (Neh. 2:18, 3:38, 6:16).

In one of the Psalms, the deeds that Yahweh does and the *'work we have done'* are mentioned in the same breath (90:16–17), and in another the view is expressed that, *'If Yahweh does not build a house in vain do its builders toil'* (127:1). In Isaiah, the skill of the farmer comes from God. He ploughs and plants in the right place *'for his God has taught him this rule and instructed him'*. Such skill is a *'gift . . . marvellous advice leading to great achievements'* (28:23–29).

Some limits, however, are set. Ecclesiastes states, *'What is*

twisted cannot be straightened, what is not there cannot be counted
(1:15). The value of work seems to depend on what is to be
done. The Psalmist is scornful of idols of silver and gold
'made by human hands' (115:3–8). Isaiah ridicules craftsmen
who make false gods (40:18–21, 44:9).

In addition to the element of blessing and of curse attached
to human work, there is a sense that work is just a normal
part of life to be got on with and done well. Without work
there will be no food. In Proverbs, the idler is reprimanded.
He should follow the example of the ant, who *'gets her food
ready, and gathers her supplies at harvest time'.* Hard workers
'get their fill'. A worker's appetite *'works on his behalf, for his
hunger urges him on'* (6:6–8, 13:4, 16:26). This point is often
made (Prov. 19:15, 20:4,13, 21:25, 28:19; Eccles. 10:18,
12:12). The truly capable woman *'does her work with eager
hands . . . She puts her back into her work . . . No bread of
idleness for her'* (Prov. 31:13,17,27). *'Whatever work you find to
do,'* urges Ecclesiastes, *'do it with all your might'* (9:10).

In Ecclesiasticus, in the Apocrypha, the value of a range
of ordinary occupations is recognized. The doctor should be
treated with *'the honour that is his due'*; the scribe has leisure
to acquire the wisdom that will lead to a good reputation
(38:1–15,24, 39:1–11). Others, however, have different roles
to play. *'How can a ploughman become wise . . . '* the writer
asks, or other workmen and craftsmen, those who engrave
seals, the blacksmith who *'concentrates on getting the job done
well'*, or the potter? But a town *'could not be inhabited without
them, there would be no settling, no travelling'.* They do not
make or interpret law, or discuss philosophy, but *'they sustain
the structure of the world, and their prayer is concerned with their
trade'* (38:25–34).

The rewards of wealth and reputation that come from hard
work are also recognized. *'Your own labours will yield you a
living,'* says the Psalmist, *'happy and prosperous will you be'*
(128:1–2). Proverbs makes the same point: *'The hand of the
diligent brings wealth'* (10:4). *'For the diligent hand, authority; for
the slack hand, forced labour'* (12:24). *'Too much haste, and all
that comes of it is want'* (21:5). *'You see someone alert at his
business? . . . Not for him the service of the obscure'* (22:29). The

works of a capable woman *'tell her praises at the city gates'* (31:31).

But even this is to be kept within limits. In Ecclesiastes, King Solomon has *'worked on a grand scale'* and amassed a fortune. He says, *'I found all my hard work a pleasure, such was the return for all my efforts'*. But reflecting on it he concludes, *'What futility it all was, what chasing after the wind!'* Someone who has *'laboured wisely, skilfully and successfully'* leaves it all to another who *'has not toiled for it at all'*. Such a man's days *'are full of sorrow, his work is full of stress and even at night he has no peace of mind'* (2:4–23). A sense of balance between the work involved and the enjoyment of the results of that work is nicely put: *'Whenever God gives someone riches and property, with the ability to enjoy them and to find contentment in work, this is a gift from God'* (5:18).

The Work of the Gospel

In the Christian Scriptures, by contrast, the word work is mostly used in a religious context. Although Jesus is a carpenter, the son of a carpenter, nothing is made of this (Mk. 6:3; Mt. 13:55).

In Luke, the Seventy-two are to be looked after by those with whom they stay, *'for the labourer deserves his wages'* (10:7). In John, Jesus speaks of his ministry as his work. In Samaria when his disciples urge him to eat, he says, *'My food is to do the will of the one who sent me, and to complete his work'* (4:34). After a healing on the sabbath he says, *'My Father still goes on working, and I am at work, too'*. The Jews are angry that this work of healing is more important to him than the sabbath rest (5:17–18). As he cures a blind man he says, *'As long as the day lasts we must carry out the work of the one who sent me; the night will soon be here when no one can work'* (9:4). These sayings fit awkwardly in their context, and John seems to be adding a theological point about the work of the gospel, rather than recording actual conversations that took place at the time.

The occupations of many of the people that Jesus meets are recorded, and he draws on ordinary life and experience

87

for many of his parables and his other teaching. But no real implications for human work as such can rightly be drawn from this. The reality of working life is there in the background as points about the kingdom and the gospel are made. The story of the workers in the vineyard, for example, may well reflect current experience, but it is told to make a point about equality in the kingdom of heaven and about the generosity of God (Mt. 20:1–16).

Paul also speaks about the work of the gospel. In 1 Corinthians, he writes, '*Are you not my work in the Lord?*' But this work is work like any other, and rest is deserved as well as pay. '*Are Barnabas and I,*' he continues, '*the only ones who have no right to stop working? . . . The Lord gave the instruction that those who preach the gospel should get their living from the gospel*' (9:1,6,14). Paul seems never to have claimed such a reward, and to have continued to support himself through his old trade of tent-making (9:15–18; Acts 18:3). The point is made again in 2 Thessalonians: '*We were not undisciplined,*' he writes, '*when we were with you, nor did we ever accept food from anyone without paying for it; no, we worked with unsparing energy, night and day, so as not to be a burden on any of you*' (3:7–8).

The work of the gospel requires commitment and support. Paul urges the Corinthian Christians to keep firm, '*always abounding in energy for the Lord's work, being sure that in the Lord none of your labours is wasted*' (1 Cor. 15:58). Epaphroditus is Paul's '*fellow-worker*' in Christ's work (Phil. 2:25,30). A Christian is to be '*a proven worker*' who '*keeps the message of truth on a straight path*' (2 Tim. 2:14–15).

Some advice is, however, given about the appropriate attitude to work in an everyday context. In Ephesians, a motive for work is given: '*Anyone who was a thief must stop stealing; instead he should exert himself at some honest job with his own hands so that he may have something to share with those in need*' (4:28). Christians are to work for their living so that they may '*earn the respect of outsiders and not be dependent on anyone*' (1 Thess. 4:12). In 2 Thessalonians, Paul is faced with Christians who are so excited about the idea of the imminent return of the Lord that they have given up all normal work. He commends his own example of hard work as a model for them to imitate, and continues,'*We urged you when we were with you not to let anyone eat who refused to work*'. He calls on people to '*go on quietly working and earning the food that they eat*' (3:10–12). In Titus, believers are urged to be '*ready to do good at every opportunity*', or as the REB translates it, '*Be ready for any honourable work*' (3:1).

It is worth noticing that these passages gain a particular significance from the context in which they are set. The early Church was anxious to avoid any idea that it was a subversive organization. Christians were honest people, who paid their way, and were ready for public service like any others. To suggest today, for example, that as a matter of general principle those who do not work should not receive any support from the community as a whole, is a misuse of the text.

In various passages work is presented as a form of service. In the Gospels, Jesus speaks of this as the real source of authority. He says to his disciples, '*Anyone who wants to become great among you must be your servant . . . just as the Son of man came not to be served but to serve*'(Mt. 20:24–28). The same point is made more fully in a famous passage in Philippians. Christ Jesus, Paul writes, '*emptied himself, taking the form of a slave . . . even to accepting death . . . And for this God raised him high, and gave him the name which is above all other names*' (2:5–10). In the household code in Colossians, slaves are advised, '*Whatever your work is, put your heart into it as done for the Lord and not for human beings . . .* ' (3:23). The same point is made in Ephesians (6:7). These codes encourage slaves, or workers – the Greek word is *doulos* – to whole-hearted obedience, unqualified respect, loyalty, willing work without argument, and honesty. They also encourage anyone who is a master, or lord – the Greek is *kurios* – to give their workers what is upright and fair, to treat them in the same spirit of respect and loyalty, and without threats or favouritism (Col. 3:22—4:1; Eph. 6:5–9; 1 Tim. 6:1–2; Titus 2:9–10; 1 Pet. 2:18).

89

Vocation

The idea of vocation also has its origins in the Bible. The sense of being called, or specially chosen, by God for a particular task occurs frequently. Abram is called to leave his country, to become a great nation, to be a blessing (Gen. 12:1–2). The children of Jacob, Moses, King David, the children of Israel are all described as God's chosen ones (1 Chron. 16:13; Ps. 105:6,43, 106:5,23, 89:3; Isa. 43:20, 65:15). Isaiah has a vision in the Temple and feels himself to be called. *'Here am I, send me'*, he responds (6:8). Amos is also called to the work of prophecy (7:15).

In the Gospels, the Twelve are appointed, or summoned and picked out (Mk. 3:14; Lk. 6:13). In Matthew, the word *'called'* is explicitly used (4:21). Jesus says to Simon and Andrew, *'Come after me'*, and to Matthew, *'Follow me'* (Mt. 4:19, 9:9). The Seventy-two are appointed and sent out (Lk. 10:1). In Acts, Paul is called in the experience of conversion on the road to Damascus, and later called to bring the gospel to Macedonia (9:3–19, 16:10).

In 1 Corinthians, Paul speaks of himself as *'called by the will of God to be an apostle'*, and of the Church as those who are *'called to be God's holy people'* and to be *'partners with his Son Jesus Christ our Lord'* (1:1–2,9). Different gifts are given by the Spirit to Christians, and different appointments made in the Church: apostles, prophets, teachers, miracle workers, healers . . . (12:4–11,28–30). In Ephesians, apostles, prophets, evangelists, pastors and teachers are mentioned (4:11). In Colossians, Christians are described as *'the chosen of God . . . called together in one body'* (3:12,15). In 2 Thessalonians, they are chosen from the beginning to be saved (2:13), and in 1 Timothy, to win eternal life (6:12). In 1 Peter, Christians are *'a chosen race, a kingdom of priests, a holy nation'* (2:9).

In each of these cases vocation is to Christian discipleship or to some role within the Christian community. It seems clear that this is the primary context in which a sense of calling is to be understood.

There is a suggestion, however, in 1 Corinthians that the

Christian calling can be worked out in an ordinary secular context. In a passage in which he encourages Christians not to use incompatibility in faith as a reason for divorce, unless they must do so, Paul says, '*Let everyone continue in the part which the Lord has allotted to him, as he was when God called him*'. Giving circumcision and slavery as examples, he urges again, '*Each one of you, brothers, is to stay before God in the state in which you were called*' (7:17,24).

The interpretation of the words paraphrased '*part*' and '*state*' in these verses from 1 Corinthians has been much disputed. The Greek seems to imply that it is the calling to be a Christian that is meant, but then there is little point in the examples given. The whole passage is set within a discussion of marriage, not discipleship. The advice to remain a slave when becoming a Christian is much more pertinent than to remain a Christian on becoming a slave. Paul may, however, be saying that the time before the end is so short that there is no sense in trying to leave any social role, however difficult for Christians. Alternatively he may be feeling that there are opportunities for Christian witness, by word and example, in secular positions. That is the point he has just made in relation to mixed marriages (7:14). It is worth noticing, too, that John the Baptist had advised tax collectors coming to baptism to '*exact no more than the appointed rate*', and soldiers to be '*content*' with their pay (Lk. 3:12–14). He did not tell them to leave their jobs.

The Reformation theologians, among them Martin Luther and John Calvin, made much of a sense of vocation in a secular job. The love of the neighbour could be expressed through such work. The Protestant ethic, or the work ethic as it is also called, seems to have been particularly suited to the development of capitalist business and industry. The hard work and the thrift of the Puritans led quickly to the increase of wealth and to prosperity, though it is true that Catholic businessmen in those days were also successful without the influence of Protestant ideas about work. In our own day, the concept of vocation is widely used in an entirely secular sense to mean little more than a craft skill acquired through a course of training.

In *The Biblical Doctrine of Work*, the former Dean of York Alan Richardson protests against what he calls 'the secularization of the biblical concept of vocation in our modern usage'. We cannot be called to be an engineer, he claims, or a doctor, a school-master, a brick-layer, an engine-driver, a machine-minder, or even 'to the Church as a profession'. We can only be called to Christian discipleship and to the ministry that is shared by all Christians (Richardson 1963: 34–35). The word 'church' itself – *ekklesia* in Greek – means that which is called out. Vocation is to faith, though that faith is also to be put into effect in ordinary life and work. In *Work and Leisure in Christian Perspective*, the American evangelical writer Leland Ryken argues that, under certain conditions, all work can be seen as a vocation. 'Work becomes a calling,' he writes, 'only if we recognize God's hand in it and view it as part of our relationship with God' (Ryken 1987: 144).

A Day of Rest

In the Bible a contrast is also drawn between work and rest. In Genesis, God rests on the seventh day after completing the work of creation (2:1–3). In Exodus, as the Israelites escape from Egypt, they are to collect a double ration of manna in the wilderness, for there will be none on the sabbath (16:22–31). In the Ten Commandments the seventh day is a sabbath for Yahweh, and no one is to do any work (20:8–11). A day of rest is enjoined on the craftsmen building the Temple in the strongest terms: '*Work must be done for six days, but the seventh day will be a day of complete rest, consecrated to Yahweh. Anyone who works on the sabbath day will be put to death*' (31:15). Every seventh year, and every fiftieth at the jubilee, the land is also to enjoy rest (Lev. 25). In Nehemiah, trading on the sabbath is roundly condemned, including the selling of food. It is prevented by the simple means of shutting the city gates to stop traders coming in on the sabbath (13:15–22).

The rest that is enjoined in these passages seems to imply doing no work. It is in other passages that a specific connection is made with religious worship. In Leviticus, the seventh day is for complete rest, but it is also to be '*a day for the sacred assembly*' (23:3). The same connection is made in relation to other festivals in further verses (23:8,21,24,27–28,35–36) and again in Numbers (28:16–18,25–26).

In a passage in Esther, recreation is also mentioned in connection with rest. After success in battle a day of rest is held and accompanied by '*feasting and gladness*'. It becomes the basis for an annual day of '*gladness, feasting and holiday-making, and the exchanging of presents with one another*' (9:17–19).

In the Gospels, Jesus seeks time to be alone, often in the mountains (Mk. 6:46–47; Lk. 6:12), and he invites his disciples to do the same: '*Come away to some lonely place all by yourselves and rest for a while*' (Mk. 6:31; Lk. 9:28). But no particular day is mentioned. In Matthew, the birds who '*do not sow or reap or gather into barns*', and the flowers which '*never have to work or spin*', are contrasted favourably with humans, who are full of worry about food and drink and clothes (6:25–34). In Hebrews, an eternal dimension appears in a passage elaborating some verses from a psalm (95:7–11) to indicate that believers will enter God's '*place of rest*' (3:7–4:11). In the vision of the new heaven and the new earth in Revelation, '*there will be no more . . . pain*' (21:4). The harshness of Adam's toil is finally overcome by the joy of the presence of God in the heavenly Jerusalem.

The Humanization of Work

In recent centuries, however, questions about work and leisure have gained a new dimension. Karl Marx has drawn attention to the phenomenon of alienation, in which the worker is distanced from his work by mass production processes and by the separation of ownership and labour. In the papal encyclical *Quadragesimo Anno*, Pius XI speaks in similar vein of bodily labour becoming an instrument of perversion, 'for from the factory dead matter goes out improved, whereas men there are corrupted and degraded' (Pope Pius XI 1931: 53).

In a famous lecture *Why Work?*, the playwright Dorothy

93

Sayers speaks out powerfully against greed and waste in the processes of production. 'Work is not, primarily,' she writes, 'a thing one does to live, but the thing one lives to do. It is, or it should be, the full expression of the worker's faculties, the thing in which he finds spiritual, mental and bodily satisfaction, and the medium in which he offers himself to God' (Sayers 1947: 55). In a more recent encyclical *Laborem Exercens*, John Paul II writes about man as 'the subject of work', and of the 'priority of labour over capital'. Work must serve to 'realize' our humanity (Pope John Paul II 1981: 20, 41).

In *Good Work*, the economist Fritz Schumacher argues against the complex, greedy, destructive and authoritarian character of modern industrial society, and in favour of smaller units and the decentralization of authority and responsibility in business organizations (Schumacher 1979: 29). He wants forms of ownership and management which allow people to share more fully in making the decisions which affect them. For him 'small is beautiful', a phrase that has become famous from the title of another of his books. In these ways something of the experience of alienation from the product and the processes of work may be overcome.

Themes

The themes that emerge from this review of work as it is reflected in the pages of the Bible and in subsequent history are these: First, **there is a basic dignity to human work**. It is regarded positively. For the Greeks, by contrast, work was degrading, something to be done by slaves. The Greek word for work – *a-skole* – means to be without leisure. In the same vein, the Latin word – *neg-otium* – means to be without ease. It is something negative. But in the Hebrew Scriptures work is creative and good. It is God-like. Human skill is inspired and its result, success and prosperity, is to be welcomed as a sign of blessing. In our own day, where human work has a strong creative element, and where it is organized in such a way that men and women can participate strongly in decision-making, it is still a source of blessing.

Secondly, **the conditions surrounding human work are often hard and unremitting, and they have great potential for degrading people**. The curse of Adam in Genesis 3 is part of everyone's experience for there is monotony and boredom and sweat in every occupation. Today, too, large impersonal organizations and authoritarian styles of management, which often lead to low morale and poor performance, have about them something of that same curse. No one works happily for a company which does not care about its employees, where no one is told what is going on or why, and where decisions are forced on people without consultation. People can be 'made', as we say, by their work, but they can also be destroyed by it.

Thirdly, **work is a means by which people can relate to God**. Something of God's nature is revealed in the world, and we can discover him as we explore it and work on it. Creative and skilled work brings us close to God. Music and art are well-known examples, and architecture too, but technology and administration that enhance human life, and open up new horizons for people, also have the divine within them. We can feel a sense of vocation not only in the calling to faith in God and to service in the work of the Church, but also in any activity which reveals God's providence and his care for people. We can love God as we love our neighbours. We can serve him not only **in** our secular jobs, as Luther said, but also **through** those jobs themselves, as Calvin put it.

Fourthly, **work needs to be balanced with periods of rest, enjoyment, fellowship and contemplation**. Work is not an end in itself; it has a purpose beyond itself. For the Jews the institution of the sabbath, and its strict observance, were a powerful witness to this truth. The first Christians seem quickly to have turned this seventh day into Sunday, the first day of the week, in order to celebrate Jesus' resurrection. It does not much matter which day is set aside for rest itself. There is nothing inherently special about Sunday for this purpose in the Christian Scriptures. What is important is that there should be a natural rhythm of work and rest, of creation and enjoyment. The early Christians chose Sunday as their day on which to assemble for fellowship and for worship.

In the cultural pluralism of our own day, different communities will look to different days to fulfil these purposes. For Christians the first day of the week is for worship; any day can be for rest, though it is convenient if the two coincide. Others will argue equally for Saturday or Friday. In this regard, much of the opposition in the Churches to Sunday trading has not been soundly based. It might be more in keeping with the biblical tradition to argue for a maximum working week for everyone – say of 48 hours as proposed within the European Community – so that work and rest can be genuinely secured for everyone, together with appropriate time off for people of faith to worship God on the days that their communities choose. The point is that work and rest should find a rhythm and balance in life, not that they should be allocated to particular days of the week.

The significance of human work is strongly reflected in the Bible. It provides for our basic needs; it enables us to use our energy and our creative skills; it is the basis of community life and of culture. It helps to make us who we are. It is a way in which we can love others. That is why unemployment is such a fearful thing for people. The cash sum that Robert received when he left the bank will help, but how long will it last, and what should his family best do with it? And what will happen to him as a person in the uncertain period before he finds another job? The fear that these questions bring with them for Robert and Jane and their children is something no society should readily tolerate.

MONEY AND POSSESSIONS

Some of the products of human work are consumed at once, like food. But others endure, like tables and chairs, and all the vast array of artifacts produced by modern industry today. The value of these products is represented by money, and accumulated over a period of time in the form of savings and capital. The products of work are possessions and money. How should they be used, and what attitude should Christians have to them?

This question became acute for Grace and George. For years Grace had looked after Emily in her large house. She was put upon mercilessly much of the time. She also turned a blind eye to the bottles of Guinness under the bed, to which Emily attributed her long life. One day, to their surprise, Grace and her husband George were left the house and a small fortune in Emily's will. It was untold wealth to them and, to start with, they hardly knew what to do with it. They went on a cruise round the world and bought a complete new wardrobe of clothes. But news got into the local paper, and begging letters started to arrive. In the end they wished they'd never had all that money; it only seemed to bring trouble.

But money and possessions are very popular with most people. The home is usually their most valuable asset. According to the government publication *Social Trends*, just over a third of all personal wealth in the United Kingdom is in dwellings. A quarter of the adult population now owns shares, a considerable increase since 1981, when it was only one in every thirteen. Marketable wealth, that is everything that can be sold, but excluding dwellings and pension rights, is quite unevenly distributed. The richest 1 per cent have nearly a fifth of it and the poorest 50 per cent have only 6 per cent between them. This general pattern of wealth distribution has changed very little in recent years. Nevertheless four-fifths of all households now have a freezer and nearly half have a microwave oven. Sixty per cent have a video and nearly a fifth a home computer (Central Statistical Office 1992: 101, 103,101, 108). Britain is not a poor country.

As with work, many people are ambivalent about money and possessions, and this uncertain attitude can be found deeply rooted in the ancient communities of which the Bible tells as well.

Wealth and its Dangers

In the Hebrew Scriptures wealth is seen as a blessing, and prosperity as a sign of God's favour, but it is fraught with danger, too. The story of the quarrel between Abel, a shepherd, and his brother Cain, an arable farmer, indicates the envy that uneven success in the accumulation of property produces. Cain is *'very angry and downcast'* that his offering is not accepted and he kills Abel. As a result he is cursed and work becomes labour for him. God says, *'When you till the ground it will no longer yield up its strength to you'* (Gen. 4:2–16). In this story the first sin seems to be the act of murder, rather than that of eating the forbidden fruit, as in Genesis 3. But in both cases disobedience lies at the heart of the matter.

In *Property and Riches in the Early Church*, the German theologian Martin Hengel notes that two theories were developed from this story. It was held, first, that private property – which led to the dispute between the brothers – came into being as a result of the fall. Before that there was no private ownership of wealth. Secondly, the idea arose that the private ownership of property had a secondary character to it by contrast with this earlier, or original state of equality. Private ownership was thus devalued. It had something sinful about it. Common ownership was superior. Hengel states that these ideas 'had great influence in the history of the Church' (Hengel 1974: 3). Negative attitudes to private wealth, therefore, have early origins.

But in the story in Genesis, Abraham became *'very rich in livestock, silver and gold'*, owning a number of slaves. He was able to offer generous hospitality to the three men who met him near the city of Sodom (Gen. 13:2, 17:6,27, 18:6–8, 18). The obligation to provide for strangers and travellers is strongly felt, and those who do not offer hospitality are condemned (Dt. 23:4–5). Hospitality cannot be extended without some wealth to make it possible.

In the Ten Commandments, stealing and coveting a neighbour's possessions are forbidden (Ex. 20:15,17; Dt. 5:19, 21). Wealth must clearly have been gained and unevenly distributed for this prohibition to have become necessary. It must have been accumulated even during the period of slavery in Egypt. In the desert, while Moses is absent, Aaron is able to collect more than enough in the form of gold rings from wives and sons and daughters to make a golden calf for the people to worship (Ex. 3:21–22, 32:2–4, 36:5–7).

In Leviticus, on the other hand, ownership is ultimately vested in God: '*Land will not be sold absolutely, for the land belongs to me, and you are only strangers and guests of mine*' (25:23). This principle lies behind the sabbatical regulation that every seventh year the land should lie fallow, and the jubilee regulation that every fiftieth year debts should be cancelled and any land that has been sold returned to the family to which it had originally been given (25:1–7,8–17). A hint that these sabbath regulations were not properly observed is contained in the following chapter. If the people are unfaithful various punishments will follow, and '*then the country will indeed observe its Sabbaths . . . It will rest, as it never did on your Sabbaths when you were living there*' (26:34–35).

In Deuteronomy, the promised land of Canaan is pictured in terms of great prosperity producing wheat, barley, vines, figs, pomegranates, olives, oil and honey. It is a land in which the people of Israel will '*eat bread without stint*' and '*want nothing*'. A warning is added, however, that when '*possessions grow great*', they are not to '*become proud of heart*' (8:7–14). They will be blessed and prosperous in every way, provided they keep the covenant faithfully with their God (28:1–14; Lev. 26:3–13).

Corruption

Something of the exploitation that often lies behind the accumulation of possessions appears in 1 Kings. Solomon's enormous wealth is carefully described, his daily provisions, his chariots and horses, his gold, his gold shields, his ivory throne, his tableware, his ships '*laden with gold and silver, ivory, apes and baboons*'. But it depended on destroying Canaanite towns and pressing foreigners into forced labour, as well as laying '*a cruel yoke*' on his own people, and eventually his kingdom is split up (5:1–8 [4:22–28 REB], 10:14–23, 9:15,21–22, 12:4).

Ecclesiasticus, in the Apocrypha, points to the practical difficulties of the business life: '*If you multiply your interests, you are bound to suffer for it . . .* ' (11:10). The different attitudes people have to rich and poor are well described. A rich man '*will make you feel small at his dinner parties and, having cleaned you out two or three times over, will end by laughing at you . . . If you are useful the rich will exploit you*' (13:2–7). The worry and the temptations of wealth are also set out: '*No one who loves money can easily avoid sinning . . . Happy the rich who is found to be blameless and does not go chasing after gold . . .* ' (31:1–11).

The prophets are very hard on those who are more interested in their own luxury than in honest dealing and the just treatment of the needy. Isaiah declares, '*Woe to those who enact unjust decrees . . . to deny justice to the weak . . . to make widows their prey and to rob the orphan*' (10:1–2). Jeremiah prophesies '*disaster for the man who builds his house without uprightness . . . who makes his fellow-man work for nothing, without paying him his wages*' (22:13). Hosea castigates merchants with '*fraudulent scales*' (12:8–9). Amos cries out against those who have '*sold the upright for silver and the poor for a pair of sandals*' (2:6). He condemns those who live in ostentatious luxury, '*lying on ivory beds*' and drinking '*wine by the bowlful*', and who can't wait to '*make the bushel-measure smaller and the shekel-weight bigger*' (6:4–6, 8:5). Micah also prophesies disaster for those who seize '*the fields that they covet*' and take over '*owner and house*' alike, '*the man himself as well as his inheritance*' (2:2). Habakkuk concludes gloomily, '*Now, surely, wealth is treacherous! He is arrogant, for ever on the move, with appetite . . . as insatiable as Death . . . Disaster to anyone who amasses ill-gotten gains . . .* ' (2:5–9).

These passages reflect the corruption that often comes with the making of money and the accumulation of possessions: idleness, greed, exploitation, the excessive concentration of wealth in few hands, lack of concern for the poor, fraud. But the basic goodness of prosperity is affirmed. Wealth is good, provided it is justly gained and all have fair access to it.

A Radical Criticism

The criticism of wealth is powerfully developed in the Gospels. Luke presents the theme most fully: Mary the mother of Jesus speaks of filling the starving with good things and sending '*the rich away empty*' (1:53). Jesus warns, '*Alas for you who are rich: you are having your consolation now*' (6:24). In the parable of the sower, some people are '*choked by the worries and riches and pleasures of life*' (Lk. 8:14; Mt. 13:7; Mk. 4:7). Jesus does not baulk at the symbolic destruction of a large herd of pigs, representing considerable wealth to their dismayed owners (Lk. 8:26–39; Mk. 5:1–20). He sends the Twelve out without staff, haversack, bread, money or spare tunic (Lk. 9:3; Mk. 6:8–9). The Seventy-two are to '*take no purse*' with them and to eat and drink whatever they are offered (Lk. 10:4–7).

Jesus refuses to arbitrate in a dispute over an inheritance. '*Watch*,' he says, '*and be on your guard against avarice of any kind, for life does not consist in possessions, even when someone has more than he needs*' (Lk. 12:13–15). The farmer who pulls down his barns and builds bigger ones is called a fool: '*This very night the demand will be made for your soul; and this hoard of yours, whose will it be then?*' The passage continues, '*So it is when someone stores up treasure for himself instead of becoming rich in the sight of God*' (12:16–21). Jesus tells his disciples to sit light to material things, for '*life is more than food, and the body more than clothing*' (12:22–23).

This theme, so critical of wealth itself as well as the attitude of over-dependence on it, continues relentlessly in Luke: '*Sell your possessions and give to those in need. Get yourselves purses that do not wear out, treasure that will not fail you, in heaven where no thief can reach it and no moth destroy it. For wherever your treasure is, that is where your heart will be too*' (12:33–34). '*None of you can be my disciple without giving up all that he owns*' (14:33). It is a profoundly challenging and uncompromising position to take.

101

The hostility to wealth is continued in more oblique terms. A father throws a feast for a son who has '*squandered his money on a life of debauchery*'; his return home far outweighs his misuse of the wealth (15:11–31). A rich man's steward is praised for letting debtors off with reduced payments (16:1–8). Money is called '*that tainted thing*', and it is to be used to win friends in case they are needed later on (16:9–12). Jesus declares roundly, '*You cannot be the slave both of God and of money*' (16:13). The Pharisees '*who loved money*' are condemned (16:14–15). A rich man suffers while Lazarus is received into Abraham's embrace in heaven (16:19–31). Jesus tells a ruler, '*Sell everything you own and distribute the money to the poor, and you will have treasure in heaven*', but he will not do so (18:18–23). He continues: '*How hard it is for those who have riches to make their way into the kingdom of God! Yes, it is easier for a camel to pass through the eye of a needle than for someone rich to enter the kingdom of God*' (18:24–25; Mk. 10:25).

Jesus sets the payment of taxes to Caesar in the context of the obligation towards God (Lk. 20:22–25; Mt. 22:15–22; Mk. 12:13–17). The widow throwing her coins into the Temple treasury is commended above the rich. They put in what they can spare, but she gives '*all she had to live on*' (Lk. 21:1–4; Mk. 12:41–44). Judas, who looks after the disciples' funds (Jn. 13:29), betrays Jesus for money (Lk. 22:3–6; Mt. 26:14–16; Mk. 14:10–11), and his death is vividly recorded in Matthew (27:3–10), and in Acts (1:15–19) also written by Luke. It is a powerful criticism of such a significant feature of everyday life.

Tithes and Alms

A more positive approach to the use of money is, however, suggested in other passages in Luke and in the other Gospels. Although Jesus has no home (Mt. 8:20; Lk. 9:58) and apparently carries no money with him (Mt. 22:19; Mk. 12:15; Lk. 20:24; Jn. 13:29), it is clear that he does not renounce material possessions altogether. Among his disciples are fishermen who own boats and employ people, and a tax official (Mk.1:20, 2:14). Although he calls them from this work, he makes no adverse comment on it. He relies on Martha and Mary, and those who follow him, for food and shelter (Lk. 10:38–40, 8:1–3). He goes to banquets with the rich (Mk. 2:15–17, 14:3–5; Lk. 7:36–37, 11:37, 14:1,12). He joins in a wedding feast (Jn. 2:1–10). He even gains a reputation 'as *a glutton and a drunkard*' (Mk. 11:19; Lk. 7:34). He knows a man with a room large enough for him to use for the passover meal with his disciples (Mt. 26:18; Mk. 14:15; Lk. 22:12). He is on familiar terms with the property-owning middle classes of his day, and by background was one of them.

Then tithes and taxes are to be paid. Tithing was a constant reminder that the land was a gift from God. Originally it involved dedicating to him the first-fruits of the fields and the first-born of the flocks and herds, and of the family. Later it seems to have been paid in money as a kind of tax. It was used to support the Levites, who did not have any land and provided the priestly functions of public worship (Num. 18:24). Every third year the tithes were to be given to support the stranger, the widow and the orphan (Dt. 14:28–29). The Pharisees were meticulous in paying tithes, a tenth part, on everything, though Jesus condemns them for neglecting '*justice and the love of God*' at the same time (Lk. 11:42, 18:12). He indicates that the Temple tax, and tribute to Caesar, are to be paid (Mt. 17:24–27).

Jesus also encourages almsgiving. Money and possessions are to be used for the poor. For Jews the giving of alms was a voluntary matter, in contrast to tithing, which was required. Proverbs gives the motive: '*Whoever is kind to the poor is lending to Yahweh, who will repay him the kindness done*' (19:17). The sense of reward or compensation for caring for those in need in this verse is reflected in the Christian Scriptures, too. The Pharisees are told to give alms from what they have, and '*everything will be clean*' for them (Lk. 11:41). Almsgiving should be done in secret and the Father '*will reward you*'. '*Your left hand must not know what your right is doing*' (Mt. 6:1–4). Those who give up everything – Luke says '*house, wife, brothers, parents or children*', and Matthew and Mark add '*sisters*' and '*land*' – will receive many times as much '*in this present age and, in the world to come, eternal life'* (Lk. 18:29; Mt. 19:29; Mk. 10:30). Salvation comes to Zacchaeus when he gives half his property to the poor and reimburses four-fold those he has cheated (Lk. 19:1–10).

There is a sense of service to those in need, as well. *'Give,'* Jesus says, *'to everyone who asks you, and do not ask for your property back from someone who takes it . . . Lend without any hope of return'* (Lk. 6:30–35; Mt. 5:42). The Samaritan who pays for the care of the man beaten up on the road to Jericho is commended (Lk. 10:29–37). In Matthew's picture of the Last Judgement the theme is well developed: those who care for the hungry, the thirsty, the stranger, those without clothing, the sick and the prisoner are told: *'In so far as you did this to one of the least of these brothers of mine, you did it to me'* (25:34–40).

Money also has other positive meanings: hidden treasure and a fine pearl are images for the kingdom of heaven (Mt. 13:44–45). In the parable of the talents in Luke, the servants who trade with the money given to them receive more, while the one who simply puts it away safely loses what was given to him (19:11–27). The hint that he might have put it in the bank and then *'drawn it out with interest'* (19:23) was subsequently used as tacit approval for usury, although this was in theory forbidden by the Church from the earliest times until the Reformation period.

The overwhelming theme of these passages, however, is one of fundamental conflict between following Jesus and owning possessions. It is not that wealth itself is rejected, but its consequences. It draws people away from God. It is a hindrance to religious commitment. The picture in the Gospels is deeply critical of the financial concerns of those in authority at the time. In this respect Jesus stands firmly in the tradition of the Hebrew prophets. Martin Hengel explains the reasoning that lies behind this radical criticism of riches like this: 'Jesus attacks mammon with the utmost severity where it has captured men's hearts, because this gives it demonic character by which it blinds men's eyes to God's will – in concrete terms, to their neighbour's needs' (Hengel 1974: 30).

Sharing Resources

The way in which the first Christians understood the implications of this powerful theme in Jesus' ministry can be seen
in Acts. All those who shared the faith *'owned everything in
common'*. They *'sold their goods and possessions and distributed
the proceeds among themselves according to what each one needed'*
(2:44–45). The whole group was *'united, heart and soul; no one
claimed private ownership of any possessions, as everything they
owned was held in common'*. Barnabas is mentioned as one of
those who sold land or houses and pooled their resources so
that *'none of their members was ever in want'* (4:32–37). The
German theologian Ernst Troeltsch used the phrase 'love
communism' to describe this practice (Hengel 1974: 31).

The sharing of resources in this way was not without its
problems. In Acts, Ananias and Sapphira try to keep something back for themselves, and the shock of being found out
leads to their death (5:1–11). What they had done broke the
fellowship.

A collection is made in Jerusalem for Judaean Christians
at a time of famine and delivered by Paul and Barnabas (Acts
11:28–30), but such collections needed careful handling. Paul
himself may have been criticized for the way things were
sometimes done (1 Cor. 9:3–14). Nor did wealthy Christians
always sell up. Some of them used their possessions in other
ways instead. Mary the mother of John Mark is mentioned
by name as one who made her home available as a meeting
place for prayer and fellowship (Acts 12:12). The love communism, influenced perhaps by the belief that the Lord was
soon to return and that possessions had little meaning in such
a context, seems not to have lasted long in the Church.

This same concern for mutual support is shown in
Romans. Paul advises, *'Share with any of God's holy people
who are in need; look for opportunities to be hospitable'* (12:13).
He mentions a generous collection made in Macedonia and
Achaea for *'the poor among God's holy people at Jerusalem'*
(15:26). In 1 Corinthians, there is a sign that almsgiving is
being put on a more formal basis. *'On the first day of the
week,'* Paul writes, *'each of you should put aside and reserve as*

105

much as each can spare' (16:2). In 2 Corinthians, the language becomes more metaphorical. Paul speaks of himself as *'poor and yet making many people rich; having nothing, and yet owning everything'*. Using the same image, he speaks of the generosity of Christ: *'Although he was rich, he became poor for your sake, so that you should become rich through his poverty'* (6:10, 8:9).

But how generous should people be? The question is considered in a number of passages. In 2 Corinthians, the Macedonian Christians have *'overflowed in a wealth of generosity'*, and made their gift *'which was not merely as far as their resources would allow, but well beyond their resources'*. Paul corrects this enthusiasm. Their giving should be so far as *'resources permit'*. They are not to relieve the needs of others and leave themselves in hardship. Twice he says, *'There should be a fair balance'*. The REB uses the word *'equality'* in its translation here. One's surplus meets another's deficit (8:1–15).

Giving should be voluntary. *'Each one'*, Paul continues in 2 Corinthians, *'should give as much as he has decided on his own initiative, not reluctantly or under compulsion, for God loves a cheerful giver'* (9:7). It should also overflow *'into widespread thanksgiving to God'* (9:11–12).

Like Jesus, Paul relies on financial help from those with enough to give (Phil. 2:25, 4:15), though he continues to support himself through his own trade (1 Cor. 9:15). He seems to have learnt to be content with whatever level of support he receives (Phil. 4:11–14). Although there were not many educated or influential people in the Church, or many from *'noble families'* (1 Cor. 1:26), there were some prominent and wealthy people involved in business and trade among them. Several are specifically mentioned: Aquila and Priscilla, Crispus a president of the synagogue (Acts 18:2–3, 8), Erastus a city treasurer (Rom. 16:23), and Philemon a slave-owner. It is clear that Paul is grateful to them for the material support they are able to give.

In 1 Timothy, the theme of contentment is also mentioned: *'We brought nothing into the world and we can take nothing out of it; but as long as we have food and clothing, we shall be content with that. People who long to be rich are a prey to trial; they get trapped into all sorts of foolish and harmful ambitions which plunge people into ruin and destruction.'* The passage continues in words that have become famous, and are often misquoted: *'The love of money is the root of all evils'* (6:7–10). It is not money itself that is condemned.

A number of other references remain to be mentioned. In Hebrews, hospitality to strangers is commended (13:2). In James, those who contemplate going off for a year trading and making money are warned of the uncertainties of life: *'Well now, you rich! Lament, weep for the miseries that are coming to you . . . '* The corruption of wealth and possessions and the exploitation of those by whose labour it has been gained is strongly put in language reminiscent of the prophets (4:13—5:6). In 1 John, almsgiving flows from love: *'If anyone is well-off in worldly possessions and sees his brother in need but closes his heart to him, how can the love of God be remaining in him?'* (3:17). Finally, in the letter to the church in Laodicea near the beginning of Revelation, relying on riches is roundly condemned (3:17–19).

The Common Good

The subsequent history of Christian attitudes to money and possessions has been rich and varied. In *Ownership: Early Christian Teaching*, The Latin American liberation theologian Charles Avila describes how the early Fathers of the Church developed these themes from the Bible. In the second century Clement of Alexandria echoed Stoic opinion in speaking of self-sufficiency – *autarkeia* in Greek. For this to be achieved, 'a standard of living enabling one to lead a life consonant with human dignity' so as not to be a burden on others, is required and an equal fellowship – *koinonia* – that 'abolishes the differentiation between the few rich who wallow in luxury and the "so many who labour in poverty" '. Clement calls these the 'twin goals of material wealth' (Avila 1983: 36, 40, 43).

In the fourth century John Chrysostom describes owning 'more than necessity demands' as a form of theft. To fail to share with the needy was to be a robber. All have an equal

107

right, he declares, to breathe the air, till the land, use water, and bask in the rays of the sun (Avila 1983: 84, 104). In the following century Augustine condemned private property as the chief enemy of peace and as the cause of wars and discords, injustices and murders. He was particularly concerned with the right use of wealth and founded monastic communities and almshouses as an organized vehicle for the sharing of goods. Augustine writes, 'He who uses his wealth badly possesses it wrongfully, and wrongful possession means that it is another's property' (Avila 1983: 121, 123, 133).

In the Reformation period the accumulation and use of wealth preoccupied Protestant minds as well. In *The Wealth of Christians*, Redmond Mullin gives some examples. Martin Luther finds it necessary to write: 'Buying and selling are necessary. They cannot be dispensed with and can be practised in a Christian manner.' Calvin was among those ready to allow the practice of usury, provided the rates of interest charged were not excessive and charity was observed. The seventeenth-century Diggers even regarded the collective manuring of common lands to help the poor, who relied on such land for food and grazing, as a religious act. John Wesley tried to resolve the problem of wealth by urging: 'Gain all you can . . . Save all you can . . . Give all you can' (Mullin 1983: 90, 92,112, 93).

In the nineteenth-century papal encyclical *Rerum Novarum*, Leo XIII argued strongly in favour of private property. 'Every man', he declares, 'has by nature the right to possess property as his own.' It 'cannot but be just'. Private ownership must be held 'sacred and inviolable'. But he also quotes Thomas Aquinas in qualification of this right: 'Man should not consider his material possessions as his own, but as common to all, so as to share them without hesitation when others are in need' (Pope Leo XIII 1891: 10, 12, 34, 20). In the encyclical *Laborem Exercens*, John Paul II summarizes Roman Catholic teaching in the blunt sentence: 'The right to private property is subordinated to the right to common use' (Pope John Paul II 1981: 51). The creation of wealth and the private ownership of possessions are permitted, but only in so far as they serve the common good and benefit the community as a whole.

Themes

Four themes emerge from this review of references to money and possessions in the Bible and the Christian tradition. First, **material prosperity is part of God's intention for humankind**. The ancient covenant relationship holds out abundance of wealth and possessions to the people of Israel, provided they are faithful to God. The earth is to be fruitful; wealth is the result of work. Jesus does not seem to question this fundamental attitude. He mixes easily with the rich of his day and relies on their hospitality and support. Many of the earliest churches are in the homes of the well-off. Without wealth human needs cannot be met, and the poor cannot be helped.

But secondly, **there is a strong awareness of the corrupting potential of money and possessions**. The prophets are loud in their condemnation of luxurious living for the rich while the poor continue to suffer. Jesus points to the harmful effects that riches can have on people. The greed, the injustice, the lack of human concern for those affected as wealth is accumulated, and the insensitivity to human need that so often accompanies it, is condemned.

The dilemma that is posed by these two conflicting forces is resolved, thirdly, by **the repeated demand that wealth should be shared**. This is partly a matter of charity, of love, but it is also a matter of justice. It is not to be left to the free choice of the individual alone; it is to be structured into the workings of the community itself. This is the significance of the ancient provision that the tithes every third year, and the produce of the land in sabbath years and at the jubilee, should be for the poor and the needy. The first Christians held their property in common and made collections to help other Christians. Everyone is to have enough for their needs. They are to be self-sufficient and to share any surplus, and such sharing is a prerequisite of fellowship. Where it is not practised, fellowship is broken. But the sharing of wealth is to be exercised with a sense of proportion; money and possessions are not to be given away to such an extent that the immediate family is left without.

Fourthly, there is a sense that **the sharing of wealth, giving it away in response to human need, is a virtuous act**. It will bring a spiritual reward. Such generosity should not lead to any enhanced personal reputation, but to the giving of thanks to God. It should turn people towards God: any reward that comes will be in secret.

In comparison with this powerful tradition Emily misused the position that her money gave her and exploited those who looked after her. But when they inherited her fortune, a new life was opened up for Grace and George. It gave them a dignity and a self-confidence they had never known before, though this was sadly darkened by the publicity, and the greed of others. Creating, using and sharing wealth is as troubled an aspect of human life and human relationships now as it has ever been.

THE POOR

What does it mean to be poor? For most of their lives Grace and George owned nothing, though they lived in a big house. They didn't feel in any way deprived. Frank, on the other hand, was a man of no fixed address and lived on the streets. When his mother died and he lost his job as a bus driver, there was nothing left for him but a life of vagrancy. He was often seen around the town, by the bus-stops, in the shopping centre, outside the railway station, in the pews of churches of all denominations. One morning he was found dead on a bench, alone, without possessions or support. Louise went to his funeral together with many others, for he had had a cheery wave and a touch of the forelock for those he knew. She felt embarrassed that they had not been able to do more for him while he was alive.

Poverty is hard to define. The famine and disaster-ridden countries of Africa and Asia know absolute poverty. People do not even have enough to supply their basic needs. For others poverty is a relative matter. The very rich often think they are poor when they have to sell a Gainsborough to pay for the upkeep of the family estate, but compared with the rest of the country, they are well-off indeed.

The sociologist Peter Townsend argues that poverty is best defined as 'relative deprivation'. In *Poverty in the United Kingdom*, he writes: 'Individuals, families and groups in the population can be said to be in poverty when they lack the resources to obtain the type of diet, participate in the activities and have the living conditions and amenities which are customary, or at least widely encouraged and approved, in the societies to which they belong.' Townsend goes into immense detail in trying to measure what he calls 'multiple deprivation', listing 60 categories under the following twelve headings: dietary, clothing, fuel and light, household facilities, housing conditions and amenities, conditions at work (severity, security, amenities and welfare benefits), health, educational, environmental, family, recreational, and social. He finds a point at which, as income diminishes, people 'drop out or are excluded' from the normal style of living of their communities (Townsend 1979: 31, 173–176, 249).

In Britain, poverty is not just a question of lack of money, it includes the exclusion, the isolation, that comes with the lack of resources. A man may, for example, enjoy a few pints of beer with his friends, but when he can no longer afford to stand his round, he stops going to the pub altogether. He loses human contact, fellowship, and the downward spiral of material poverty gains an additional and vicious social twist. Frank knew the reality of this. People may have greeted him hurriedly in the street, but no one really knew where he spent the night, or felt able to enquire.

Oppression

A variety of words are used in the Hebrew Scriptures to refer to the poor. In *A Theology of Liberation*, the Latin American theologian Gustavo Gutierrez gives the details. The most frequently used word – *ani* in Hebrew – means 'the bent over one, the one labouring under a weight, the one not in

111

possession of his whole strength and vigour, the humiliated one'. Then there is *ebyon*, meaning 'the one who desires, the beggar, the one who is lacking something and awaits it from another'. Other words include *dal*, 'the weak one, the frail one, the poor of the land' (Gutierrez 1974: 291, 303).

These three words alone appear 189 times, so great was the ancient Hebrew concern about the poor. They suggest oppression, deprivation, powerlessness. They indicate that poverty is an economic and social matter. Its existence raises questions about justice, about the way society is structured. Poverty is not a personal failing; it is primarily a failure of community.

In Exodus, the commandment not to steal is uncompromisingly stated (20:15), and much else follows from it. Freedom and human dignity are not to be stolen from people. Slaves are to be freed after seven years, widows and orphans are not to be ill-treated, the poor are not to be cheated of their rights at law, the alien is not to be oppressed (21:2, 22:21, 23:6–9). The poor, and wild animals, are to have whatever the land produces naturally in a sabbath year (23:11). At the jubilee people are to return to their ancestral property, and in between, families are to have the first right of redemption over any land sold (Lev. 25:13,24–25). In this way poverty is not to be institutionalized in society. Every so often the slate is to be wiped clean.

There is also a general duty to help the poor so that the covenant community is not broken: '*If your brother becomes impoverished and cannot support himself in the community, you will assist him as you would a stranger or guest, so that he can go on living with you*' (Lev. 25:35). If a fellow-Hebrew has to sell himself to work for another because of poverty, he is not to do the work of a slave, but to be treated '*like an employee or guest*', and released at the jubilee (25:39–41). In Deuteronomy, particular groups are to receive special help. At the end of every three years the tithe is to go to '*the foreigner, the orphan and the widow*' in the community, as well as to the Levites (14:28–29). A sheaf overlooked at harvest-time, as well as olives and grapes, are to be left for these same groups (24:19–21; Lev. 19:9–10). Crops at the field-edges are also for *'the poor and the stranger'* (Lev. 23:22). It is a simple form of wealth distribution in favour of the poor, that avoids any patronizing relationship between giver and receiver.

Debt

The problem of debt seems to have been particularly worrying in ancient Israel, and various provisions are made about it. Charging interest on loans to fellow-countrymen is forbidden. Exodus states: *'If you lend money to any of my people, to anyone poor among you, you will not play the usurer with him: you will not demand interest from him'* (22:24). The passage continues: *'If you take someone's cloak in pledge, you will return it to him at sunset. It is all the covering he has; it is the cloak he wraps his body in; what else will he sleep in?'* (22:25–26). Leviticus states, *'Fear your God, and let your brother live with you. You will not lend him money on interest, or give him food to make a profit out of it'* (25:35–37). Deuteronomy also includes the prohibition of usury within the community, but adds that charging interest on loans to foreigners is allowed (23:20–21).

The human concern for a fellow-member of the community is such that the full rigours of debt are to be softened. In Deuteronomy, debt is to be remitted at the end of every seven years: *'Any creditor holding a personal pledge obtained from his fellow must release him from it; he must not exploit his fellow or his brother . . . '*, though *'a foreigner you may exploit'* (15:1–3). But lending is, nevertheless, still encouraged. Deuteronomy continues: *'Is there anyone poor among you . . . Do not harden your heart or close your hand against that poor brother of yours, but be open handed with him and lend him enough for his needs'* (15:7–10). The objective is clear: *'There must, then, be no poor among you.'* These provisions are necessary because, as a practical reality, *'there will never cease to be poor people in the country'* (15:4,11).

Detailed rules are also set out in Deuteronomy to control loans, and wages: *'No one may take a mill or a millstone in pledge; that would be to take a life itself . . . If you are making your brother a loan on pledge, you must not go into his house and*

113

seize the pledge . . . You must stay outside, and the man . . . must bring the pledge out to you . . . If the man is poor, you must not go to bed with his pledge in your possession; you must return it to him at sunset so that he can sleep in his cloak and bless you . . . You must not exploit a poor and needy wage-earner, be he one of your brothers or a foreigner resident in your community. You must pay him his wages each day . . . You must not take a widow's clothes in pledge . . . ' (24:6,10–15,17).

Nehemiah records an incident where debt has clearly got out of hand. During a famine when the walls of Jerusalem are being rebuilt, some people were pledging their sons and daughters and mortgaging their fields, vineyards and houses '*to get enough grain to eat*'. Others were borrowing on their fields and vineyards '*to pay the royal tax*'. Even selling children into slavery is being contemplated. Nehemiah protests: '*What you are doing is wrong . . . Let us cancel these pledges . . .* ' The creditors agree. '*We shall make restitution . . . We shall claim nothing more from them*', they say (5:1–12).

In the Christian Scriptures Jesus teaches his disciples to pray, '*Forgive us our debts . . .* ' (Mt. 6:12; Lk. 11:3–4), though this may have a broader reference to sins in general. Debt is forgiven in the story of the crafty steward who lets his master's debtors off with partial payments (Lk.16:1–8). The same point in reverse is made in Matthew, where an unforgiving debtor is punished for failing to be generous to a fellow-servant who owed him a small sum (18:23–35).

In *Families in Debt*, the Jubilee Centre states that in prohibiting interest within the community, though not outside it, Israel was 'unique among societies in the Ancient Near East' (Hartropp 1988: 142). In keeping with this tradition, however, interest was officially banned on loans within the Christian community and then, from the fourth century, on all loans, though ways were found of getting round this. In the fifteenth century Calvin was prominent among some reformers who permitted interest. Times had changed. He writes, 'Usury is not now unlawful except in so far as it contravenes equity and brotherly union' (Hartropp 1988: 145). But he was still against taking interest from the poor.

Usury was finally made legal in England in 1572, though

the Roman Catholic Church continued to oppose it until 1854. Now no Christian Church argues for a total ban on this practice, though there are often strong demands that Third World debt should be written off or re-scheduled, and that interest-free loans should be made. Usury was resisted in Israel because it tended to reinforce poverty and enslave people once again. God had, after all, brought his people out of slavery in Egypt. It also deprived them of the fullness of God's blessing on their labours, and it divided society into rich and poor, powerful and powerless. It split the covenant community. Although extending credit to people makes business and industry possible for those who do not have capital, and not just for the rich who do, debt can still have the same damaging effects on society today as it did in ancient times.

Injustice and Exploitation

The causes of poverty are clearly indicated in numerous passages. Job, for example, reflects current experience in one of his speeches: '*The wicked move boundary-marks . . . They drive away the orphan's donkey, as security, they seize the widow's ox . . .* ' As a result of such corruption and heartlessness the needy find themselves '*searching from dawn for food . . . They go about naked, lacking clothes, and starving while they carry the sheaves . . .* '. Even '*the child of the poor is exacted as security . . .*' (24:2–9).

It is fair to note, however, that certain personal attitudes also help to cause poverty. Proverbs observes: '*A little folding of the arms to lie back, and poverty comes like a vagrant and, like a beggar, dearth*' (6:10–11). The same point is made again and again: '*A slack hand brings poverty . . . Poverty is the undoing of the weak . . . Idle talk brings only want . . . Pleasure-lovers stay poor . . . In autumn the idler does not plough, at harvest time he looks – nothing there!*' (10:4,15, 14:23, 21:17, 20:4).

In the Psalms, poverty is a question of justice. The king is to '*ride on in the cause of truth, gentleness and uprightness*', and God is asked to endow the king with '*fair judgement*' so that he can *'judge the poor of the people'* with justice, and *'save the children of the needy and crush their oppressors'* (45:3, 72:1–3).

The prophets turn their attention ferociously to denouncing injustice to the poor. In a powerful passage Isaiah cries, *'Cease doing evil. Learn to do good, search for justice, discipline the violent, be just to the orphan, plead for the widow'* (1:16–17). He continues: oppressors pillage and extortioners rule, vineyards are ravaged, and the *'spoils of the poor'* are in their houses. *'By what right,'* Yahweh asks, *'do you crush my people and grind the faces of the poor?'* (3:12–15). *'Woe to those who enact unjust decrees . . . to deny justice to the weak,'* the prophecy continues, *'and to cheat the humblest of my people of fair judgement . . . '* (10:1–2). Is not the sort of fast that pleases Yahweh: *'to break unjust fetters, to undo the thongs of the yoke, to let the oppressed go free, and to break all yokes? Is it not sharing your food with the hungry, and sheltering the homeless poor; if you see someone lacking clothes, to clothe him, and not to turn away from your own kin?'* (58:6–7). Isaiah's message of restitution itself indicates how the poor were treated: *'The spirit of Lord Yahweh is on me . . . He has sent me to bring the news to the afflicted, to soothe the broken-hearted, to proclaim liberty to captives, release to those in prison, to proclaim a year of favour from Yahweh and a day of vengeance for our God, to comfort all who mourn . . . '* (61:1–2). Jeremiah, too, cries out for fair treatment, and an end to the exploitation of the stranger, the orphan and the widow (7:5–6, 22:3).

Other ways in which the poor are exploited are condemned in passage after passage in the prophetic writings. Fraudulent commerce is denounced (Jer 5:27–28; Hos. 12:8; Amos 8:5; Mic. 6:9–12), as well as the hoarding of land (Mic. 2:1–3), dishonest courts (Isa. 5:23, 10:2; Amos 5:12; Mic. 3:9–11), the failure to pay workers' wages (Jer. 22:13), the violence of rulers (Amos 4:1; Mic. 6:12), selling the poor into slavery (Amos 2:6, 8:6), and imposing unjust taxation (Amos 5:11). The passages that protest against the oppression of the poor are as colourful as any in the Bible.

The Humble

There is, however, another word for the poor – *anaw* in Hebrew – which has a more religious meaning, 'humble before God' (Gutierrez 1974: 291, 303). It is used 25 times. Moses is said to be *'extremely humble, the humblest man on earth'* (Num. 12:3). The Messiah will be *'humble and riding on a donkey'* (Zech. 9:9). In the Psalms, the close relationship between Yahweh and the spiritually poor, the humble, is often reflected: *'Yahweh is near to the broken-hearted, he helps those whose spirit is crushed'* (34:18). The opposite is wickedness, not wealth (37:10–11), and arrogance (86:1,14). In Isaiah, Yahweh says, *'My eyes are drawn to the person of humbled and contrite spirit, who trembles at my word'* (66:2).

Because of Israel's repeated infidelity, the prophets develop the idea of a small, faithful remnant, with whom there will be a new covenant. Then the law will be written on people's hearts (Jer. 31:33). In Ezekiel, Yahweh says, *'I shall give you a new heart, and put a new spirit in you'* (36:26–27). In Zephaniah, this remnant is the poor: *'Seek Yahweh all you humble of the earth, who obey his commands. Seek uprightness, seek humility . . . '* The prophecy continues in the voice of Yahweh, *'In you I shall leave surviving a humble and lowly people, and those who are left in Israel will take refuge in the name of Yahweh'* (2:3, 3:12–13). In these passages poverty is the opposite of pride, rather than of riches. It is a pre-condition for approaching God.

The Poor and the Poor in Spirit

These two understandings of poverty also appear in the Christian Scriptures. The one who is materially poor – *ptokos* in Greek – is the 'one who does not have what is necessary to subsist, the wretched one driven into begging' (Gutierrez 1974: 291, 303). The word appears 34 times.

Concern for the poor in this sense occurs throughout the Gospels. It is the fact that *'the good news is proclaimed to the poor'* that indicates the status of Jesus as the Messiah (Mt. 11:5; Lk. 72:22). The disciples want the alabaster jar of

117

expensive ointment sold and '*the money given to the poor*', though Jesus resists this and says, echoing Deuteronomy 15, '*You have the poor with you always, but you will not always have me*' (Mt. 26:8–11; Mk. 14:4–7; Jn. 12:4–8). In the great vision of the Last Judgement in Matthew, those who have helped the hungry, the thirsty, the stranger, the naked, and who have visited the sick and the prisoner are those who receive the kingdom as their heritage. When this is questioned the king says, '*In so far as you did this to one of the least of these brothers of mine, you did it to me* ' (25:31–46).

A rich young man is urged to sell what he owns and '*give the money to the poor*' (Mk. 10:21; Lk. 18:22). A poverty-stricken widow casting two small coins into the Temple treasury is commended (Mk. 12:41–44; Lk. 21:1–4). In Luke, the most socially concerned of the Gospels, it is '*the poor, the crippled, the lame, the blind*' who are to be invited to a party. And one of Judas' functions, as keeper of the disciples' purse, is assumed to be giving to the poor (Jn. 13:29).

The theme of compensation, apparent in Matthew 25, also appears here. Commending the host who invites such people, the passage continues mysteriously, '*Then you will be blessed, for they have no means to repay you and so you will be repaid when the upright rise again*' (Lk. 14:12–14,16–24). The poor man Lazarus goes to Abraham's embrace when he dies, while the rich man languishes in Hades (16:19–31). It is to the poor that Zacchaeus gives back what he has wrongly taken from them (Lk. 19:8).

From the earliest days in the Church the poor, and widows, are helped through the sharing of possessions and the making of collections in time of need (Acts 2:44, 4:32–35, 6:1, 11:28–30; Rom. 15:26; 2 Cor. 8:1–3). In Galatians, Christians are reminded to help the poor (2:10). In James, '*pure, unspoilt religion, in the eyes of God*' is said to be '*going to the help of orphans and widows in their hardships*' (1:27). In the religious community the poor are to be given just as much notice as the wealthy, and the openness of the poor to the gospel is contrasted with the arrogance of the rich (2:1–9).

An echo of the distinction between those who are economically poor and those whose poverty is to be understood as

118

humility appears in the Beatitudes. In Matthew, these words are used: '*How blessed are the poor in spirit: the kingdom of heaven is theirs. Blessed are the gentle: they shall have the earth as inheritance*' (5:3–4). The word translated gentle – *praus* in Greek – matches the Hebrew word *anaw* in the psalm which is being quoted (37:11). The poor in spirit are those who are humble before God, completely open to him and dependent on him. The version in Luke, however, says simply, '*How blessed are you who are poor: the kingdom of God is yours*' (6:20).

Luke's emphasis on the blessedness of material poverty fits well with the condemnation of riches found so often in this Gospel. In his interpretation of this passage Gustavo Gutierrez says that the poor are blessed, 'because the coming of the Kingdom will put an end to their poverty by creating a world of brotherhood' (Gutierrez 1974: 298). Earlier, in the synagogue, Jesus had said, quoting from Isaiah 61: '*The spirit of the Lord is on me, for he has anointed me to bring good news to the afflicted . . . liberty to captives, sight to the blind, to let the oppressed go free . . .*' (Lk. 4:18). The link between faithful dependence on God, and liberation from material poverty and oppression, which is made so often in the Bible, gives Luke's version of these words a particular power.

The theme of spiritual humility or meekness – *tapeinos* in Greek – occurs in other passages. Anyone who would enter the kingdom of heaven is to make himself '*as little*' as a child (Mt. 18:4). Jesus says, '*Anyone who raises himself up will be humbled, and anyone who humbles himself will be raised up*' (Mt. 23:12; Lk. 14:11, 18:14). The same word is used in a significant passage in Philippians on the self-emptying of Christ in the incarnation. '*He emptied himself,*' Paul writes, '*taking the form of a slave . . . he was humbler yet, even to accepting death . . .*' (2:7–8). In 2 Corinthians, Paul uses the word of his own attitude, calling himself '*the one who is so humble when he is facing you . . .*' (10:1). Such gentleness is one of the fruits of the Spirit (Gal. 5:22–23). The theme occurs again and again (Gal. 6:1; Eph. 4:2; Col. 3:12; 1 Tim. 6:11; 2 Tim. 2:25; Titus 3:2; Jas. 1:21, 3:13, 4:10). 1 Peter, quoting Proverbs (3:34), urges humility because '*God opposes the proud but accords his favour to the humble*' (5:5).

119

A Bias to the Poor

In the subsequent history of the Church both these ideas find a continuing place. On the one hand, concern for the materially poor has made charity a major Christian virtue. The provision of immediate help to relieve suffering, and of medical care and education, and the long struggle to abolish slavery, so significant in Victorian times, have all had their roots in this theme from the Bible. The contemporary concern with aid for developing countries, and for those suffering from famine and other disasters, also finds its motivation here.

In the last 30 years liberation theology has put a powerful new emphasis on the poor and their place in God's concern. Gutierrez identifies the poor in wider, more political or economic terms. He writes: 'The "poor" person today is the oppressed one, the one marginated from society, the member of the proletariat struggling for his most basic rights; he is the exploited and plundered social class, the country struggling for its liberation' (Gutierrez 1974: 301). In the papal encyclical *Solicitudo Rei Socialis*, John Paul II writes of 'the option or love of preference for the poor . . . a special form of primacy in the exercise of Christian charity' (Pope John Paul II 1988: 84).

The report of the Archbishop of Canterbury's Commission on Urban Priority Areas, *Faith in the City*, gives a detailed analysis of poverty and deprivation in Britain, and makes a large number of recommendations under the following eight headings: urban policy, poverty, employment and work, housing, health, social care and community work, education and young people, and order and law. The report concludes, 'A growing number of people are excluded by poverty or powerlessness from sharing in the common life of our nation . . . The present situation demands an urgent response from the Church and from the government' (Church of England ACUPA 1985: 359). Through the Church Urban Fund, set up as a result of the report, and similar funds in other Churches, numerous projects have

120

been started in inner city areas and on housing estates. The poor are being 'empowered', and not just offered charity.

On the other hand, the sense of uncertainty about wealth and the tradition of humility and openness to God have also found a place. From the earliest times the monastic movement has given expression to the desire to renounce personal material possessions and to live a life of sharing and fellowship. In the Reformation period the adoption of a simple lifestyle by the Puritans, and by other sectarian groups, has also sprung from this same motive. The call today to adopt a less stressful, more ecologically aware, less materially wasteful way of living, and to resist excessive consumerism, also finds its roots here. Poverty, simplicity and openness, when they are willingly embraced, enable an uncluttered appreciation of God.

Themes

Three themes emerge from the many references to the poor in the pages of the Bible. First, **material poverty is unacceptable**. It is oppressive and divisive when it is forced on people. It splits families and breaks the cohesion of the community. It is a denial of the national unity and the prosperity that belongs to the covenant relationship with God. It is not for some to keep excessive wealth to themselves, or to take it for themselves, while others suffer with nothing.

Gutierrez makes the same point for our own day in these words: 'The existence of poverty represents a sundering both of solidarity among men and of communion with God. Poverty is an expression of sin, that is, a negation of love . . . Poverty is an evil, a scandalous condition . . . To eliminate it is to bring closer the moment of seeing God face to face, in union with other men' (Gutierrez 1974: 295–296). The Scottish Churches' report *Just Sharing* puts it in similar words: 'Fair sharing encourages love and community; unfair distribution is disruptive of fellowship' (Forrester and Skene 1988: 80). In the early Church the concept of fellowship – *koinonia* in Greek – is clearly more than a spiritual one; it involves economic equality and the practical sharing of possessions as well. It goes well beyond earlier provisions for correcting gross inequality and for softening the full rigours of poverty, when it arose.

Secondly, **poverty is to be dealt with as a matter of justice, through formal arrangements that are part of the structure of society, and not merely by individual charity on a voluntary basis**. Certain groups in the community are singled out for special provision: the stranger, the orphan, the widow, those who are in debt, the starving, those suffering from famine, the prisoner. Without formal help such relatively powerless groups might well suffer greatly. The poor have a dignity as persons like everyone else; they are not to be driven mercilessly into the ground. The pressures which produced poverty in ancient Israel are constantly criticized by the prophets. The hint that sabbath and jubilee provisions were not observed also indicates the persistent and deep-seated reluctance of people to share what they have, instead of keeping it all for themselves. Without public provision poverty can destroy people.

Thirdly, **concern for the poor stretches beyond the care of the immediate family or group**. Although there is a constant emphasis on looking after their own poor, the whole nation was the covenant community in ancient Israel. Everyone within its borders, even the stranger and the visitor, was embraced within the structure of social care. In the early Church support was offered to the needy, regardless of where the congregation was to be found. Those early Christian congregations extended their concern for the poor beyond national boundaries, though they were as yet too fragile to extend it much further. But it was not many centuries before Church and state were one and the same structure, and the care of the whole community fell on the Church. Christians who stand in this tradition have no cause to restrict their concern today to members of their own religion or of their own nation. The whole world is now one interdependent community in a way that it has never been before. Christian love knows no boundaries.

The tragedy of Frank lies in the fact that his real aloneness, his deprivation, was masked by the familiarity of his presence around the town and in the pew. Christian fellowship is to extend beyond the cheery wave into a structured sharing of resources, so that no one is ever in need while others have more than enough. And the example that is set within the community of the Church is to be a pattern for the world as a whole. Our God is not a 'tribal' deity; he is the God of the whole creation, and his love extends to all.

5.

THE NATURAL ENVIRONMENT

In one of his poems Tennyson has some words that have become famous. He writes about man,

> Who trusted God was love indeed
> And love Creation's final law—
> Tho' Nature, red in tooth and claw
> With ravine, shriek'd against his creed—

For Tennyson the violence of the natural world seems to contradict the idea of a God of compassion and love (*In Memoriam*: Canto lvi). If God loves his creation, why has he made it like this? The view that nature is 'red in tooth and claw' is also sometimes quoted to support the opinion that if this is how things are, human beings should not be expected to be any different.

The apparent brutality of nature has been amply illustrated by regular popular wildlife programmes on television. One by one every creature seems to prey upon another, and be preyed upon in its turn. In one shocking programme whales were seen eating seal pups after beating them to death on the beach.

What sort of attitude should Christians have, then, to the natural environment? Should we 'go green', join conservation groups, use unleaded petrol, recycle our newspapers and our bottles? Should we seek to get rid of factory-farming and ban blood sports? People often get very emotional about these things and the need to think them through carefully is important. In this chapter, therefore, I want to look at the whole matter of ecology, and then at the treatment of animals.

124

ECOLOGY

A growing number of people go into the countryside at weekends to get fresh air and peace. John, for example, likes to go on long-distance walks with Christopher. One Saturday in Great Monk Wood, he was moved by the size of the trees and their obvious age, and by the atmosphere created by shafts of sunlight glancing through the leaves. The pollarding of hornbeams had produced gnarled tree-trunks with slim branches like fingers reaching towards the sky. Satanic rituals were thought to take place in this part of the forest, but John felt more of a shudder going through him from the shadows and the shapes of the trees. It was a place of splendour, of mystery, even of religious awe. Great Monk Wood is well named.

The popular attitude to the environment is full of contra-dictions. People love to walk in the woods, but trees are being cut down world-wide at an alarming rate. They go out into the fields with their children, but the relentless demand for houses and roads, and economic growth, buries those fields under tarmac and concrete. In *Seeing Green*, the environmentalist Jonathon Porritt, former director of Friends of the Earth, has called the process of industrial development, spurred on by the desire for efficiency and productivity, a 'system without a soul' (Porritt 1984: 93). Without doubt there is now a higher standard of living in Western countries than ever before, but at what cost? And is it worth it? And can it continue?

In *This Common Inheritance*, the government's bulky White Paper on Britain's environmental strategy, the problems have been set out in detail: a world population set to go up by 13 per cent to six billion in the last thirteen years of this century; an area of tropical rain forest about one-and-a-half times the size of England cut down or burnt each year; a third of the 50 million living species on the earth extinct in 30 years' time; the ozone layer damaged by man-made chemicals increasing the incidence of skin cancer; global warming as a result of greenhouse gases emitted when fossil fuels are burnt in power stations and motor vehicles increasing the level of

125

the sea, altering the climate and damaging crops; the rapid growth of commercial and domestic building threatening green areas; more than 40,000 hectares of derelict land in Britain, half of it contaminated by chemicals; the over-production of food; acid rain, pollution, waste . . . It is a sorry litany. The White Paper declares: 'We may not be seeing the end of Nature, but Nature is certainly under threat . . . We have a moral duty to look after our planet and to hand it on in good order to future generations.' In a telling phrase, the White Paper observes, 'We must put a proper value on the natural world: it would be odd to cherish a Constable but not the landscape he depicted' (Secretary of State for the Environment and others 1990: 9–10).

Dominion

The word 'ecology' is derived from the Greek word *oikos*, meaning a house. Concern about the proper treatment of the natural environment is basically, therefore, a concern about housekeeping. Growing rich through the efforts of business and industry, while at the same time damaging the world from which those products ultimately come and in which they have to be enjoyed, is simply bad management. The sense of unease that many people feel about the way we 'keep house' in the world around us has ancient origins.

In the first creation story in Genesis (1:1–2:4a), each stage of the process in which the world comes to be formed is declared to be good: day and night, earth and heaven, land and sea, plants and trees, sun and moon, marine life and birds, and then land animals and human beings. Indeed the whole creation is said to be '*very good*'. But then a distinction is made. Men and women are created in the image and likeness of God. They are blessed and told, '*Be fruitful, multiply, fill the earth and subdue it. Be masters of the fish of the sea, the birds of heaven and all living creatures that move on earth*' (1:28). In this story human beings are apart from nature. They alone have the divine image and the position of '*dominion*', as the AV translates it, over nature.

But the creation of humankind is not the culmination of

126

the process. This is reserved for the sabbath. In *Creating a Just Future*, the German theologian Juergen Moltmann describes it like this: 'After action comes letting things be, and after creation comes existence . . . If God has created this world to dwell and rest in it, then the sabbath day with the rest of God is in fact the goal of the whole work of creation. God creates in order to arrive at this rest; he does not rest in order to create again.' He concludes, 'The sabbath is the consummation of creation; without it creation is incomplete . . . ' (Moltmann 1989: 84–85). Resting on the sabbath does not mean relaxing or being idle. It means letting things be what they are, enjoying creation for its own sake, not intervening to change things any further. This is what is blessed about the final day of creation.

The second creation story (2.4b–25), probably earlier in origin, gives a different picture. Here God works on material which already exists; he *'shaped man from the soil of the ground and blew the breath of life into his nostrils and man became a living being'* (2:7). The word translated man – *adam* in Hebrew – means 'of the earth' and it is from this same source that *'every kind of tree'* also comes (2:9). Then the man is put in the garden of Eden *'to cultivate and take care of it'* (2:15). The picture is one of common origin with the rest of nature and of a God-given responsibility to look after it, to nurture it, to be a good steward or trustee. It is almost as if taking care of the earth is one of the purposes for which human beings have been created.

In the story of the fall (3:1–24), the relationship between humankind and God is broken and there is also a break with nature. The snake is cursed and there is enmity between it and the woman and her offspring. The soil is cursed and is to yield food for the man with pain as long as he lives. The man and his wife are expelled from the garden. But the sense of common origin itself is still there. Yahweh says, *'For dust you are and to dust you shall return'* (3:19).

Two pictures emerge from these ancient stories. One is of human beings separate from nature and masters of it. The other is of humankind continuous with nature and responsible for caring for it. It is the desire of men and women to

127

over-reach themselves that leads to the break with nature and the consequences continue throughout the generations.

The idea that human beings have dominion over nature, instead of being part of it, has justified much reckless excess. Nature has been thought to be there for human purposes alone. To have dominion has come to mean to exploit, to use up, to lay waste. Industrial and technological advance has gained support from this idea, and in some places it has forged ahead almost regardless of the consequences. The creative image of God in humankind has been seen in unrestrained economic growth rather than in conservation.

The fundamental idea that the land belongs to God, however, and not to human beings to do what they like with, is further developed in Exodus. The people are instructed: *'For six years you will sow your land and gather its produce, but in the seventh year you will let it lie fallow and forgo all produce from it.'* The same applies to vineyards and olive groves. The poor and the wild animals are to have whatever food grows naturally. This sabbath rest every seventh year both for the labourer and for the land is closely tied to faithfulness to the covenant with God (23:10–13; Lev. 25:1–7).

When seven times seven years have passed there is to be a year of jubilee, and instructions are given in Leviticus about this (25:8–55). People are to return to their ancestral property. The price of any land sold in intervening years should reflect the period left until this reversion at the jubilee. It is a form of leasehold sale. The reason for this is clearly set out. God says, *'Land will not be sold absolutely, for the land belongs to me, and you are strangers and guests of mine'* (25:23). It is only the harvest, the produce of the land, that can be fully sold.

Everyone had a share, in proportion, at the beginning and this heritage should not be taken away (Num. 26:52–56), although there is some doubt about whether the jubilee was ever fully observed (Lev. 26:34–35). The evil of accumulating houses and fields and concentrating ownership in ever fewer hands, and the decline in the productivity of the land that might come with it, is starkly put in Isaiah (5:8–10). If this did not happen the prophets might not have found it necessary to rail against it.

Respect for Nature

A basic respect for the natural world – because it belongs to God – is reflected in numerous places in the Hebrew Scriptures. Trees are not to be destroyed during a siege (Dt. 20:19). A profound knowledge of the natural world is a notable aspect of the wisdom of King Solomon (1 Kgs. 5:13). Water pollution is thought to cause death and miscarriages (2 Kgs. 2:19–22). Job contains a magnificent passage about the intimate relationship between God and creation. *'Where were you,'* says Yahweh, *'when I laid the earth's foundations . . .? Who pent up the sea behind closed doors when it leapt tumultuous from the womb, when I wrapped it in a robe of mist and made black clouds its swaddling bands . . . ? Has the rain a father? Who begets the dewdrops? What womb brings forth the ice, who gives birth to the frost of heaven . . . ?'* (38:1–38). The effect of this long, poetic passage is powerful. God is a mother to nature itself. Nature is God's new-born child.

The Psalms are full of imagery of the same sort. The Psalmist gives praise to God and speaks about the heavens *'shaped by your fingers . . . '* (8:3). Other Psalms declare: *'You visit the earth and make it fruitful . . . The meadows are covered with flocks, the valleys clothed with wheat; they shout and sing for joy'* (65:9,13); *'Let the countryside exult, and all that is in it, and all the trees of the forest cry out for joy'* (96:12); *'May Yahweh find joy in his creatures!'* (104:31); *'Praise him, sun and moon . . . mountains and every hill, orchards and every cedar . . . '* (148:3–9). Similar themes appear again and again (19:1, 24:1–2, 77:16, 89:5,11, 95·4–5, 97:6, 98:8, 103:22, 104:1–4, 139:7–8, 147:15–18). It is an impressive witness to the idea that God and nature have an intimate relationship with each other, quite separate from any intervention by humankind, and that nature rejoices in this relationship.

In Proverbs, the figure of Wisdom, later merged with that of the Spirit of God, is pictured present at creation (3:19–20). In the book of Wisdom, in the Apocrypha, the spirit of the Lord *'holds everything together'*. The writer declares, *'Your imperishable spirit is in everything!'* (1:7, 12:1). In the Song of the Three, an addition in Greek to the book of Daniel, also in the Apocrypha, the elements are called to praise God in a canticle that has come to be known as the Benedicite or The Song of Creation: *'Bless the Lord, all the Lord's creation: praise and glorify him for ever!'* (Dan. 3:57 NJB; The Song of the Three: 3:35 REB).

How is this paean of praise from the Psalms and the wisdom literature to be understood? Four points can be made. First, it is poetry, some of it for chanting in the Temple. Liturgy is not the same as reasoned argument, and it should not be interpreted as any sort of scientific or historical statement. These tender words about nature have more to do with religious emotion than with science. Secondly, they are to be seen in the context of competition with Canaanite religion which found spirits everywhere, in hills and trees and natural forces. In contrast to this the followers of Yahweh emphasize that it is their God who creates the universe and who is intimately involved in it.

Thirdly, although God is understood to reveal himself in the events of Israel's history, he is also to be found in the natural environment. Too great an emphasis on a God of history can obscure the world of nature as a source of revelation. Animist religions, and in our own day some aspects of the 'new age' movement, have a valuable reminder to offer in this regard. And fourthly, these words and ideas come from a pre-scientific age, when the workings of nature were understood differently. It seemed natural to attribute the weather or the seasons to the direct intervention of God in a way that is incomprehensible to the modern mind. But the sense that the natural environment is a vital part of God's concern, and that, in its own way, it can offer praise to him, is an enduring insight.

The prophetic literature adds its own perspectives. In Isaiah, as in Psalm 72 (1–9), God's judgement will affect the earth (24:1,4–5). When the spirit of God is poured out, *'Fair judgement will fix its home in the desert, and uprightness live in this orchard'* (32:15–16). The magnificence and power of God is strongly contrasted with that of the idols (40:12,19–22). The prophet's vision of restoration is on a cosmic scale: *'Look, I am going to create new heavens and a new earth'* (65:17).

In Jeremiah, human faithlessness affects nature; the progression of the seasons is damaged. *'Your misdeeds,'* he says, *'have upset all this.'* The land is in mourning, grass is withering, and creatures are dying *'as a result of the wickedness of the inhabitants'* (5:24–25, 12:4). A similar point is made in Joel (1:10,16), and Amos (4:7–9). Micah's vision is one of harmony and fruitfulness restored: *'Each man will sit under his vine and fig tree with no one to trouble him'* (4:4). The religious context of these passages is clear. Those who break the covenant of faithfulness with Yahweh will pay the price with ecological as well as human disaster.

A Cosmic Vision

The Christian Scriptures pick up these themes and add to them. In the Gospels, Jesus finds the natural world a rich source of analogy with which to illustrate the points he wants to make. God clothes the flowers of the field without them having to worry (Mt. 6:28–30; Lk. 12:28). The kingdom of heaven is like a sower who went out to sow, or a man who sowed good seed in his field, or a mustard seed, or yeast, or treasure hidden in a field, or a merchant looking for fine pearls, or a drag-net cast in the sea. It is a vineyard owner's son who is killed by wicked tenants (Mt. 13:3–52, 21:33–46). A rich man pulls down his barns and builds bigger ones, and a dishonest steward forgives debtors owing oil and wheat (Lk. 12:16–21, 16:1–8). The sense of imminent judgement is strong, too, in these stories.

Something of the divinity of Jesus is revealed by his power over nature. He stills the storm, feeds the crowd with loaves and fishes, walks on the water (Mt. 8:23–27, 14:13–21,22–33; Mk. 6:30–52; Jn. 6:1–21). *'Whatever kind of man is this,'* his disciples wonder, *'that even the winds and the sea obey him?'* (Mt. 8:27). He plucks ears of corn on a sabbath walk through the fields with his disciples and is reprimanded by the Pharisees. *'The Son of man is master of the Sabbath'*, he says (Mt. 12:1–8; Mk. 2:23–28; Lk. 6:1–5).

It is significant, too, that Jesus goes into the wilderness or the mountains for important moments in his life and minis-

try: for the temptation (Mt. 4:1; Mk. 1:13; Lk. 4:1), for the
transfiguration (Mt. 17:1–8; Mk. 9:2–8; Lk. 9:28–36), for
prayer (Mt. 14:23; Mk. 6:46), for the appointment of the
Twelve (Mk. 3:13–19; Lk. 6:12–16).

The doctrine of the incarnation also implies a positive
attitude to the natural world. John begins his Gospel with
this theological theme: '*In the beginning was the Word: the Word
was with God and the Word was God . . . Through him all things
came into being . . . The Word became flesh, he lived among us,
and we saw his glory . . .* ' (1:1–14). The word translated flesh
– *sarx* in Greek – is an earthy word. John uses it to counter
any idea that the material world is evil and only the spirit is
good. It is the world that God loved (3:16). The same point
is made later in the Gospel through the use of the earthy
image of the vine, the vinedresser and the branches (15:1–8).
God's identification with the world in the person of Jesus
makes a powerful statement about the value of the material
creation itself.

The idea in the Hebrew Scriptures that land and possessions belong to God can be seen in the early Christian
practice of holding everything in common. Acts notes that
'*no one claimed private ownership of any possessions*' (4:32–35).
Barnabas and Paul echo the Psalms and the prophets when
they speak of '*the living God who made sky and earth and the
sea and all that these hold*' (14:15). In his speech before the
Areopagus council Paul repeats the point: '*The God who made
the world and everything in it is himself Lord of heaven and earth*'
(17:24).

In Romans, Paul declares, '*Ever since the creation of the world,
the invisible existence of God and his everlasting power have been
clearly seen by the mind's understanding of created things*' (1:20).
The existence of God can be known to human reason alone,
and it is through the natural creation that God reveals himself. There can be no 'natural theology' without nature.

The flowering of Paul's thinking is to be found later in
Romans in a vision of cosmic salvation. '*The whole creation,*'
he writes, '*is waiting with eagerness for the children of God to be
revealed . . . With the intention that the whole creation itself might
be freed from its slavery to corruption and brought into the same*

glorious freedom as the children of God.' He continues, *'We are well aware that the whole creation, until this time, has been groaning in labour pains . . . Waiting with eagerness for our bodies to be set free'* (8:19–23). This broad vision occurs again: *'Everything there is comes from him and is caused by him and exists for him'* (11:36; 1 Cor. 8:6). *'In Christ,'* he is able to say, *'there is a new creation: the old order is gone and a new being is there to see'* (2 Cor. 5:17).

The vision of cosmic reconciliation and unity, overcoming the rupture between humankind and nature and God described in Genesis 3, is put in impressive words in Ephesians: God *'has let us know the mystery of his purpose . . . That he would bring everything together under Christ, as head, everything in the heavens and everything on earth'* (1:9–10). And again in Colossians: *'In him were created all things in heaven and everything on earth . . . He exists before all things and in him all things hold together . . . And through him to reconcile all things to him, everything in heaven and on earth'* (1:15–20). It is a magnificent passage, a cosmic vision of fullness, of completion or perfection, of the realization of the potential that is in the creation as a whole.

The ancient picture of the natural environment and its relationship to God is thus complemented in significant ways in the Christian Scriptures. Nature and natural events are appropriate vehicles through which the gospel can be communicated. Flowers, seeds, vineyards, cornfields all reveal something of God and his purposes. The value of the material, the earthy, is firmly stated. God is the creator and the redeemer of the whole of creation. The salvation brought by Christ is on a cosmic scale.

The Earth Community

This sensitivity towards nature has not been typical of the Christian Churches until recent times. In *To Care for the Earth*, the Irish Roman Catholic missionary priest Sean McDonagh quotes a lecture given in 1966 by Lynn White, the American historian, in which he attacks 'the Christian axiom that nature has no reason for existence but to serve

133

man'. In a memorable phrase White speaks of an 'orthodox Christian arrogance towards nature'. In exploring the development of this attitude, McDonagh blames Francis Bacon, René Descartes and Isaac Newton for promoting a mechanical view of nature. They 'de-sacralized' and 'objectified' it, taking away its 'vital forces'. They understood it according to 'abstract mathematical principles' rather than as a living system. All the mystery was taken out of it; nature was simply a machine (McDonagh 1986: 137,68–73).

More recently, however, a different approach has emerged. In *Gaia: a New Look at Life on Earth*, the scientist James Lovelock has developed the idea of the earth as an open, continuous, self-regulating system. 'The Gaia hypothesis', he writes, 'implies that the stable state of our planet includes man as a part of, or partner in, a very democratic entity' (Lovelock 1979: 145). He argues for peaceful co-operation with nature. Something of this sense of respect is reflected in Sean McDonagh's term 'earth community' (McDonagh 1986: 73), and in Juergen Moltmann's words: 'It is not its individual parts but the community of creation as a whole which reflects God's wisdom and God's beauty' (Moltmann 1989: 56).

Themes

Three themes dominate the wealth of material about the natural environment in the Bible. First, there is a strong sense that **human beings have a responsibility to act as stewards of the environment in which they are set**. The idea of dominion over nature may have seemed appropriate in primitive times. The natural world was hostile, powerful, in need of placating. If humans did not master it, they would be overcome by it. To tame nature may have seemed to be a way of acting in the image of God, bringing order where there was only void or chaos. It was to make a garden where previously there was only wilderness. But the strength of science and technology is now so great that it is in our power not just to subdue, but to destroy. Conservation and a proper respect for the natural world is the form in which dominion is best exercised today.

Secondly, **there is a general truth in the pre-scientific idea that there was a direct link between human sin and natural disaster**. Although God does not directly punish individuals or communities through natural events, causes do have effects. If we do not exercise a responsible care for the natural world, there will be harmful ecological consequences. If we continue to pollute the soil and the atmosphere through the over-use of chemicals, food will not grow, the earth will get warmer, the sea level will rise, the environment will be damaged. Humankind has to live in harmony with nature, to till the garden and care for it, or suffer the consequences. In this sense, human evil and natural disaster are part of the same phenomenon.

Thirdly, **the idea that humankind is part of nature, sharing with it in a common origin and a common destiny, puts a permanent question mark against some forms of economic growth in our own day**. It suggests a different basis on which to evaluate industrial and economic development, a more communal, less individualistic one.

Rain forests in South America, for example, are cut down to make way for cattle ranches to supply beef to hamburger shops in Europe. Hill-farmers in Britain feel the effects of radiation dispersed into the atmosphere as a result of an accident at a Russian nuclear power station. The interdependence of the natural and the economic world is clear. We are all affected. As the World Council of Churches has emphasized, justice and peace are interwoven with the integrity of creation. The green agenda in the West, therefore, does not just mean a lower standard of living for everyone, or slower economic development in the Third World. It is not some kind of rich world plot to keep the rest of the world poor. In principle it is a response to an ecological threat on a global scale. We are all poorer if we do not recognize this dependence one on another. No one owns the sky; we all share it. In the end there is more value and joy in the song of a skylark than in any number of cheap fast-food shops.

135

The sense of mystery that John felt in Great Monk Wood echoes the understanding of nature to be found in the pages of the Bible. In *The Greening of the Church*, Sean McDonagh quotes Francis of Assisi's famous poem in which he reflects the sense of human kinship with nature. He speaks of brother sun, sister moon and stars, brothers wind and air, sister water, brother fire, and of sister earth our mother (McDonagh 1990: 172). John and Christopher, walking through the forest, knew what he meant and both are closer to God as a result.

ANIMALS

To mention Francis of Assisi is to turn at once to the subject of animals. They, too, are part of the natural world. Millions of dogs and cats share our homes and are much loved household companions. But there is also much cruelty. Many domestic pets are abandoned by their owners or mistreated. Farm animals are reared intensively in restricted conditions. Wild animals are hunted as much for sport and pleasure as for the control of their numbers. Other animals are used in laboratories to test drugs and cosmetics before they are sold for human use, or to entertain in zoos and safari parks or in the circus ring.

On a walk in the country Eleanor and Jean come across an animal cemetery alongside a large house on a country estate. The headstones stretch back to the beginning of this century and bear a rich variety of names. Some are diminutive human names – Katy, Bob, and perhaps Holly. Others – Sonny and Lassie – suggest that domestic animals are part of the family like little sons and daughters. One name, however, indicates something more: it is Psyche, the Greek for soul or spirit. To call a dog or a cat by this name is to suggest that humans and animals are two of a kind.

It is easy to become emotional about animals. They appear in every children's book endowed with appealing human characters. The soft eyes of a calf move the heart. The gambolling of a lamb in the fields in springtime delights young children. No connection is made with the leather shoes on the feet, or the roast joint on the Sunday dinner table. The processes that come between the piglet in the sty and the bacon on the breakfast plate are simply overlooked.

In *Christianity and the Rights of Animals*, the theologian Andrew Linzey has summarized the position in stark words. 'We eat, ride, shoot, fish, wear, trap, hunt, farm and experiment upon billions of animals world-wide every year', he writes. 'Even if we only grant animals some minimum moral status, it could be seriously claimed that in terms of pain, suffering and deprivation alone, the treatment of the non-human ranks among the most important moral issues confronting the human species' (Linzey 1987: 99).

But what is the status of animals? Are they there for humans to use? Do they share in God's love equally with us? Is the limit of our responsibility towards them one of compassion and humane treatment, or can animals have rights over us?

A Common Origin

The Hebrew Scriptures speak positively about animals and their relationship with humankind. In the first creation story in Genesis (1:1 — 2:4a), marine life and birds are created on the fifth day and blessed and told, '*Be fruitful, multiply . . .*' (1:20–23). Then wild animals and farm animals are created on the next day, the same day as men and women. In the story they are not blessed, though they share the same stage of creation as human beings, and both share the assessment that all God has made is '*very good*'. Food for humans is to be seed-bearing plants and fruit, and for animals the foliage of the plants (1:24–31). No meat is to be eaten. In this liturgical text for chanting in worship, there is a sense that animals and humans are on a level with each other, although they are not said to be made in the image of God, like human beings.

The second creation story (2:4b–25), pictures man shaped '*from the soil of the ground*' and animals and birds similarly fashioned '*from the soil*'. They have a common origin. Then

137

Yahweh God says, '*It is not right that the man should be alone. I shall make him a helper*' and it is wild animals and birds that first fulfil this role. They are his companions. The power that the man has over the animals is symbolized by the naming that follows. This relationship is not fully satisfactory, however, and woman is fashioned as man's helper or partner (2:7,18–22).

Humans and animals also share the same spirit. When the man was created, Yahweh God '*blew the breath of life into his nostrils, and man became a living being*' (2:7). The word translated living being – *nephesh* in Hebrew – is also used of sea and land creatures (1:21,24). In Job the same word is translated soul (12:10).

Furthermore, the word used of the spirit of God in creation, and translated divine wind – *ruach* in Hebrew – is used of animals and of humans (Gen. 1:2, 7:21–22). The same word appears in a significant passage in Ecclesiastes. '*The fate of the human and the fate of the animal*,' the writer declares, '*is the same: as the one dies, so the other dies; both have the selfsame breath . . . Who knows if the human spirit mounts upward or if the animal spirit goes downward to the earth?*' (3:19,21). It is clear from the language used here, obscured though it is by the translation, that the same spirit is thought to inhabit both animal and human. Andrew Linzey puts the point like this: 'Whatever hope there may be for a future life for humans applies equally to animal life as well.' He uses the word 'spirit-filled creatures' for both (Linzey 1987: 37,112).

In the story of the flood in Genesis, human sin has consequences for animals and for nature as a whole. Creeping things and birds, though not sea creatures, are destroyed along with humans. Animals board the ark in pairs with Noah, '*to preserve their species throughout the earth*' and every species is included (7:2–3,14–16).

After the flood, God blesses Noah and his sons, and repeats the command to '*breed, multiply and fill the earth*'. But then a new, harsher note appears. God says: '*Be the terror and the dread of all the animals on land and all the birds of heaven, of everything that moves on land and all the fish of the sea; they are placed in your hands.*' Now the eating of meat is sanctioned:

138

'*Every living thing that moves will be yours to eat, no less than the foliage of the plants*', though the eating of flesh with the life, that is the blood, in it is not permitted (9:1–4).

Then God makes a covenant with humankind and with the animals, and the inclusion of '*every living creature*' and '*all living things*' is constantly repeated. The rainbow is to be the sign of the covenant between God '*and the earth*' (9:8–17). Enmity between humans and animals is not part of the original state of blessedness in these ancient stories; it seems to come as a consequence of human sin (3:14–15).

The Welfare of Animals

This state of hostility can be seen, for example, in the ease with which Saul cuts a yoke of oxen in pieces in his fury (1 Sam. 11:7). But it is tempered by numerous references to kindness to animals. Some are clearly a matter of good husbandry, but in others more is also implied. The wilful killing of animals, for example, is condemned in the same breath as murder under the influence of rage (Gen. 49:6). Oxen, donkeys and other animals are not to work on the sabbath (Ex. 20:10, 23:12; Dt. 5:13–14). Stray animals are to be returned to their owners (Ex. 23:4; Dt. 22:1–2). Passers-by are to help even their enemies if their animals have fallen under a heavy load (Ex. 23:5). Cattle and wild animals are to benefit along with humans from whatever the land produces in a sabbatical year (Lev. 25:7). The unequal yoking of ox and donkey is forbidden (Dt. 22:10). An ox is not to be muzzled when it is treading out corn (Dt. 25:4).

Concern for the welfare of animals sometimes has a more profound significance. Rebekah and Laban feed Eliezer's camels and this is seen as a sign that she is a suitable wife for Isaac (Gen. 24:4,10–14). Moses helps some girls to water their flocks, and marries one of them (Ex. 2:16–21). Balaam is reprimanded by his donkey for beating him when he turns off the road. But the animal has a greater sense of the presence of God's angel in front of them than his owner does (Num. 22:22–35). Nathan's story of the theft of a ewe lamb enables him to confront King David with his sin (2 Sam. 12:1–7). In

Jonah, a great fish plays a part in the salvation of Nineveh, and animals share in the public repentance for evil and violence. In response to Jonah's personal protest, God says that he is concerned about the animals in the city as well as the humans (2:1, 3:7–8, 4:11).

Some of the most beautifully expressed and powerful passages about animals appear in the book of Job. There is a sense of natural theology in one of the early speeches. '*You have only to ask the cattle*', Job says, '*for them to instruct you . . . There is not one such creature but will know that the hand of God has arranged things like this!*' (12:7–9). In a magnificent passage towards the end of the book, Yahweh speaks from the heart of the tempest about the creator's wisdom revealed in nature: '*Who endowed the ibis with wisdom and gave the cock his intelligence . . . ?*' and more follows about the lioness, the raven, about mountain goats, deer in labour, the wild donkey, the wild ox, the ostrich, the horse, the hawk, and the eagle. Imaginative and well-observed passages follow about Behemoth the hippopotamus and Leviathan the crocodile (38:36—39:30, 40:15—41:26). Job is a skilled naturalist and a poet, who sees God's power and splendour in nature and in animals. His response to these marvels of Yahweh is to '*repent in dust and ashes*' (42:6).

The idea that animals have no wisdom or rationality, however, also appears in Job. The ostrich leaves her eggs on the ground to be crushed. '*God, you see,*' the passage explains, '*has deprived her of wisdom and given her no share of intelligence*' though she can make fools of horse and rider if she '*uses her height*' (39:17–18). The same idea is found in one of the Psalms: '*Be not like a horse or a mule; that does not understand bridle or bit . . .* ' (32:9). But this does not seem to be a general indication that animals have no powers of reason. In Proverbs, the idle are advised to learn wisdom from the ant: '*No one gives her orders, no overseer, no master, yet all through the summer she gets her food ready . . .* ' (6:6–8).

In the Psalms, God's care for animals as part of his creation comes again and again. He supports '*both man and beast*' (36:6). He knows '*every bird in the air*' (50:11). He provides wild animals, birds, cattle with their food. He has a direct relationship with them all and they exist for purposes he decides. He made Leviathan *'to sport with'*. If he turns his face from them, they *'panic'*. The breath – *ruach* – that gives them life comes from him. *'May Yahweh find joy in his creatures'*, the Psalmist concludes (104:10–31). God's *'tenderness'* embraces all his creatures and with a *'generous hand'* he satisfies their desires (145:9,16). In Proverbs, compassion for animals is a sign of uprightness (12:10).

Animals can worship God. *'Praise Yahweh from the earth,'* says the Psalmist, *'sea monsters . . . wild animals and all cattle, reptiles and winged birds'* (Ps. 148:7,10). Isaiah makes the same point: *'The wild animals will honour me . . . '* (43:20). In the Song of the Three, in the Apocrypha, every kind of creature in the waters, in the air and on land joins in thanksgiving to God (Dan. 3:79–81 NJB; The Song of the Three: 57–59 REB).

Much is also made of the analogy of the shepherd, a theme that is to be taken up later in the Christian Scriptures. In 2 Samuel, Yahweh promises David that he is to *'shepherd my people Israel and be leader of Israel'* (5:2). In the Psalms, *'Yahweh is my shepherd, I lack nothing . . . '* (23:1–4; 95:7). In Isaiah, Yahweh is *'like a shepherd feeding his flock . . . '* (40:11). In Ezekiel, faithless shepherds are reprimanded at length (34:1–31).

Human Sin and Sacrifice

The idea that animals share in the consequences of human sin, touched on in Genesis, is further reflected in the prophetic and wisdom literature. In Jeremiah, Yahweh's anger at the worship of foreign gods will be poured down on *'man and beast'* (7:20). Stork, turtledove, swallow and crane understand migration, but *'my people do not know Yahweh's laws!'* and disaster is the result (8:7,13–14). In Hosea, Yahweh in his anger at his unfaithful people will be like a lion, or a leopard, or a *'bear robbed of her cubs'* and will *'tear them to shreds'* (13:7–8). The same image occurs in 2 Samuel (17:8) and Proverbs (17:12). In Joel, the *'flocks of sheep bear the punishment too'* (1:18–20). In Zephaniah, *'humans and animals, the birds of the air and the fish of the sea'* are all punished as a result of human faithlessness (1:2–3).

It is through the practice of ritual sacrifice that animals share most obviously in the effects of human sinfulness. Animal sacrifice played an important part in ancient religious life. Noah, for example, offers a sacrifice after coming out of the ark and it is pleasing to God (Gen. 8:20–21). The regulations for conducting animal sacrifices on various occasions are set out in Exodus (29:10–42) and in Leviticus (1:3–17). The ceremony of transferring the sins of the people on to the head of a goat and sending it out into the wilderness on the annual day of expiation is also described in Leviticus (16).

Some degree of compassion towards animals is shown, however, in the regulation that a sacrificial victim should not be taken from its mother until the eighth day (Ex. 22:29), and that no animal should be *'slaughtered on the same day as its young'* (Lev. 22:27–28). But there is little doubt that the practice was brutal. Leviticus gives a description involving pouring blood over the altar, skinning, quartering, washing entrails, wringing off the head of a pigeon or a turtledove, squeezing the blood out and dismembering it (1:5–17). It was also done on a large scale. Solomon, for example, sacrifices huge numbers of animals in dedicating the Temple (1 Kgs. 8:62–64).

Human sacrifice also took place. Abraham is prepared to offer up Isaac, though his place is finally taken by a ram (Gen. 22:1–19). Jephthah sacrifices his daughter (Jgs. 11:30–40). Ahaz and Manasseh, and the Israelite people as a whole, sacrifice their children to foreign gods (2 Kgs. 16:3, 17:17; 2 Chron. 28:3, 33:6; Ps. 106:37). In Leviticus, child sacrifice of this sort is forbidden (18:21), and in Deuteronomy, Israel is told not to copy such a *'detestable'* practice (12:31, 18:10). But it seems to have continued. It was roundly condemned by the prophets (Isa. 57:5; Jer. 7:31, 19:4, 32:35; Ezek. 16:20–21, 20:26; Mic. 6:7).

In *Replenish the Earth*, the American animal welfare writer Lewis Regenstein comments on the practice of human and animal sacrifice like this: 'Placing a value on a human life, and substituting an animal for a human in offering a sacrifice, was a major step forward for these ancient people, however barbaric it may seem to us today' (Regenstein 1991: 46).

From an early time ancient voices spoke strongly against the practice, regarding it as superseded by more spiritual forms of worship. The point is made in 1 Samuel: '*Truly, obedience is better than sacrifice, submissiveness than the fat of rams*' (15:22), in the Psalms (40:6, 50:8–14,23), and in Proverbs (15:8, 21:3). In Isaiah, Yahweh says, '*I am sick of burnt offerings of rams and the fat of calves . . . Cease doing evil. Learn to do good, search for justice . . .* ' (1:11–17), and the same theme appears again and again in the other prophets (Jer. 6:20, 7:22–23; Hos. 6:6; Amos 5:21–24; Mic. 6:6–8). After the exile, the practice seems to have declined in the face of growing concern with observing the details of the Law and with the worship of the synagogue. In the Christian Church it is fully superseded by the sacrifice of Christ on the cross, the lamb of God. The theme of sacrifice, however, continues in a spiritual as well as a personal sense.

The final vision in the Hebrew Scriptures is one of harmony. One day humans and animals will live together in peace. Job declares, '*You will have a pact with the stones of the field, and live in amity with wild beasts*' (5:23). Isaiah puts it in words that have become famous. '*The wolf*', he prophesies, '*will live with the lamb, the panther lie down with the kid, calf, lion and fat-stock beast together, with a little boy to lead them. The cow and the bear will graze, their young will lie down together. The lion will eat hay like the ox. The infant will play over the den of the adder; the baby will put his hand into the viper's lair. No hurt, no harm will be done on all my holy mountain, for the country will be full of knowledge of Yahweh as the waters cover the sea*' (11:6–9). Looking to the future Hosea adds, '*When that day comes I shall make a treaty for them with the wild animals, with the birds of heaven and the creeping things of the earth . . . and I will let them sleep secure*' (2:20). It is a major reversal of the hostility between human and animal described in Genesis 3.

Animals as Symbols

The Christian Scriptures contain a number of references to animals, though they are mainly incidental or used as illustrations in making theological points. In Mark, Jesus is '*with the wild animals*' during his temptation in the desert (1:13). The birds in the sky '*do not sow or reap or gather into barns*' and human beings are worth '*much more than they are*' (Mt. 6:26; Lk. 12:24). Sparrows are cheap to buy, '*yet not one falls to the ground without your Father knowing*' (Mt. 10:29; Lk. 12:6). A man will rescue a sheep from a pit, and water an ox or a donkey on the sabbath (Mt. 12:11; Lk. 13:15). Jesus compares his desire for Jerusalem to a hen gathering her chicks under her wings (Mt. 23:37; Lk. 13:34).

The theme of the shepherd and the sheep recurs. Shepherds visit Jesus after his birth (Lk. 2:8). Jesus sends his disciples to '*the lost sheep of the House of Israel*' (Mt. 10:6). A man goes after one sheep that is lost, leaving the 99 others behind (Lk. 15:4–7). A comparison is made between Jesus and the good shepherd who sacrifices himself for his sheep (Jn. 10:1–18). Jesus tells Peter, after the resurrection, to feed his lambs, his sheep (Jn. 21:15–17). The animal world is a useful source of analogy in the Gospels as points are made about God's love for his people.

The story of the Gadarene swine, however, seems to suggest a different, darker view. Jesus responds to the devils' request and allows them to enter the pigs. '*At that,*' the story continues, '*the whole herd charged down the cliff into the lake and perished in the water.*' To allow such apparently pointless destruction, and on such a large scale, might seem to reflect a lack of concern for the animals, as well as for those who owned them and suffered financially as a result of their loss. But the story is full of symbolism – the priority of the troubled man's salvation, the power of Jesus that is displayed, the Jewish rejection of pigs that are acceptable to gentiles, the allusion to the other side of the lake beyond Jewish territory, the rejection of Jesus himself and its consequences. In view of this, the story cannot be read as any sort of comment on animal welfare. Indeed it is the devils who bring about the destruction of the pigs; Jesus merely permits them to have their way (Mt. 8:28–34; Mk. 5:1–20; Lk. 8:26–39).

Criticism of the system of animal sacrifice also continues in the Gospels. Jesus cleanses the Temple of sacrificial animals and dealers (Mt. 21:12; Mk. 11:15; Lk. 19:45; Jn. 2:14–16). A scribe tells Jesus that the love of God and of the neighbour is *'far more important than any burnt offering or sacrifice'* (Mk. 12:33), a detail not there in Luke's account (10:25–28). Jesus quotes Hosea (6:6) to the Pharisees: *'Mercy is what pleases me, not sacrifice'* (Mt. 9:13).

In John, Jesus is described as *'the lamb of God that takes away the sin of the world'* (1:29). The same point is made at length in Hebrews (3—10). In a passage about the priesthood of Christ and the superiority of the new covenant over the old, the writer explains, *'But now Christ . . . has entered the sanctuary once and for all, taking with him not the blood of goats and bull calves, but his own blood, having won an eternal redemption'* (9:11–12). *'Worthy is the Lamb that was sacrificed . . .'* declares Revelation (5:12). Here the higher sacrifices himself for the lower. It is a complete reversal of the ancient system. The dominion of Christ is worked out in terms of service and self-sacrifice.

Animals again have a symbolic significance in Peter's dream in a house in Jaffa. He sees a sheet containing *'every kind of animal, reptile and bird'* and a voice says to him, *'What God has made clean, you have no right to call profane'* (Acts 10:12,15). The acceptance of the gentiles into the Church, and their baptism, follows this experience.

Perhaps with his tongue in his cheek, 1 Timothy quotes Deuteronomy, *'You must not muzzle an ox when it is treading out the corn'* to support the payment of *'double reward'* to elders in the Church (5:17–18).

Animals have a place of honour in the vision of God's kingdom at the end of all things in Revelation. Creatures looking like a lion, a bull and an eagle join a human face around the throne praising God (4:7–11). Elsewhere in Revelation, however, images of other creatures, a dragon (12:3), a beast part leopard, bear and lion (13:1–2), and white horses (19:11,14) also appear with more sinister or warlike significance. In a great feast, birds eat the flesh of generals, heroes and others (19:17–18), reversing the permission to eat animals given to humans in Genesis 9.

It is easy to be carried away by references like these in the Scriptures. In many cases they are simply metaphors taken from the natural world, and no significance can be read into them for the treatment of animals themselves. If Jesus is compared with a lamb, this does not mean that lambs have a special place in God's concern. The lamb in the image is, in any case, killed in a sacrifice. But the frequent use of such metaphors does suggest an easy inter-relationship between human and animal. The images are appropriate. An angry man can be like a bear deprived of her cubs. God does care for all of his creation, sparrows as well as humans.

Reason and Rights

The idea, however, that animals are little more than property for human use occurs frequently in later Christian thought. Lewis Regenstein gives some examples: Augustine writes: 'He that kills another's ox sins, not through killing the ox, but through injuring another man in his property.' Thomas Aquinas develops the hint that animals have no understanding, no rationality, and draws a distinction between animal and human souls. He still recommends the kind treatment of animals, not for its own sake but rather 'to dispose men to pity and tenderness towards one another' (Regenstein 1991: 73, 72). The idea that animals exist for human use could not be more clearly put. Regenstein quotes a nineteenth-century edition of the *Catholic Dictionary* which states: 'As the lower animals have no duties . . . so they have no rights . . . It must also be lawful to put them to death or to inflict pain on them, for any good or reasonable end, such as the promotion of man's knowledge, health, or even for the purposes of recreation . . . ' One limitation is allowed: 'It is never lawful for a man to take pleasure directly in the pain given to brutes, because in doing so, man degrades and brutalizes his own nature' (Regenstein 1991: 114).

With the nineteenth-century scientist Charles Darwin

146

comes a different view, a sense of kinship with animals. Darwin writes: 'Various emotions and faculties, such as love, memory, attention, curiosity, imitation, reason, etc., of which man boasts, may be found in an incipient, even sometimes in a well-developed condition, in the lower animals.' In this century Albert Schweitzer has argued for reverence for life. 'A man's religion', he writes, 'is of little value unless even seemingly insignificant creatures benefit from it' (Regenstein 1991: 95, 149).

But cruelty to animals persists. The British government's Ministry of Agriculture (MAFF) has found it necessary to issue *Codes of Recommendations* and a *Code of Practice* for the care and welfare of livestock. Animal welfare organizations campaign relentlessly against specific abuses.

The welfare approach, however, depends on the goodwill of humans. It assumes that it is for us to determine how animals are to be treated, and as we think best. The animal rights approach, on the other hand, is more robust and uncompromising. It assumes that a certain level of moral treatment is required, whether it pleases humans or not. In *Policies on Animal Welfare*, the RSPCA has adopted a Declaration of Animal Rights which includes the sentence: 'We believe in the evolutionary and moral kinship of all animals and declare our belief that all sentient creatures have rights to life, liberty and natural enjoyment' (RSPCA 1984: 1). Andrew Linzey argues for what he calls 'theos-rights' for animals – God's right 'to have what he has given honoured and respected'. He goes on to set out a programme of 'progressive disengagement from exploitation' in every form. 'Animals', he writes, 'have a God-given right to be animals' (Linzey 1987: 71, 104, 112).

Themes

Three themes come strongly out of the many references to animals in the Bible. First, it is significant that **animals and humans share the same stage of creation**. Even though they do not share the image of God, the same spirit animates them and gives them life. They are from the same soil. They

147

have the same origin as us. They are our partners in the world. Even the wild animals are to be our companions, not just domestic or farm animals, cats and dogs, or cattle. It is also clearly stated that God can reveal himself through the animal world, as well as through human history. Animals can respond to God in their own way, just as humans can. Although there is hostility and fear in the relationships that so many animals have with humans, the final vision in the Scriptures is one of harmony and peace. We are to do more than have a proper respect for animals, as we are for the rest of the natural environment. We are to share the world with them. It is a powerful idea, and it requires much re-thinking, in our own times, of attitudes and practices.

Secondly, **the partnership between animals and humans suggests that more than just kindness and compassion is required**. Animals have rights that need to be respected. Cruelty to animals in all its forms, at home, on the farm, in the field, is clearly a violation of this relationship. It is neither loving nor just.

In our own day, intensive farming methods that severely restrict animal movement, and mutilation such as the de-beaking of hens to stop them pecking each other in battery cages, cannot be supported by the Christian conscience, even though they may contribute towards the production of cheap food. Hunting animals for pleasure, or for exercise, is also inappropriate. Farmers who claim that field sports make a major contribution to conservation in the countryside need to find another motivation for their commendable concern for the natural environment. Coverts may be carefully tended and pheasants reared safely for the shoot, but kindness does not justify killing for sport. The use of animals in laboratories to test drugs for humans, except where there is genuinely no alternative, is also impossible to justify. The display of animals, or their use in entertainment, in settings that are not remotely connected with their natural environment or behaviour, is patronizing and demeaning, even though it may evoke a sense of wonder in those who look on.

Thirdly, **the continued and unrestrained use of animals for food needs careful examination**. Eating meat

was not part of the original vision in Genesis 1. Vegetarianism is growing in popularity, especially among young
people, and much more is known now about how to provide
what is necessary for a healthy diet without recourse to meat.
Vegetarianism may not be for everyone, but the challenge
to begin to live out the vision of harmony presented in the
Scriptures is a serious one. Progressive disengagement from
eating meat ought to be on the agenda of every Christian
household.

The headstones that Eleanor and Jean found on their walk
carry a greater significance than they realized at first. To call
an animal Psyche, and to give it a decent burial, is to reflect
a sense of kinship between earth's creatures that has very
ancient origins.

6.

POLITICS AND VIOLENCE

There is a marvellous moment towards the end of Act I in Beethoven's opera *Fidelio*, where a group of political prisoners emerge from their dungeon into the daylight. They sing movingly about their temporary freedom. Later, Fidelio, who is really Leonora disguised as a man, rescues her husband Florestan from the deepest dungeon. Then, on the arrival of the minister Don Fernando, the others are granted a general pardon and released. They had all been put there unjustly as political prisoners. The story ends with a scene of great rejoicing. Written around the time of the French Revolution, the opera explores political power and political liberation as much as a woman's courage and personal heroism.

What degree of authority should the state be able to exercise? In what circumstances, and under what conditions, should it be allowed to punish people, or even to take them into war? Should it be able to pass the death penalty on people? And what attitude should Christians have towards politics? In this chapter I want to look at the questions raised by the authority of the state, and then at war and peace, and at capital punishment.

THE STATE

The modern secular state, with its complicated system of local and county councils and its national parliament, was unknown in ancient times. The Greeks had a city-state – a *polis* – in which all adult men took part. It was the original 'democracy', rule by the people. Involvement in public affairs, politics, was natural, and anyone who chose not to be involved was an 'idiot', someone who kept himself to himself. In ancient Israel, the political and the religious communities were one and the same thing. Israel was a 'theocratic' state, ruled by God. The early Christians, however, had an ambivalent attitude both to the Jewish and to the Roman state under which they lived. They were often uncertain whether to accept or to resist political authority over them.

This ambivalence is still around today. Reginald and Marjorie, for example, are pillars of society. They live in a fine eighteenth-century house in a conservation village. He is patron of a number of voluntary organizations in the county, and she is a magistrate on the local bench. They think that the Church should keep out of politics, and they say so in no uncertain terms at a Deanery Synod meeting. The local council is there to deal with political matters, not the local church. A murmur of agreement goes round the hall as this view is expressed.

A Covenant Community

In the Hebrew Scriptures the point is constantly made that Israel is a nation under God. The Ten Commandments, and a great deal of other law in Exodus, Leviticus and Deuteronomy, order both religious and community life. It is quite clear where political authority comes from. During the period of the monarchy, the kings are anointed to office by God and at the hands of a prophet. Samuel, for example, takes a phial of oil and pours it on Saul's head, kisses him and says, '*Has not Yahweh anointed you as leader of his people Israel? You are the man who is to govern Yahweh's people and save them from the power of the enemies surrounding them*' (1 Sam. 10:1). The books of Samuel, Kings and Chronicles are full of stories about these rulers and their faithfulness or otherwise to God. Sinful ones suffered disasters, or lived short lives, and were rejected by God. Eventually the people

151

were taken off into exile and power in society came increasingly to be centred on the Temple and the priesthood.

The subordination of temporal authority to God is clearly illustrated in the story of King David and the prophet Nathan in 2 Samuel. David takes Bathsheba and arranges the death of her husband Uriah in battle. Nathan confronts him with this by telling the dramatic story of a beloved ewe lamb stolen by a neighbour as a meal for a visitor. David is angry, but the prophet makes him realize that he has behaved in just the same way, stealing someone else's property and killing the owner, and he is overcome with remorse. '*I have sinned against Yahweh*', he says. As a consequence, the story continues, David's house will never be free of the sword, his wives will be taken from him, and his first child is to die. His second child Solomon, however, succeeds him as king in due course (12:1–24).

The same point is made in the story of Elijah and King Ahab in 1 Kings. Ahab tries to get Naboth to give him his ancestral vineyard, but without success and his wife Jezebel taunts him, '*Some king of Israel you make!*' She arranges for Naboth to be falsely accused of cursing God and king and stoned, so that Ahab can take the vineyard. When Elijah confronts him with this, he repents and the dire punishment predicted for his whole house is staved off until his son's days (1 Kgs. 21).

In both these stories the temporal power of the ruler is subject to the power of God. A man's right to life, property, wife, land and animals is guaranteed by God, it is not for the king to usurp it in any way. In *Christians and the State*, the American theologian John Bennett summarizes the significance of these stories like this:'The righteousness of God is above the state. That righteousness is on the side of elemental human rights. The prophet takes freedom to challenge the king and his lawless use of power. The king recognizes that he is under God, that his power and his will are not ultimate' (Bennett 1958: 115)

The same point is made again and again by the prophets as they oppose religious unfaithfulness and political corruption wherever they find it. Amos, for example, prophesies

'*Disaster for those so comfortable in Zion* . . . *Lying on ivory beds and sprawling on their divans, they dine on lambs from the flock, and stall-fattened veal; they bawl to the sound of the lyre and, like David, they invent musical instruments; they drink wine by the bowlful, and lard themselves with the finest oils, but for the ruin of Joseph they care nothing. That is why they will now go into captivity, heading the column of captives. The sprawlers' revelry is over!*' (6:1,4–7).

Protest and Submission

In the Gospels the tension between religious and secular authority can be found in an altogether different social and political context. Jesus and his followers are seen, wrongly, as political agitators. Simon is a Zealot, a member of an anarchist group active at the time (Mk. 3:18). Simon Peter's name '*son of Jonah*' (Mt. 16:17), may not just mean son of John, for it is 'terrorist' in another ancient language, and he has a sword with him in the garden of Gethsemane and is not afraid to use it (Jn 18:10). James and John, the sons of Zebedee, are nicknamed '*sons of thunder*' and they want to call down fire on an unwelcoming Samaritan village (Lk. 9:54). They also want political power and status when Jesus is in '*his glory*' (Mk. 10:35–40). Judas' name '*Iscariot*' may be a word derived from *sicarius*, the Latin for a cut-throat (Mk. 3:19). Jesus himself is seen as '*one of the rebellious*' (Lk. 22:37). Even Paul is accused of being an agitator when he is arrested in Jerusalem. An official asks him, '*Aren't you the Egyptian who started the recent revolt and led those four thousand cut-throats out into the desert?*' (Acts 21:38).

These references indicate something of the political insecurity of the time. Roman power, whether exercised directly or through the Herodian kings, was constantly threatened by protest groups, sometimes of a violent nature, and it is not surprising that the Romans mistook the movement around Jesus for a political one. The possibility of turning to the sword was always there (Mt. 10:34; Lk. 22:36), but Jesus resists the temptation (Mt. 26:52). '*Mine is not a kingdom of this world*', he says (Jn. 18:36). The tension between

153

violence and peace can be seen in a number of brief allusions in the Gospels (Mt. 11:22; Lk. 16:16; Jn. 6:15, 10:8,18).

Jesus does not seem to have had any great respect for the authorities, however. He lists tax collectors, who collaborated with the Romans, together with sinners, gentiles and prostitutes (Mt. 9:10, 18:17, 21:31). He calls King Herod *'that fox'* (Lk. 13:32). With some sarcasm, he refers to the title *'Benefactor'* given to gentile kings and rulers, and says to his disciples, *'With you this must not happen'*. The leader must behave *'as if he were the one who serves'* (Lk. 22:24–27). Authority for Jesus is exercised in service not in domination.

The first three Gospels all record the famous episode in which Jesus is asked about paying taxes to Caesar. The question is put as a trap: *'Is it permissible to pay taxes to Caesar or not?'* Jesus calls for a coin and asks, *'Whose portrait is this? Whose title?'* The answer comes, *'Caesar's'*, to which he replies, *'Pay Caesar what belongs to Caesar – and God what belongs to God'* (Mt. 22: 15–22; Mk. 12:13–17; Lk. 20:20–26). The precise meaning of this enigmatic saying has troubled commentators ever since. If Jesus had said 'Pay', he would have shown himself up as a collaborator, like the Herodians, and upset his more fiery companions. If he had said 'Don't pay', he would have identified himself with current political protest groups, with dire consequences.

In *The State in the New Testament*, the Swiss theologian Oscar Cullmann explains the saying like this: Jesus 'merely recognizes that within its sphere the State can demand what belongs to it: money, taxes. But it is not placed on the same level as God. Give God what is his! That means: your life, your entire person' (Cullmann 1957:35–36). Caesar's image is impressed on a coin, but God's image is in human beings. The implication is that the state, and particularly a totalitarian state, should not be given more than its due. Cullmann continues, 'In the background we hear the challenge: if ever the State demands what belongs to God, if ever it hinders you in the proclamation of the Kingdom of God, then resist it' (Cullmann 1957: 37).

Jesus' position in the Gospels is a sensitive one. He attracts people who have good cause to oppose the political regime of the day, but he also welcomes some who collaborate with it, like Matthew the tax collector, into his circle. The kingdom he preaches is seen by some to be a political one, and he realizes the implications of this, but he denies that he is a threat to the authorities. He does not want to accept the title *'the Christ'* publicly; its overtones are too political (Mk. 8:29–30). He pays the Temple tax (Mt. 17:24–27). He resists the way of violence. But in the end, it is as a political agitator that he is charged (Lk. 23:2) and put to death on a cross. If his crime had simply been blasphemy, he would have been stoned by the Jews, merely with Pilate's ratification. An inscription is fixed to the cross giving the offence, *'King of the Jews'* (Jn. 19:19). At face value, it is a misunderstanding, but underneath, it is a profound truth.

This apparent attitude of critical acceptance, provided the state keeps within its limits, seems to be radically contradicted in a famous passage in Romans 13. Here no resistance or opposition is allowed. *'Everyone is to obey the governing authorities,'* Paul writes, *'because there is no authority except from God and so whatever authorities exist have been appointed by God. So anyone who disobeys an authority is rebelling against God's ordinance.'* Paul goes on to advise his readers to live honestly, for the state is there *'to serve God for you and for your good'*. It is there as God's avenger, *'to bring retribution to wrongdoers'*. Christians in Rome should be obedient, and pay their taxes, *'because the authorities are all serving God as his agents, even while they are busily occupied with that particular task'* (13:1–7).

Similar points are made in 1 Timothy: petitions, prayers, intercessions and thanksgiving are urged for kings and others in authority, *'so that we may be able to live peaceful and quiet lives with all devotion and propriety'* (2:1–2). Titus has the same theme: *'Remind them to be obedient to the officials in authority . . . to be peaceable and gentle'* (3:1–2). And so does 1 Peter: *'For the sake of the Lord, accept the authority of every human institution: the emperor, as the supreme authority, and the governor as commissioned by him to punish criminals and praise those who do good . . . Have respect for everyone and love for your fellow-believers; fear God and honour the emperor'* (2:13–17).

In all these passages, which may have come from a

155

common source, the state is clearly to be obeyed and the Christian is to be submissive. Behind temporal authority lies divine authority. The purpose of the state is to secure honest dealing, to punish criminals, to raise taxes in a fair way, to secure peace and social order, and to promote the individual and the common good. Within the state, honour is due at each level because authority flows down from God to the emperor, and then on to lower officials. In the early Church the critical attitude of Jesus seems to have been severely tempered by practical experience in a hostile world.

How can this radically altered approach be understood? Originally the Church had gained a reputation as a subversive organization; its leader had been executed and his followers imprisoned or persecuted. If it was to continue at all, it had to promote the idea that Christians were law-abiding citizens with no political agenda. In any case, it was a very small group, and challenging the mighty Roman empire was hardly a realistic option. The early Church also lived in the strong expectation that the end of all things was imminent. In this context, political opposition had little point; the state had at best a temporary existence. In as much as it provided order and security, even a corrupt and oppressive regime was working under the authority of God, and it deserved support for this at least.

Two further passages indicate that Paul did not intend Christians to accept the authority of the state without qualification in every respect. In 1 Corinthians, they are advised to sort out their quarrels among themselves, without being 'so brazen as to seek judgement from sinners and not from God's holy people' (6:1–8). In Philippians, Paul writes, 'Our homeland is in heaven' (3:20). The RV translates the word more pointedly, our 'citizenship'.

It is important to understand that the early Church had a strong view of the presence of angelic and demonic powers at work behind persons and institutions in the world. Various terms are used in the Scriptures, none of them easy to interpret today. 'It is not against human enemies that we have to struggle,' says the letter to the Ephesians, 'but against the principalities and the ruling forces who are masters of the darkness in this *world, the spirits of evil in the heavens'* (6:12). Other terms along with these appear frequently (Rom. 8:38–39; Eph. 1: 21; Phil. 2:10; Col. 1:16). With such a world view, it is easy to understand how the state can be seen as the agent of God, until it oversteps the mark. When it demands that its citizens should show their loyalty by worshipping Caesar, as Nero's state was doing at the time of some of these writings, it has become the agent of Satan (2 Thess. 2:9).

Quite a different approach again can be found in Revelation 13. This highly symbolic passage is full of obscure imagery, echoing the vision in Daniel 7. *'Then I saw a beast emerge from the sea,'* it begins. *'It had seven heads and ten horns, with a coronet on each of its ten horns, and its heads were marked with blasphemous titles.'* The beast makes war against the saints. It is given power over every race, people, language and nation. All people will worship it. Then a second beast emerges, working miracles, even *'calling down fire from heaven'*. It persuades people to put up a statue in honour of the first beast and breathes life into it. Anyone who refuses to worship it is put to death. It compels everyone, *'small and great alike, rich and poor, slave and citizen'* to be branded on the right hand or on the forehead (13:1–18).

It seems clear that the Roman empire is being described here, and the worship of Caesar's statue. Perhaps we can also hear echoes of the creation story and of Noah's descendants in Genesis (2:7, 10:31), and of the baptismal formula in Galatians (3:28). The state has clearly exceeded its divine remit and become demonic. Resistance even to death is envisaged. *'Those for captivity to captivity,'* the writer continues, *'those for death by the sword to death by the sword'* (Rev. 13:10). It is quite a different attitude from that of Romans 13.

Democracy

Christian theologians through the centuries have picked up these various strands and developed them for their own time. Martin Luther, for example, sees the state as 'an agent of God, symbolized chiefly by the sword, with authority to defend society against enemies from without and to punish crime and sedition within' (Bennett 1958: 37–38). Luther separates God's redemptive work through the Church and the political responsibilities of the secular order into two realms or kingdoms. The consequences of this Lutheran doctrine, separating Church and state, seem to have hindered the Church in Germany from dealing adequately with the rise of the Nazi threat in the 1930s. Calvin, on the other hand, has a more integrated view. He says that the authority of kings and governors is 'not a consequence of the perverseness of men, but of the providence and holy ordinance of God, who has pleased to regulate human affairs in this manner' (Bennett 1958: 41).

Both these theologians of the Reformation speak strongly about submission even to tyrants, though a loophole is left for resistance by lower authorities to those above them. Bennett summarizes the point: 'A minimum of order is a pre-condition of life itself' (Bennett 1958: 72).

More recent theologians have struggled with the complex nature of modern democratic societies. What is the common good? How can society be protected from human sin and selfishness, without at the same time infringing human freedom? What should happen when the law that applies to everyone comes into conflict with the conscience of the individual? In *The Children of Light and the Children of Darkness*, Reinhold Niebuhr argues in favour of democracy in words that have become famous. 'Man's capacity for justice makes democracy possible', he writes; 'but man's inclination to injustice makes democracy necessary' (Niebuhr 1966: xiii). In *Christianity and Social Order*, William Temple wants the Church to supply its members with 'a systematic statement of principles' carrying with it 'a denunciation of customs or institutions in contemporary life and practice which offend against those principles' (Temple 1976: 43).

Liberation theologians argue for something much more robust. God is not to be seen at work behind order and obedience, but in the struggle for justice and the liberation of the poor. In *Toward a Christian Political Ethics*, José Miguez Bonino writes: 'God's power, therefore, is his active presence – those "powerful acts" of liberation, protection, vengeance, or punishment that correspond to his faithfulness to his people and to the whole of humankind. In other words: God's power is his "justice" in action' (Bonino 1983: 96).

Themes

Three themes emerge from this review of the material in the Bible on the state and its authority, and the hints we have noted of the discussion it has helped to inform. First, **the state plays a fundamental role in preserving order and enabling people to go about their business in peace**. It is a natural expression of human society. It is what happens when people come together into something corporate, a community, a nation. As such it should gain the willing consent of most of its citizens. This positive attitude encourages a basic respect and support for its officers, its policies and its programmes. It also encourages Christian people, today, to stand for office and to regard the political life as a means of Christian service.

Secondly, **no secular authority, no parliament, no political leader, or judge, has any absolute status**. Honour and respect may be due, but in the end even the highest in society is subject to a higher authority still, that of God. Where natural justice is infringed, or human rights are denied, or the common good is not served, or the poor suffer, the state loses its authority. God is no longer behind it. In the language of ancient times, it has become enslaved to Satan.

Thirdly, **the Church stands in critical solidarity with the state**. It should watch it carefully to see where legitimate authority is being over-stepped. When this happens, the Church has a clear mandate to intervene – to interfere as William Temple puts it – to lobby, to pass resolutions of opposition, to protest, to march, even to defy and to take the consequences, if that seems, as it has done to some, to be what conscience requires. And the state should be glad of this. It is an opposition that emerges out of a basic support, not always offered by others. It is an opposition with the good of the state and the people as its objective.

159

Reginald and Marjorie are shocked by the idea that the state might become evil in some of its policies and actions, in Britain at least, and that there may be a Christian responsibility to resist it even to death. But they know that this is what happened in Germany in the time of Hitler. In July 1944, members of the Confessing Church, including Dietrich Bonhoeffer, plotted to assassinate their head of state. In the event they did not succeed, and the graves of some of them can be seen in an east Berlin graveyard. More recently, Reginald and Marjorie have seen the horrific abuse of political power in Romania and in Iran. Revelation 13 must have had a powerful meaning for Christian people in situations such as these.

Our two pillars of society have a point in wanting the Church to keep out of politics, in as much as well-meaning amateurs may be trespassing into technical areas they know little about, or even because the gospel may be compromised by the realities of power. But in the end all political leaders and all political power are subordinate to the higher authority of God himself. The Church has to be involved in politics and to keep this vision alive.

WAR AND PEACE

The state may have the right to ask for the willing support of its citizens, provided it keeps within its proper bounds, but has it the right to require them to take up arms and fight? If so, on what conditions? And should a Christian really be prepared to kill? Isn't that to go beyond any reasonable limit?

William feels this acutely. On leaving school, he went to Sandhurst and then into the Army. He was trained to obey orders, to defend his country, to uphold peace. As an officer he found the camaraderie of the Mess, and the sense of common purpose, deeply rewarding. But as the cold war came to an end, and communism collapsed, he began to be very uneasy about the deadly capability of modern high-technology weapons systems. The Falklands conflict in 1982 and the Gulf war in 1991 seemed to justify fighting on a

160

limited scale, but the possible use of nuclear weapons looked more and more unacceptable. So he took his chance when he reached 40 and left the Army. Now he has a job in personnel management and a company car. He is happy to be out of it.

Holy War

The Hebrew Scriptures, however, record battles and fighting, and mass destruction on page after page, and God seems to be behind it. In Exodus, Yahweh strikes down all the first-born in Egypt and this persuades Pharoah to let the Israelites go (12:29–33). After their escape, they sing in Yahweh's honour: '*He has covered himself in glory, horse and rider he has thrown into the sea . . . Yahweh is a warrior.*' By his right hand, he wins glory, shatters his foes, fells his assailants, unleashes his fury (15:1–7). In Numbers, there is mention of a '*Book of the Wars of Yahweh*' (21:14). The land of Canaan is taken and all opposition wiped out (21:1–3, 33–35). A war of vengeance is conducted against the Midianites. Twelve thousand men '*equipped for war*' from the twelve tribes of Israel take part. They put every male to death, kill the kings and slaughter all the women, sparing only the young girls '*who have never slept with a man*', keeping them for themselves (31:1–18).

In Deuteronomy, there are several examples of a holy war, in which whole populations are devoted to Yahweh and completely destroyed. Seven nations are conquered and put '*under the curse of destruction*'. There is to be no treaty with them, no mercy shown, no inter-marriage, no serving of other gods (Dt. 7).

Some limitations are, however, put on the conduct of war. Those who have just built a house '*and not yet dedicated it*', who have planted a vineyard '*and not yet enjoyed its fruit*', have got engaged to be married, or who are '*frightened or faint-hearted*', are to be excused from taking part. Peace terms are to be offered before any attack is made on a town. Except in a holy war, there is no requirement that everything should be destroyed: women, children, livestock and spoil may be

161

taken as booty. Fruit trees are not to be destroyed in a long siege (Dt. 20:5–20, 24:5). It is clear that all-out war is not permitted, and that the conduct of war is subject to conditions springing from religion.

But the warlike, avenging character of Yahweh is still put in powerful terms: '*Vengeance is mine, I will pay them back . . . When I have whetted my flashing sword, I shall enforce justice . . . I shall take vengeance on my foes. I shall make my arrows drunk with blood, and my sword will feed on flesh: the blood of the wounded and the prisoners, the dishevelled heads of the enemy!*' (Dt. 32:35–42).

The ruthless conquest of Canaan is further portrayed in Joshua. Jericho is encircled and captured, following the blast on the trumpet and the collapse of the wall. The '*curse of destruction*' is enforced on everything there, except the prostitute Rahab, who has helped the spies (6:1–25). Achan, who violates the curse by helping himself to some of the spoil, is stoned, and possibly his family with him (Josh. 7). Other towns are also destroyed in this way (Josh. 8—12).

The slaughter continues in Judges. Ten thousand Moabites are beaten (3:29). Sisera's army, with nine hundred iron chariots, is overcome and the result is celebrated in a gruesome victory song, one of the most ancient passages in the Bible (4:12–16, 5). Later, the Benjaminites are put to the sword, '*people, livestock and everything else*' (20:48). In 1 Samuel, wars against the Philistines and the Amalekites are recorded. David slays the Philistine champion Goliath. Eighty-five priests of Nob are killed for conspiracy (1 Sam. 13—15, 17, 22). David's prowess is celebrated in dance with the words, '*Saul has killed his thousands, and David his tens of thousands*' (18:7, 21:12, 29: 5). The fighting continues in 2 Samuel (5, 8, 10—12, 21), 1 Kings (11, 22), 2 Kings (3, 6—7, 10, 17—18) and 2 Chronicles (20, 25, 32). In one night, during Sennacherib's attack on Jerusalem, '*Yahweh went out and struck down a hundred and eighty-five thousand men in the Assyrian camp*' (2 Kgs. 19:35).

War, often brutal, though with some constraints, seems to be a normal part of Israelite life, and Yahweh is intimately involved in it. But what is the purpose of all this bloodshed?

Holy wars have a religious motivation. They are intended to remove all possible opposition to the exclusive covenant between Yahweh and his people. The destruction of whole communities roots out any temptation there might be to worship other gods and to break the covenant by disobeying the Law. A holy war is intended to secure the religious purity that is required of Yahweh's people.

War has other purposes, too. The theme of punishment for disobedience and unfaithfulness occurs frequently. In attacking Israel, Assyria is an agent of divine anger, sent against a godless nation, commissioned by Yahweh against a people who enraged him *'to pillage and plunder at will'* (Isa. 10:5–6). Invasion from Babylon, destruction and exile are seen as punishment for sin. In the streets of Jerusalem, says Jeremiah, there is not *'one individual who does right and seeks the truth'*, and swearing by gods *'that are not gods at all'* is rife (5:1,7).

There is no doubt that the ancient world was unruly, violent and warlike. Samuel *'hewed Agag in pieces'* without apparent hesitation (1 Sam. 15:33 REB). The Psalmist could write at a moment of despair about the exile in Babylon, *'Daughter of Babel, doomed to destruction, a blessing on anyone who treats you as you treated us, a blessing on anyone who seizes your babies and shatters them against a rock!'* (137:8–9). In his paper *The Concept of Peace in the Old Testament*, the biblical scholar Andrew Chester concludes: 'The sheer weight of evidence is concentrated not on peace but on vindictive destruction, bloodthirsty retribution, and wholesale slaughter of peoples, including women and children; and it would be idle to pretend otherwise.' By way of explanation, he continues: 'The violent destruction and military disaster that overtakes a nation, especially Israel, is linked directly with injustice, oppression and idolatry within that society, and interpreted theologically as divine judgement upon it' (Chester 1989: 468, 473).

Peace with Justice

This emphasis on war is, however, matched with a concern for peace, providing certain conditions are fulfilled. The

163

Hebrew word for peace – *shalom* – is a rich concept including faithfulness and prosperity as well as the absence of conflict. '*If you live according to my laws,*' Yahweh says in Leviticus, '*I shall give peace in the land*' (26:3,6). In Numbers, Aaron and his sons are to use these words of blessing: '*May Yahweh bless you and keep you. May Yahweh let his face shine on you and be gracious to you. May Yahweh show you his face and bring you peace*' (6:24–26).

Isaiah speaks of a time when military boots and clothing will be burnt and people '*will hammer their swords into plough-shares and their spears into sickles. Nation will not lift sword against nation, no longer will they learn how to make war*' (2:4). Micah has the same vision (4:3). Joel, however, exactly reverses the idea. '*Prepare for war . . .* ' he says, '*Hammer your ploughshares into swords, your billhooks into spears*' (4:9–10 [3:9–10 REB]). In Isaiah, the Messiah is called '*Prince-of-Peace*'. He will '*extend his dominion in boundless peace, over the throne of David and over his kingdom to make it secure and sustain it*' (9:4–6 [9:5–7 REB]). It will be a time of harmony. '*The wolf will live with the lamb . . .* ' he writes, '*no hurt, no harm will be done on all my holy mountain*' (11:6–9, 65:25). Peace will flow over Jerusalem '*like a river*' (66:12).

In a passage full of the imagery of sheep and shepherd, Ezekiel speaks of a '*covenant of peace*'; the people will be secure, the land will be prosperous, there will be no slavery, no foreign aggression, no famine, no insults from other nations (34:25–31). In Zechariah, the figure of the Messiah will '*banish chariots from Ephraim and horses from Jerusalem; the bow of war will be banished. He will proclaim peace to the nations . . .* ' (9:10).

The vision of peace is intimately linked with justice and with concern for the poor. The Psalms make this point well: '*Turn away from evil and do good, seek peace and pursue it*' (34:14). Peace and justice are constantly set alongside each other (72:1–4,7), and '*Saving Justice and Peace embrace*' (85:10). In Isaiah, the kingdom will be sustained '*in fair judgement and integrity*' (9:6 [9:7 REB], 11:4). '*The product of uprightness will be peace*' (32:17). In Jerusalem, Yahweh says, '*I shall make Peace your administration and Saving Justice your government*'

(60:17). The same link is also made in other passages (Jer. 22:3; Amos 1:3—2:16).

The theme of false prophecy of peace also occurs. In Jeremiah, Yahweh will stretch his hand over greedy and fraudulent prophets and priests who say ' *"Peace! Peace!" whereas there is no peace'* (6:14, 8:11; Ezek. 13:10,16) In Micah, Yahweh speaks of prophets who lead people astray: *'So long as they have something to eat they cry "Peace". But on anyone who puts nothing into their mouths they declare war'* (3:5).

In ancient Israel, it is clear that another of the purposes of war is the securing of peace and prosperity. The vision seems to apply to Israel at first, but there is a growing sense of something much wider. Without justice on an international level, there can be no real abiding peace for anyone.

Military Images

In the Christian Scriptures there is no longer any picture of God as a warrior leading his people to victory over their enemies. But the presence of the military is often to be found, and some violent images are used.

Soldiers appear in the Gospels. In Luke, they are among the crowds around John the Baptist. They are told, *'No intimidation! No extortion! Be content with your pay'* (3:14). The servant of a centurion is healed (7:1–10; Mt. 8:5–13). Soldiers are present when Jesus is arrested, and at his trial. They are there at the foot of the cross. One of them says, *'In truth this man was Son of God'* (Mk. 15:39; Mt. 27:54). In Luke, he calls him simply *'an upright man'* (23:47).

War and destruction are referred to directly in a number of passages. Matthew includes the obscure remark, *'Since John the Baptist came, up to this present time, the kingdom of heaven has been subjected to violence and the violent are taking it by storm'* (11:12). No one knows exactly what events are referred to here. In passages which also seem to reflect the later experience of the Church, Jesus says, *'Do not be afraid of those who kill the body but cannot kill the soul; fear him rather who can destroy both body and soul in hell'* (10:28), and again, *'When you hear of wars and rumours of wars, do not be alarmed;*

165

this is something that must happen, but the end will not be yet. For nation will fight against nation, and kingdom against kingdom . . . ' (Mk. 13:7–8). Endurance is encouraged when these things happen.

In Luke, there is an occasion when the disciples want to call down fire from heaven to burn up an unwelcoming Samaritan village, but Jesus rebukes them (9:51–55). His power over Beelzebub is illustrated in terms of weapons and defence. *'So long as a strong man fully armed guards his own home,'* Jesus says, *'his goods are undisturbed; but when someone stronger than himself attacks and defeats him, the stronger man takes away all the weapons he relied on and shares out his spoil'* (11:21–22). *'What king marching to war against another king,'* he says again, *'would not first sit down and consider whether with ten thousand men he could stand up to the other who was advancing against him with twenty thousand?'* (14:31).

The cleansing of the Temple is also a violent act with a symbolic significance. In John's account, Jesus makes a *'whip out of cord'* and drives out the cattle, sheep and doves and those selling them, and the money changers. He puts this event at the start of Jesus' ministry (2:13–16). The other Gospels do not mention the whip, and put the story at the end, before his arrest and trial (Mt. 21:12; Mk. 11:15; Lk. 19:45).

There are a number of references to the sterner side of God's nature. In Matthew, Jesus says, darkly, that it would be better for anyone who causes the downfall of little ones to be *'drowned in the depths of the sea with a great millstone round his neck'* (18:6). In the vision of the Last Judgement, those who do not care for the needy are told, *'Go away from me, with your curse upon you, to the eternal fire prepared for the devil and his angels'* (25:41). Luke refers obliquely to *'weeping and grinding of teeth'* (13:28). In Hebrews, God is *'a consuming fire'* (12:29).

In the letters, there is specific reference to God's 'wrath' – *orge* in Greek. In Romans, in the NJB translation, *'the retribution of God'* against ungodliness and injustice is mentioned, and it is the *'stubborn refusal to repent'* which stores it up (1:18, 2:5). The same theme comes in Ephesians (5:6), Colossians

166

(3:6) and 1 Thessalonians (2:16). Retribution indicates the meaning more clearly than the word wrath, used in the AV. It is not some personal response of anger. It is cause and effect. As Paul puts it in Romans, *'The wage paid by sin is death'* (6:23). The one follows inexorably from the other.

The Sword

Much has been made of a number of references to the sword. In Matthew, Jesus says to his disciples, *'It is not peace I have come to bring, but a sword'* (10:34; Lk. 12:51). *'If you have no sword,'* he says again before they set out for the garden of Gethsemane, *'sell your cloak and buy one'*. They say, *'Lord, here are two swords'*; and he answers, *'That is enough!'* (Lk. 22:36–38). As Jesus is betrayed by Judas, the disciples call out, *'Lord, shall we use our swords?'* One of them strikes the high priest's servant and cuts off his ear. Again Jesus replies, *'That is enough'* and heals him (22:49–51). In Matthew's account, the healing is omitted and Jesus says, *'Put your sword back, for all who draw the sword will die by the sword'*. He claims that he could have more than twelve legions of angels to defend him, but he does not want this (26:51–54). Simpler versions of the same episode are given by Mark (14:47) and John (18:10–11).

In Romans, the sword appears again in a passage on obedience to the civil authorities. *'It is not for nothing'*, Paul writes, *'that the symbol of authority is the sword: it is there to serve God, too, as his avenger to bring retribution to wrongdoers'* (13:4). Ephesians, quoting Isaiah (59:17), uses a military metaphor to good effect: *'Put on the full armour of God so as to be able to resist the devil's tactics.'* Truth is to be a belt, uprightness a breastplate, faith a shield, salvation a helmet, and the Spirit, the word of God, a sword. Among these defensive weapons, there are also shoes, *'the eagerness to spread the gospel of peace'* (6:11–17). The same metaphor comes in Romans (13:14) and in 1 Thessalonians (5:8). In Hebrews, the word of God *'cuts more incisively than any two-edged sword'* (4:12).

Finally, there is a symbolic reference to war in Revelation:

167

'*War broke out in heaven.*' The beast is allowed '*to make war against the saints*' and '*against the Lamb*' (12:7, 13:7, 17:14).

These passages seem to permit the use of military force, or at least to accept that it is inevitable in some circumstances. It cannot fairly be claimed, however, that, in advising the restrained use of force, and contentment with army wages, or that in healing a centurion's servant, the military profession as a whole is approved. Jesus seems to resist the use of force. He will not allow the Samaritan village to be destroyed for its lack of hospitality, and the whip, though a violent instrument, is hardly a weapon of death. More than once he says '*enough*' to the use of the sword when it is proposed. The disciples may have been urged to buy swords for defence out in the darkness of the hillside. Peter's use of his sword was more an impetuous act of temper than a deliberately authorized attack.

The argument that armed aggression leads to armed retaliation is less of a justification for military action that a statement of fact. Violence breeds violence. For Paul, the sword is a symbol of the role of the state in keeping order and punishing wrong-doing. There is no necessary military implication. Armour is for defence, not for attack. The early church was, in any case, too fragile an organization to have very strong views about military service, and no great weight can really be put on these incidental references. For its first 400 years, the Church seems to have been substantially pacifist. This was how it understood the implications of the Christian Scriptures on this matter.

Forgiveness and Non-resistance

The theme of peace, however, is often mentioned. In a passage in Luke that has become the Benedictus, Zechariah, the father of John the Baptist, sings about the Messiah, who will '*guide our feet into the way of peace*' (1:79). In the Beatitudes in Matthew, peace requires positive action. '*Blessed are the peacemakers,*' says Jesus: '*they shall be recognized as children of God.*' It is the poor in spirit, the gentle, those who mourn, and who hunger and thirst for uprightness, the merciful, the pure in heart, and the persecuted who are blessed, not the violent or the warlike (5:3–10).

In the farewell discourses, placed by John in the context of the last supper, Jesus says, '*Peace I bequeath to you, my own peace I give you, a peace which the world cannot give . . .* ' (Jn. 14:27). After his resurrection, Jesus appears to the disciples and says, '*Peace be with you*' (Jn. 20:19,21,26). It is the basic Christian greeting.

Jesus often urges forgiveness rather than retaliation, fundamentally challenging the normal response to aggression in the Mosaic law (Gen. 9:6). In the Lord's Prayer, forgiveness of debt, or of sins, is central (Mt. 6:12,14–15; Mk. 11:25; Lk. 11:3–4). In answer to Peter's question about how often to forgive, Jesus says, '*Not seven, I tell you, but seventy-seven times*' (Mt. 18:21–22; Lk. 17:3–4). At the crucifixion, Jesus prays for his executioners, '*Father, forgive them; they do not know what they are doing*' (Lk. 23:34).

In Matthew, Jesus quotes the law of retribution, '*an eye for an eye . . .* ' and replaces it with a new standard: '*But I say this to you: offer no resistance to the wicked. On the contrary, if anyone hits you on the right cheek, offer him the other as well . . . Love your enemies and pray for those who persecute you*' (5:38–44). Luke gives a stronger version, adding positively, '*Do good to those who hate you . . . Treat others as you would like people to treat you . . . Love your enemies and do good to them*' (6:27,31, 35). To hit someone on the right cheek would mean striking him with the back of the hand, adding insult to injury. To offer the other cheek as well would be doubly forgiving. But Jesus is not here suggesting an entirely passive response to personal aggression. He offers an alternative, that of active love, which seeks the good of the aggressor, not his punishment.

Love is central. '*This is my commandment*', Jesus says: '*love one another, as I have loved you. No one can have greater love than to lay down his life for his friends*' (Jn. 15:12–13). Although this passage has been used to support military action in defence of family and country, this cannot have been in Jesus' mind at the time. Before Pilate, he specifically renounces

169

such a method. '*If my kingdom were of this world,*' he says, '*my men would have fought to prevent my being surrendered to the Jews*' (Jn. 18:36).

In Romans, Paul urges, '*Be at peace with everyone. Never try to get revenge . . . As scripture says: Vengeance is mine – I will pay them back, the Lord promises*' (12:18–19). Christian people are to seek '*the ways which lead to peace*' (14:19). For Paul, there is an underlying theological basis for true peace. '*Now that we have been justified by faith,*' he writes in Romans, '*we are at peace with God through our Lord Jesus Christ*' (5:1). In 2 Corinthians, he considers the work of Christ in bringing about a new creation: '*It is all God's work; he reconciled us to himself through Christ and he gave us the ministry of reconciliation*' (5:18). '*Try to grow perfect,*' he continues: '*encourage one another; have a common mind and live in peace, and the God of love and peace will be with you*' (13:11).

In Galatians, peace is part of the fruit of the Spirit (5:22). In Ephesians, Christ is the peace between God and man (2:14). A strong passage in Colossians declares that through Christ God wanted '*to reconcile all things to him . . . by making peace through his death on the cross*' (1:20).

The theme continues in other letters. Hebrews urges, '*Seek peace with all people*' (12:14). In James, the '*wisdom that comes down from above*' is '*peaceable*', and the '*peace sown by peace-makers brings a harvest of justice*' (3:17–18). In 1 Peter, the theme of submission (2: 13,17) is further developed. Retaliation within the Christian fellowship is forbidden. '*Never repay one wrong with another,*' the author writes, '*or one abusive word with another; instead, repay with a blessing*' (3:9). The passage continues with a quotation from Psalm 34, '*Turn away from evil and do good, seek peace and pursue it*' (3:11). Suffering is to be endured rather than resisted. '*Blessed are you if you have to suffer for being upright . . . And if it is the will of God that you should suffer, it is better to suffer for doing right than for doing wrong*' (3:14,17).

Pacifism and the Just War Tradition

The tension between war and peace, between resisting evil and enduring it, between taking up arms for defence and putting them aside, was apparently resolved without much difficulty in the early Church. A Christian could not kill, nor could he serve in the armed forces. In *The Politics of Love*, the biblical scholar John Ferguson quotes some words from the second-century African theologian Tertullian: 'How shall the Christian wage war, no, how shall he even be a soldier in peace-time, without the sword which the Lord has taken away? For although soldiers had come to John and received the form of their rule, although even a centurion had believed, the Lord afterwards in disarming Peter, ungirded every soldier' (Ferguson 1973: 60). The shedding of blood that was involved, the unconditional military oath which conflicted with allegiance to Christ, and the pagan religious worship that played an important part in military life, made such service impossible for Christians.

By the fourth century, however, as Christianity became officially recognized by the state, attitudes changed. Attention turned to the attempt to contain war, which seemed an inevitable part of life, within some moral boundaries. Augustine and, later, Thomas Aquinas, developed the doctrine of the 'just war'. This theory, perhaps better called the limited or justified war, is based on a presumption in favour of peace, and it accepts the legitimacy of war only in self-defence.

In their pastoral letter *The Challenge of Peace*, the American Catholic Bishops describe the conditions that need to be met if going to war is to be justified – *jus ad bellum* in Latin. There must be a just cause, 'to protect innocent life, to preserve conditions necessary for decent human existence, and to secure basic human rights'. War must be declared by competent authority, by 'those with responsibility for public order, not by private groups or individuals'. There must be comparative justice; it must be clear that 'the rights and values involved justify killing'. There must be right intention; war must be 'legitimately intended only for the reasons

171

set forth'. It must be a matter of last resort; 'all peaceful alternatives must have been exhausted'. There must be probability of success, to 'prevent irrational resort to force or hopeless resistance'. And there must be proportionality; 'the damage to be inflicted and the costs incurred by war must be proportionate to the good expected by taking up arms' (Roman Catholic Church U.S. Bishops 1983: 26–29).

Two conditions must be met in the conduct of war – *jus in bello*. These are proportionality and discrimination (Roman Catholic Church U.S. Bishops 1983: 29). In a way that was unimaginable when the just war doctrine was first developed, it is all too easy for a modern war to escalate out of all apparent control, even if it is carefully and responsibly entered into in the first place. It is almost certain that those not directly involved, innocent non-combatants, will be killed as a secondary consequence of, say, a bombing raid on a more limited military target. The Bishops write of the possibility of 'total war' and of the use of 'weapons of horrendous destructive potential'. In such a situation they admit the practical difficulty of applying the just war criteria. They see the validity of the way of non-violence. Nuclear war, they conclude, seems to be ruled out by these criteria, because of the impossibility of placing any effective limits on the consequences of the use of such weapons. The Bishops declare: 'As a people, we must refuse to legitimate the idea of nuclear war' (Roman Catholic Church U.S. Bishops 1983: 38).

But how can nuclear war be prevented? Here resort is made to the theory of deterrence: threatening so convincingly to loose off nuclear weapons in response to any first strike, that the enemy is deterred from attacking at all. Although threatening to do what is immoral is just as immoral, this theory is acceptable to the Bishops only because it seems to have been effective in preventing the outbreak of nuclear war. They describe their uncomfortable moral position on this as 'a lack of unequivocal condemnation of deterrence' (Roman Catholic Church U.S. Bishops 1983: 56).

In *War and the Christian Conscience*, written 30 years ago, the American theologian Paul Ramsey accepts the legitimacy

172

of limited war, thinking of it as a work of love in resisting the indiscriminate killing of the defenceless and the innocent. But he writes, more strongly, that nuclear war and deterrence 'by the mightiest means' cannot provide 'a feasible umbrella under which international relations can be conducted'. He continues, 'There is no policy *more* feasible than dismantling the era of immoral terror' (Ramsey 1961: 190, 270–271). More recently, however, Ramsey has withdrawn a little from this uncompromising opposition to deterrence as a way of keeping peace.

On the other hand, it is argued by pacifists that the way of love rules out any killing. Love is the only power by which evil can be overcome. It is through suffering that evil is conquered and the world redeemed. Violence only leads to more violence. They add that in practice the just war criteria, strictly applied, rule out most armed conflicts in the highly sophisticated and technologically advanced warfare of today. John Ferguson writes: 'Christ showed us a new way, a way of life, a way of changing the world. It was politically relevant. It was in its own way revolutionary. It was the way of love, the way of the Cross, the way of non-violence . . . It is still the way. He seeks to fulfil it in us' (Ferguson 1973: 115).

Themes

The themes which come strongly out of this review of war and peace in the Scriptures, and the Christian tradition of thought about the morality of war, are these: First, there is a sense that, **whatever happens, God is involved in the affairs of his people and his creation**. Both war, when it breaks out, and peace, as it is longed for, reveal something of God and his character and will. This is far from justifying fighting and killing. It does not make war right to say that people of faith are able to find the hand of God somewhere at work within it. But it does give hope that human life, even at its worst moments, is not beyond all redemption.

Secondly, **a clear connection is made between peace and justice**. There is no real peace where people are

173

exploited and human rights are denied. The mere absence of armed conflict is but a pale shadow of the harmony and prosperity envisaged in the Hebrew Scriptures. The brutality and the ruthlessness of war in those ancient times was not an end in itself; it was always subject to religious and humanitarian conditions. War can only be justified, therefore, if its objective is a lasting peace and security which is rooted in justice. Peace is not kept by weapons; it is made by removing injustice and by reconciling people and nations with each other. Only when people have no reason to go to war at all will peace be a reality.

Thirdly, **there is no room for the 'first use' of weapons, for initiating any form of attack on others**. Nor is there any justification for the use of means that are out of all proportion to the size, or the significance, of the target under attack. In our own day, the use of obliteration bombing that destroys innocent people not involved in the conflict, or nuclear weapons that destroy vast areas, is clearly prohibited. Nor is there a place for militarism, or for glorying in battle or in victory. Paul Ramsey notes that down to about the year 1000, 'a private soldier had to do 40 days' penance for fighting in any war, however just' (Ramsey 1961: 115). To celebrate victory was a feature of ancient Israel, but it does not fit well with a Christian approach. Repentance and humility are a more appropriate response.

Fourthly, there is a conviction in the Christian Scriptures that **fighting as a way of solving disputes is not the way of Christ**. Non-violence is better than violence. There is thus a strong incentive to find every way possible of preventing such fighting. Jesus calls people to be peacemakers, actively to meet violence with love, so that it is overcome and peace is made possible.

In 1930 the Lambeth Conference of Anglican bishops expressed the view that 'war as a method of settling international disputes is incompatible with the teaching and example of Our Lord Jesus Christ', and this judgement has been repeated frequently since then (Anglican Consultative Council 1988: 221). Similar views have been expressed by the leaders of other Churches, too, on many occasions. War is unacceptable to Christian people.

When William left his regiment, he did so with mixed feelings. To fight with such terrifying power could not be right, but to refuse to play a part in defending the innocent from attack could not be right either. He feels strongly the tragic nature of so much in human relationships. The importance of international understanding, of fair trading relationships, and of closer links between countries formalized in treaties and in joint regulations of every sort, seems to him to be essential if the tragedy of war is to be prevented. One day he hopes to find a job that will enable him to contribute to this process more fully himself.

CAPITAL PUNISHMENT

There may be occasions when the state can justifiably ask its citizens to take up arms, knowing that some of them will die. But has the state the right to take away the lives of individuals in peace-time? It is sometimes argued that murderers and terrorists forfeit their own right to life when they wilfully kill other people. For them the severest of punishments seems no more than they deserve.

That, at least, is Stephen's view. As an MP he regrets the abolition of the death penalty in the mid–60s. In the House of Commons in June 1988 and again in December 1990 he voted to restore hanging. But the vote was lost by a majority of well over a hundred on each occasion. It isn't enough, in his view, just to have capital punishment in Britain for treason and hijacking on the high seas. It should be imposed on those who kill police officers, as well as for murders involving the use of fire-arms, explosives and offensive weapons. He also wants the power to impose the death penalty for any murder to be given to the Appeal Court. Murders have got to be stopped, he tells a Constituency meeting, to general applause.

175

Blood-Vengeance

Stephen's attitude seems to receive some support in the Hebrew Scriptures. In Genesis, capital punishment for murder is clearly laid down: '*He who sheds the blood of man, by man shall his blood be shed*' (9:6).

In Exodus, the death penalty is prescribed for a range of crimes. '*Anyone who by violence causes a death*', provided it is done with '*deliberate planning*' and not by accident, is to '*be put to death*'. The same applies to anyone who strikes father or mother, who abducts a person who is a slave or a former slave, who curses father or mother, who beats a slave to death, who causes a woman to have a miscarriage and then to die as a result of a brawl, or who fails to keep under control an ox which gores a man or a woman having already done so before. The death penalty also applies if it gores a boy or a girl, though not a slave (21:12–32).

In some cases it seems that a money ransom can be paid instead (Ex. 21:30). The death penalty appears to be a maximum sentence rather than one that is invariably imposed. One limitation is, however, specified. Where a thief is '*caught breaking in and is struck a mortal blow*' at night, vengeance is not permitted, though it is if the break-in takes place during the day (22:1–2). The death penalty can also be imposed on someone for being a sorceress, having intercourse with an animal, sacrificing to other gods, or for working on the sabbath (22:17–19, 31:15).

Similar points are made in Leviticus. Capital punishment is prescribed for those who engage in child sacrifice (20:2), as well as those who curse their parents. Both parties can be put to death in cases of adultery with a neighbour's wife, or intercourse with a father's wife or with a daughter-in-law, or '*with a man in the same way as with a woman*', as well as for marrying a woman and her mother, and for having intercourse with an animal. Women are to lose their lives for this last offence, too. Marrying a father's or a mother's daughter is also liable to this penalty (20:2,9–17). Lesser penalties are prescribed for other similar sexual offences (20:18–21). Anyone who '*blasphemes the name of Yahweh*', or

176

who '*strikes down any other human being*' is to be put to death (24:16–17).

In Numbers, a man caught gathering wood on the sabbath is to be stoned (15:32–36). In Deuteronomy, a prophet or a dreamer of dreams, who urges people to follow other gods, is to be put to death, and the same applies to a brother, son, daughter, spouse or intimate friend, who counsels such apostasy (13:6–7,10). Worshipping other gods, or '*the sun or the moon or any of heaven's array*' is also subject to the death penalty (17:2–7). A son who is '*stubborn and rebellious*' and who will not listen to his parents and who is a '*wastrel and a drunkard*' is to be put to death (21:18–21). Adultery is also a capital offence, as well as rape in certain circumstances: '*If a virgin is engaged to a man, and another man encounters her in the town and has sexual intercourse with her*', they are to be stoned. But if it is in the open country, she is to be let off, for '*the betrothed girl may have called out, without anyone's coming to her rescue*' (22:22,23–27).

The theme of deterrence is also reflected in Deuteronomy. A passage on the penalty for apostasy concludes, '*All Israel, hearing of this, will be afraid, and none of you will do such a wicked thing again*' (13:12). The same deterrent effect is intended in the punishment imposed for other offences (17:13, 19:20, 21:21).

It seems that relatives were often left to put a punishment into effect and to avenge crimes (Num. 35:11–12; Dt. 19:6, 10,12). Capital punishment was mostly imposed by stoning, outside the camp, and the whole community was involved, the accuser casting the first stone (Lev. 24:14,16; Dt. 13:10). Hanging seems not to have been used as a method in Israel, though there may be a reference to this practice in Deuteronomy (21:22–23). It was, however, used in surrounding countries, such as Egypt (Gen. 40:19) and Persia (Esth. 2:23). The bodies of prominent people were sometimes hanged on trees after they had been put to death (Josh. 8:29, 10:26, 2 Sam. 4:12), or dismembered and left outside for a period (2 Sam. 21:1–14).

Divine punishment, or retribution, was also recognized. It might come in the form of death or other disaster, and sin

177

was its basic cause. In Genesis, for example, Abraham tries to save the city of Sodom if even a few upright men can be found in it, but without success (18:20–32). It might also come through natural disaster (Num. 16:30), or the death of children (2 Sam. 12:14; Jer. 11:22), or famine, conquest in battle, or disease (2 Sam. 24:12–15). In Jeremiah, it is Israel's unfaithfulness to Yahweh that makes the prophet cry out: '*So, hand their sons over to famine, abandon them to the edge of the sword. Let their wives become childless and widowed. Let their husbands die of plague, their young men cut down by the sword in battle . . .* ' (18:21).

What was the reason for this severe and apparently brutal punishment in ancient Israel? Blood-vengeance seems to have been a major feature in the life of the community. Bloodshed was thought to defile the land. Abel's blood, for example, cried out to Yahweh from the ground (Gen. 4:10), and expiation was required. But in addition to this, the protection of the people from contamination by foreign religious practices, and the maintenance of the covenant relationship with Yahweh was of primary importance, and this outweighed any other prohibitions against the taking of life. Crime brought its own consequences, and the severity of them must have served to discourage others from offending too.

Other punishments for lesser offences included 'cutting-off', outlawing or excommunication, from the covenant community (Gen. 17:14; Lev. 20:5,18), restitution, full as well as two-, four-, five-, or even seven-fold (Ex. 21:37– 22:14; 2 Sam. 12:5–6; Gen. 4:15,24; Lev. 26:18; Prov. 6:30–31), as well as fines (Ex. 21:32; Dt. 22:19,29), and flogging, probably on the soles of the feet, with no more than 40 strokes being allowed (Dt. 25:1–3). Remand in prison before sentencing is also mentioned (Lev. 24:12; Num. 15:34; 1 Kgs. 22:27), together with imprisonment (Jer. 38:9), and putting people in the stocks in prison (2 Chron. 16:10).

Excessive revenge, however, was not permitted. The law of retaliation – *lex talionis* in Latin – is mentioned in relation to inadvertently causing death after a miscarriage: '*You will award life for life, eye for eye, tooth for tooth, hand for hand, foot for foot, burn for burn, wound for wound, stroke for stroke*' (Ex.

178

21:23–25), and again in Deuteronomy at the end of a passage on giving false evidence in a case of alleged apostasy (19:16, 21). A restriction on vendettas is also found in Deuteronomy as part of a passage on the protection of the individual: '*Parents must not be put to death for their children, nor children for parents, but each must be put to death for his own crime*' (24:16). The same point is made in Ezekiel. '*Why do you keep repeating this proverb in the land of Israel*', Yahweh says: '*The parents have eaten unripe grapes; and the children's teeth are set on edge? . . . Look, all life belongs to me . . . The one who has sinned is the one to die*' (18:1–4).

Much has been made of this, but in reality, these words are a restriction on the lengths to which revenge should go, rather than a justification for capital punishment. The principle of 'proportion' is found again in Leviticus in relation to more modest matters: '*Anyone who injures a neighbour shall receive the same in return, broken limb for broken limb, eye for eye, tooth for tooth. As the injury inflicted, so will be the injury suffered*' (24:19–20).

Mercy and Forgiveness

Mercy and forgiveness, however, match the sternness of Yahweh. In Genesis, Cain ought to lose his life for murdering Abel, but instead he is cursed and banned, the land will not '*yield up its strength*' to him and he is to be a wanderer. But he finds even this too much to bear and Yahweh puts a mark on him to protect him from being killed in revenge (4:11–15). In Exodus, in spite of punishment passing on through the generations, Yahweh says, '*I act with faithful love towards thousands of those who love me and keep my commandments*' (20:5–6). Yahweh is a '*God of tenderness and compassion, slow to anger, rich in faithful love and constancy, maintaining his faithful love to thousands, forgiving fault, crime and sin, yet letting nothing go unchecked, and punishing the parent's fault in the children and in the grandchildren to the third and fourth generation!*' (34:6–7; Num. 14:18; Dt. 5:9–10).

This theme is given practical expression in Numbers in the setting aside of six cities of refuge, '*where those who*

179

have accidentally committed manslaughter can take sanctuary'. The passage continues, *'These towns will afford you refuge from the avenger of blood, so that the killer will not be put to death before standing trial before the community'* (35:10–15). The rules are laid down in some detail. If an object *'meant for killing'* has been used, and the deed has been done *'out of enmity'*, it is murder and vengeance is appropriate. But if it happened *'by chance'*, and the killer bore his victim *'no malice'*, then *'the community will decide'* between them. The killer may stay in the place of sanctuary for a period. More than one witness is needed to sustain a capital charge, and no ransom will be acceptable as an alternative (35:16–30). Again the reason is given: *'Blood profanes the country and, for the country, the only expiation for the blood shed in it is the blood of the man who shed it'* (35:33).

Similar provisions are described in Deuteronomy, although those who kill in a feud are not allowed to use the sanctuary arrangement. The passage concludes, *'You must banish the shedding of innocent blood from Israel, and then you will prosper'* (19:1–13). This concern is taken to considerable lengths. A parapet, for example, should be built round the roof of a house to prevent people falling off, so that it will not *'incur blood-vengeance'* (22:8).

The prophets also promote the concept of mercy, even though they are implacable in their opposition to crime. Their vision is one of restoration, forgiveness and release. Isaiah says that he has been anointed *'to proclaim liberty to captives, release to those in prison'*, and *'to proclaim a year of favour from Yahweh and a day of vengeance for our God'* (61:1–2). In Jeremiah, Yahweh says, *'I shall not make an end of you, only discipline you in moderation, not to let you go quite unpunished'* (30:11). The broken relationship with God is to be restored. Under the new covenant envisaged by Jeremiah, Yahweh declares, *'I shall forgive their guilt and never more call their sin to mind'* (31:34).

Other prophets reflect the same theme: *'I will not give rein to my fierce anger . . . '* says Yahweh in Hosea, *'for I am God, not man'* (11:8–9, 14:5). *'Hate evil, love good . . . '* says Amos, and '*it may be that Yahweh, God sabaoth, will take pity on the remnant of Joseph*' (5:15).

In some passages, repentance is required if forgiveness is to be granted. This theme comes in the Psalms: '*I said, "I shall confess my offence to Yahweh." And you, for your part, took away my guilt, forgave my sin*' (32:5). Again, '*Sacrifice to God is a broken spirit, a broken, contrite heart you never scorn*' (51:17). Yahweh '*forgives all your offences*' (103:3).

The possibility of repentance and forgiveness is profoundly significant. In *Punishment in the Bible*, the former principal Methodist prison chaplain Arthur Hoyles writes: 'The conventional view was that wrongdoing would be punished. Retribution was built into the natural order of things. Divine justice demanded it . . . That this cycle could be upset by the cancellation of deserved penalty was a staggering discovery or a shocking revelation' (Hoyles 1986: 37–38).

Love your Enemies

In the Christian Scriptures, the theme of forgiveness is strongly presented. In Matthew, Jesus says, '*Love your enemies and pray for those who persecute you*'. God '*sends down rain to fall on the upright and the wicked alike*' (5:43–45). The king who forgives the servant with an enormous debt, and who asks for time to pay, '*felt so sorry for him that he let him go and cancelled the debt*'. When he fails to treat a fellow-servant in the same merciful way, the king hands him over to be tortured (18:23–35).

In a long passage in Matthew, Jesus points to the spirit behind the Law, although his actions seem to break the Law itself. '*Do not imagine*', he says, '*that I have come to abolish the Law or the Prophets. I have come not to abolish but to complete them.*' Jesus affirms the Law in detail in strong words, but then continues: '*You have heard how it was said to our ancestors, You shall not kill . . . But I say this to you, anyone who is angry with a brother will answer for it before the court . . . Come to terms with your opponent . . .*' The underlying motive is emphasized all through the chapter in relation to adultery, divorce, breaking an oath, retaliation, and love of the Jewish

181

neighbour alone and not the foreigner as well. The way of perfection for Jesus is summed up in the words, '*Love your enemies*' (5:17–48).

In Luke, the ministry of Jesus begins in the synagogue with the reading of the passage from Isaiah 61. Jesus tells his hearers that the theme of '*liberty to captives*' and of '*a year of favour from the Lord*' is '*being fulfilled*' even as they listen to him. Significantly, Isaiah's final words about a day of vengeance are omitted (4:16–22).

Repentance and forgiveness come again and again in Luke. The three stories of the lost sheep, the lost coin and the lost son press home the point: '*There will be more rejoicing in heaven over one sinner repenting than over ninety-nine upright people.*' While the son is still a long way off, his father sees him and is '*moved with pity*' (15:4–32). The same theme comes in the story of the crafty steward who lets his master's debtors off with reduced payments of oil and wheat (16:1–8). Even as he is crucified, Jesus prays in Luke, '*Father, forgive them . . .*' (23:34). In a striking passage in John, Jesus refuses to accept the death penalty for a woman caught in adultery. He says to the crowd: '*Let the one among you who is guiltless be the first to throw the stone at her.*' No one does, and he continues, '*Neither do I condemn you. Go away, and from this moment sin no more*' (8:3–11).

The further idea that there is a direct relationship between sinful actions and quite unrelated disasters is firmly challenged by Jesus. In Luke, some Galileans '*whose blood Pilate had mingled with that of their sacrifices*' and eighteen people '*on whom the tower of Siloam fell*' are not more guilty than anyone else. Everyone needs to repent (13:1–5). The idea that illness is a punishment is also rejected in the story of the man born blind (Jn. 9).

These passages represent a major development in thinking about sin, or crime, and punishment. The inevitability and the rightness of retribution, both human and divine, in the Hebrew Scriptures is radically reversed in Jesus' approach to the matter.

There is little else in the rest of the Christian Scriptures about capital punishment itself. In Acts, Saul witnesses the stoning of Stephen, and it makes a great impression on him. He '*approved of the killing*', and then '*began doing great harm to the Church*', arresting people and sending them to prison (7:55—8:3). In Romans, Paul is able to write, '*Bless your persecutors; never curse them, bless them . . . Never pay back evil with evil . . . Never try to get revenge: leave that, my friends, to the Retribution . . .* ' Vengeance is for God not for men (12:14–19; 1 Thess. 4:6).

The themes of guilt and punishment, of sacrifice, of blood-vengeance, and of repentance, forgiveness and mercy, play an important role, however, in the attempt to understand the death of Christ on the cross (Rom. 5—6; Gal. 3:10–14; Eph. 2: 1—10; Heb. 2—10; 1 Jn. 1:6—2:2). As so often in the Bible, practical aspects of daily life in ancient Israel are taken up and used to illuminate a profound theological point.

Sitting in Judgement

The idea of never paying back evil with evil was taken to considerable lengths in the early Church. In the second century, Tertullian declares: 'As to the duties of civil power the Christian must not decide on anyone's life or honour – about money it is permissible; but he must bind no one, nor imprison and torture any' (Hoyles 1986: 126). But in later centuries, this early response changed. Under Constantine the Church was allowed to set up its own courts, and mercy was often shown to offenders. In the sixth century, cities of refuge were allowed to shelter criminals, though this arrangement was often abused. In Britain the laws about sanctuary were repealed in 1604, and all rights of refuge removed in 1623 (Hoyles 1986: 128).

In cases of heresy and witchcraft, however, the mediaeval Church showed no mercy. It has been reckoned that there were more than 341,000 victims of the Spanish Inquisition between 1481 and 1808, of whom 32,000 were burned. In the sixteenth and seventeenth centuries, 200,000 witches were put to death, 30,000 of them in Britain alone. Witchcraft became a felony in England in 1541 and the last trial took place in 1712 (Hoyles 1986: 130–131).

Themes

Four themes emerge from this review of the evidence about the death penalty in the Bible. First, **against the background of often uncontrolled violence in the ancient world, the law of retaliation was a considerable advance**. In spite of the Mosaic law, and later of the efforts of judges and kings to promote justice, and of the prophets to keep them to it, there was constant disobedience. Judges notes that '*everyone did as he saw fit*' (17:6, 21:25). The brutal story of the rape of the Levite's concubine and its aftermath is specifically given as an example of this lawlessness (Jgs. 19). The law of retaliation brought some order into a system of revenge and retribution that might affect whole families, generation after generation, for the crime of one person. The idea of a life for a life, an eye for an eye, was not intended to authorize capital punishment, but to limit it, to bring retaliation and revenge under control.

Secondly, **anything that infringed the covenant with Yahweh, particularly sexual behaviour that undermined family identity, and apostasy that broke the religious bond, was to be met with the severest of penalties**. Sexual unfaithfulness and religious apostasy are regularly mentioned together, and the imagery of the one is easily transferred to the other. It is not always the acts done – many are relatively trivial matters in themselves – but the lack of faithfulness to the covenant that is so serious. For Jesus, however, working or carrying wood on the sabbath, and even adultery, are no longer capital crimes. He puts a new emphasis on the heart, rather than the nation, as the basis of faithful community life.

Thirdly, **retaliation is increasingly tempered by recourse to mercy and forgiveness**. Retaliation, even if limited, is not an end in itself. God longs for the sinner to be reconciled with him, to come back into the fold, to keep the covenant. Mercy expresses the character of God just as much as judgement.

In ancient Israel sin was not only met with punishment; it was also dealt with by the ritual of animal sacrifice and, once a year, by the scapegoat. In this ceremony, the sins of the people were laid on the head of a goat, which was then sent off into the desert to *'bear all their guilt away into some desolate place'* (Lev. 16:5–10,20–22). This image is taken up powerfully in the Christian Scriptures in relation to the sacrifice of Jesus on the cross (Rom. 3:25; 1 Jn. 2:2, 4:10). There is a powerful sense of dealing with sin by repentance and restitution, and not just by punishment.

Fourthly, **the law of retaliation is itself undermined by the prophets and by Jesus**. Forgiveness and compassion are better than vengeance. No one is without fault. Enemies are to be loved, not pursued. Vengeance is left to God; it is not for human beings to take into their own hands. It is clear that capital punishment is quite out of keeping with this spirit. Even if a charge of murder can be sustained, and the difficulty of this is recognized in the Hebrew Scriptures, capital punishment holds out no opportunity of forgiveness, nor of any restitution to the community.

Reflecting eighteenth-century criticisms of penal policy Arthur Hoyles writes: 'Punishment for its own sake whether or not it brings benefit to the individual or society offends against the dignity of man. It could fairly be described as useless cruelty. When the purpose of punishment is less than an exercise which produces good effects on human beings it must be pronounced both immoral and irrational' (Hoyles 1986: 116).

In the same way, it seems that imposing severe punishment in order to deter others also needs to be questioned. Although the deterrent effect of punishment is mentioned a number of times in the Hebrew Scriptures, to punish one so that others may not act in similar ways does seem to infringe the law of retaliation itself, let alone the more profound vision of the prophets and of Jesus. An eye for an eye implies that punishment must fit the crime, not serve purposes over and above it.

Stephen's feeling, then, that killing should be met with killing, that a murderer has forfeited his right to life, and that the severest punishment will serve to deter others, is hardly a Christian one. In today's terms, the rehabilitation and resettlement of offenders, and not just their punishment, would seem to match most closely the spirit of the tradition that unfolds in the Bible. It is certainly more loving.

7.
LIFE AND DEATH

Detective stories are immensely popular. The best of them deal in a fascinating way with the subject of murder and death. Characters such as Adam Dalgleish, Maigret, Miss Marple, Morse, Hercule Poirot, Reg Wexford, who live on our television screens and in bookshops, are almost as real to people as politicians and other figures in public life. There is endless scope for argument and disagreement about human relationships, or the environment, or politics, but there is much less scope when it comes to the difficult problems of life and death. Where abortion, for example, or suicide is concerned, the subject is either alive or dead.

As a result, questions about life and death are among the most hotly debated of all moral issues. Exaggerated language is often used. Those against abortion say they are 'pro-life' and those in favour 'pro-choice'. The words *You shall not kill* from Exodus (20:13) seem to be clear-cut, but particular cases often turn out to be not quite so simple. I want to look now, therefore, at some of the questions raised by our treatment of life in the womb, at research on embryos, and at abortion, and then at suicide and euthanasia, and how to die well.

LIFE IN THE WOMB

Alan and Joan long to have a child. Although she has a spinal condition which makes childbirth risky, they feel that their family is not complete without children of their own. They have heard about *in-vitro* fertilization, and eventually arrange, through their doctor, to get on to a programme. Joan is worried abut whether such a thing is moral or not. Will they be 'playing God' by using medical techniques to stimulate fertilization? Do 'spare' embryos have souls, and will their destruction amount to murder? But they are keen to go ahead in the hope of having a much-wanted child.

Rosie is faced with a different question. On holiday in Spain she meets a local boy and goes out with him every evening. The warm nights and the lap of the water on the rocks near the beach are romantic and seductive. Some weeks later she finds she is pregnant. A desperate phone call to Spain meets with no response. A visit to a clinic is arranged and her pregnancy is terminated. That autumn she goes back to college as if nothing had happened. But secretly she weeps every night over her lost child. She thinks of him by name, and tells herself that he is with the angels in heaven.

These two matters – embryo research and abortion – need to be carefully distinguished. Techniques to help people conceive, and research designed to combat disease or handicap, take place in the very earliest days, and they are intended positively to enhance life. Abortion, on the other hand, involves the ending of a life already some months old.

Assisting fertilization for childless couples is a relatively recent concern. The first 'test-tube' baby, Louise Brown, was born in July 1978 and is now a teenager. There has been great uncertainty about the exact legal position of the processes involved and the children brought into life. In the *Report of the Committee of Inquiry into Human Fertilization and Embryology*, published in 1984, the whole matter is discussed in detail. All the techniques then known were examined by the Committee, chaired by Dame Mary Warnock, including artificial insemination by husband (AIH) and by donor (AID), *in-vitro* fertilization (IVF), egg donation, embryo donation, and surrogate motherhood, as well as the freezing and storage of embryos, and other matters to do with research.

The Warnock report maintains, as a starting point, that 'infertility is a condition meriting treatment'. It also recommends that 'the embryo of the human species should be afforded some protection in law', that some research on embryos 'up to the end of the fourteenth day after fertilization' should be permitted, and that there should be 'a new statutory licensing authority' to regulate all these procedures (Warnock 1984: 10, 63, 69, 75).

Shortly after the report was published, commercial agencies arranging surrogacy for a fee were banned. But a Bill in 1985 to outlaw all embryo research failed to get through Parliament. Public uncertainly about this whole matter was so great that it was not until April 1990 that a Bill went before the House of Commons to set up the licensing authority and to regulate the other matters. MPs voted by a majority to accept the Warnock recommendation that, under strict control, research on embryos should be permitted during the first fourteen days after conception.

Early in 1991, there was further uproar over the practice of offering artificial insemination to single women, so that they could have children without the need for sexual intercourse. The press spoke luridly about 'virgin births'. Some psychologists claimed that the biological need to have children was independent of the need for a sexual relationship. An article in *The Times* declared abruptly, 'Getting semen from a bank screened for the Aids virus was better than searching singles bars for a stud' (12 March 1991: 2).

The termination of a pregnancy, on the other hand, raises a number of quite different questions. The development of the law on abortion is summarized in the House of Lords' *Report of the Select Committee on the Infant Life (Preservation) Bill*, published in 1988. In 1861 an Act of Parliament made it a crime to use drugs or instruments with intent to procure a miscarriage, unless it was done to save the mother's life, and unless a jury considered that the probable consequence of the continued pregnancy would be to make the woman 'a physical or mental wreck'. Another Act in 1929 set out the offence of child destruction, where a child 'capable of being born alive' was caused to die 'before it has an existence independent of its mother', provided this was not done in good faith to preserve the mother's life. The Act also said that a period of 'twenty-eight weeks or more' was enough

189

to prove that the child was capable of being born alive (House of Lords 1988: 4–5).

The 1967 *Abortion Act* went on to permit the termination of a pregnancy if two doctors thought its continuance would 'involve risk to the life' or 'risk of injury to the physical or mental health' of the woman, or greater 'risk of injury to the physical or mental health of any existing children of her family' than would be the case without the termination. It also allowed abortion where there was a substantial risk that if the child were born 'it would suffer from such physical or mental abnormalities as to be seriously handicapped' (House of Lords 1988: 5).

Following these changes in the law, the number of abortions has greatly increased. In 1986 the total number in England and Wales was 172,286, all but 29 within the first 24 weeks. The vast majority were on grounds of risk to the mother's health (House of Lords 1988: 9, 8).

The 1990 *Human Fertilization and Embryology Act*, although it was mainly about embryo research, also contained a hotly-debated clause relating to abortion. MPs voted on a range of options and approved by a majority the reduction of the legal time limit from 28 to 24 weeks. But in cases of serious abnormality, this limit was removed altogether. The life of a child in the womb that is capable of being born alive, although seriously handicapped, may now be legally taken away. As the Archbishop of York said in the debate in the House of Lords, in allowing this they were 'crossing a moral divide' (*Church Times*, 26 October 1991).

The Mystery of Personal Origins

There is little about any of these matters in the Bible. Bio-ethical research was unknown in ancient times, though abortion has probably been a feature of every age. A number of passages, however, do speak of life and its origins, and treat them with tenderness and concern.

In the first creation story in Genesis (1:1—2:4a), men and women are made '*in the image of God*' and this gives a basic status to human life (1:26–27). In the second story (2:4a–25),

190

the same point is made in different words: '*Yahweh God shaped man from the soil of the ground and blew the breath of life into his nostrils, and man became a living being*' (2:7). The origin and the animation of humankind are attributed to God himself.

When Eve conceives and gives birth to Cain, she says, '*I have acquired a man with the help of Yahweh*', and when another son is born, she calls him Seth, '*because God has granted me other offspring*' (Gen. 4:1,25). In the new covenant with Noah, the regulation about blood-vengeance is made, and account is to be demanded for human life, '*for in the image of God was man created*' (9:4–6). It is the image that gives human beings their fundamental value and dignity, and their right to life.

The problem of childlessness is also mentioned in Genesis. Abram bemoans his lot to Yahweh. '*What use are your gifts*', he says, '*as I am going on my way childless? . . . Since you have given me no offspring . . . a member of my household will be my heir*' (15:2–3). Sarai, his wife, says to him, '*Since Yahweh has kept me from having children, go to my slave-girl. Perhaps I shall get children through her.*' But Hagar's pregnancy leads to strife with her mistress and she runs away, eventually returning to give birth to Ishmael (16:1–16). Then, following the covenant with Abraham, Sarah conceives in her old age and gives birth to Isaac. Both sons are blessed, though the covenant relationship is continued through Isaac not through Ishmael (17:2,16–21, 21:1–3). A similar story appears later in Genesis where Rachel and Leah both give sons to their husband Jacob through their slave-girls Bilhah and Zilpah (30:1–13).

These early examples of a form of surrogacy prove successful. But they also reflect conditions in a patriarchal society where men have several wives, and where male heirs are given a high status.

Ancient societies generally had a very pragmatic view of human life. Infants were frequently exposed to die, particularly girls. In Exodus, because of the growing strength of the Israelite people, and as a notable exception to normal practice, Pharoah tells the Hebrew midwives to kill the boys at birth and to let the girls live. When they refuse to do this, he gives the command: '*Throw every new-born boy into the*

191

river, but let all the girls live.' The midwives' resistance is specifically said to be because they were *'God-fearing women'* (1:15–22).

Birth took place on to the lap or the knees (Gen. 30:3, 50:23; Job 3:12), and it often happened in the open fields. The practice of leaving girls unattended to die seems to be reflected in a passage in Ezekiel, in which God rescues the city of Jerusalem from this fate (16:4–6,22). People were sometimes prepared to offer their children up in sacrifice for various purposes (Gen. 22:1–19; Jgs. 11:30–40). Although the practice is forbidden (Lev. 18:21), the prophets persistently feel it necessary to condemn it (Jer. 32:35; Mic. 6:7). Whole communities were also put under the *'curse of destruction'* and *'babe and suckling'* were put to death along with all the rest (1 Sam. 15:1–3).

The basic value of human life is, however, reflected in Exodus in the commandment, *'You shall not kill'*, or as the REB translates it more accurately, *'Do not commit murder'* (20:13). A later verse puts it in fuller words: *'Do not cause the death of the innocent or upright . . . '* (23:7).

Exodus also contains the only reference in the Hebrew Scriptures to a miscarriage caused by human agency. If a woman is hurt as a result of a brawl and suffers a miscarriage, a fine is to be paid. But if *'further harm is done'*, the judges are to award *'life for life'* (21:22–25). The passage seems to suggest that a fine is all that is needed when a miscarriage is caused: the father has simply been robbed of offspring. But if the woman is also harmed and dies, the penalty should be death.

These verses have been much discussed. The Septuagint, a Greek version of the Hebrew Scriptures from the third century before the Christian era, understood the harm done, or not done, to apply to the child, and introduced into its translation a distinction between an unformed and a formed fetus. This distinction was of great significance in further thought about the status of life in the womb. The General Synod report *Personal Origins*, notes Augustine's claim, seven centuries later, that the principle of a life for a life did not apply if the fetus was unformed. Augustine writes, 'There

192

cannot yet be said to be a live soul in a body which lacks sensation when it is not yet formed in flesh and so not yet endowed with sense' (Church of England General Synod BSR 1985: 24).

As a result in the early Church, causing a miscarriage in the first few weeks was not considered to be homicide, though it was still wrong. The distinction persisted. In the thirteenth century Thomas Aquinas accepted Aristotle's view that the fetus was formed or vivified 'at 40 days for a male child and 90 for a female' (Church of England General Synod BSR 1985: 25). This distinction was challenged, however, by later theologians. Although they were prepared to accept abortion in order to save the mother's life on the grounds that killing in self-defence was acceptable, they were not prepared to accept it in any other circumstances. In 1869 Pope Pius IX dropped any reference to the 'ensouled fetus' and all abortions then effectively came under official prohibition in the Roman Catholic Church.

The idea that everything in life, even barrenness and handicap, comes from God can be found in a number of other passages in the Hebrew Scriptures. In Exodus, Yahweh asks Moses, '*Who makes a person dumb or deaf, gives sight or makes blind? Is it not I, Yahweh?*' (4:11). In 1 Samuel, Hannah has no children because '*Yahweh had made her womb barren*' and this is a cause of grief and resentment. When she does give birth, she makes her son over to Yahweh '*for the whole of his life*' (1:6,16,28).

Job, regretting that he was born at all, says, '*Why was I not still-born . . . Put away like an abortive child, I should not have existed, like little ones that never see the light*' (3:11–12,16). The REB uses the gentler term '*untimely birth*' here. The reality of a miscarriage, spontaneous or induced, is thought to be a better state than that of the misery Job later endured. But in another of his speeches Job says to Yahweh, '*Your hands having shaped and created me . . . Did you not . . . clothe me with skin and flesh, and weave me of bone and sinew? In your love you gave me life, and in your care watched over my every breath*' (10:8,10–12). Protesting that he has never infringed

193

the rights of any slave, he declares, '*Did he not create them in the womb like me, the same God forming us in the womb?*' (31:15).

There are several references in the Psalms which seem to imply an understanding of the moment at which an embryo becomes a person, though the thought is not at all clear. At one point, the Psalmist says, '*I was born guilty, a sinner from the moment of conception*' (51:5), but at another: '*You created my inmost self, knit me together in my mother's womb . . . My being held no secrets from you, when I was being formed in secret, textured in the depths of the earth. Your eyes could see my embryo. In your book all my days were inscribed . . .*' (139:13–16). In his paper 'Using the Bible in the Debate about Abortion', John Rogerson notes that the word translated embryo – *golem* in Hebrew – appears here only. Its use outside the Bible indicates that it means 'a rolled up, shapeless mass . . . a shapeless or lifeless substance' (Rogerson 1985: 91). The processes of conception and growth in the womb were clearly a mystery to the ancient world. Ecclesiastes puts the situation bluntly: '*You do not understand . . . how the embryo grows in a woman's womb: no more can you understand the work of God, the creator of all*' (11:5).

Isaiah, on the other hand, speaks of Yahweh '*who formed you in the womb*' and declares: '*Yahweh called me when I was in the womb, before my birth he had pronounced my name*' (44:24, 49:1). '*Woe to anyone*', he states, '*who asks a father, "Why are you begetting?" and a woman, "Why are you giving birth?"* ' (45:10). Jeremiah records Yahweh's call: '*Before I formed you in the womb I knew you; before you came to birth I consecrated you*' (1:4–5). This verse expresses the prophet's deep sense of vocation, rather than any idea that his soul had some pre-existence before he was even conceived.

The same themes occur in the Gospels. In Luke, when Elizabeth hears that her cousin is also pregnant, the expressive phrase is used, '*The child leapt in her womb*'. She goes on to say, '*The moment your greeting reached my ears, the child in my womb leapt for joy*' (1:41,44).

It is worth noting, also, the general obligation in both the Hebrew and the Christian Scriptures to care for the needy and the innocent, and to support the weak. It is part of the character of God to save the needy from death, to *'rescue the weak and the needy'* (Ps. 72:12–13, 82:4). Special concern is to be shown for widows and orphans, and collections made for those in need (Acts 6:1, 11:28–30; Jas. 1:27).

These few references do not amount to any considered view of the nature of life in the womb. The most that can be said is that life itself is seen to come from God, and to have about it something of his image and his spirit. As such it is to be treated with respect. There seems to be a view that personal identity does exist in the womb, and not just from the moment of birth, though there are only the smallest hints, perhaps no more than poetic licence, to indicate whether this is thought to begin at conception, at the quickening at sixteen weeks or so, at birth, or even that it pre-dates conception itself.

Personal Identity

How is this material to be understood? The whole question seems to hang on what is meant by the concept of a 'person'. This needs careful thought. Clearly the embryo is alive; it is not dead tissue. It is also human; it is not animal or other tissue. But sperm and ova, and kidneys or a heart used in a life-saving operation, are also human and alive, and no anxiety is caused when they are lost or destroyed. But at what point does it become a person? As the Warnock report explains, within the first two weeks of its life, an embryo can still divide into twins, two separate persons. It cannot feel any pain until about the twenty-second day, and the brain is not formed until about six weeks. Until it implants in the mother's womb it cannot begin to develop in any way. Some of the procedures involved in treating infertility, for example, take place in a glass dish – *in vitro* in Latin – and the mother is unaware of the embryo's existence. No relationship, or bonding, has yet begun. Nor is it viable apart from its mother until about 20 to 22 weeks. It seems, therefore, that we cannot say that the embryo, at this very early stage, is a person according to any of the usual criteria by which we recognize persons: it has no separate individual

195

existence, it feels no pain, it has no capacity to reason or think, and it is involved in no relationships with others.

An embryo can, however, be described as a 'potential person', but so can the countless fertilized eggs that are lost naturally, perhaps as many as three-quarters of all those produced as a result of sexual intercourse. It can also be called 'a person with potential', but we all have potential at every stage of life, providing other necessary favourable conditions are there, such as food and shelter, and this is not any different from calling it a person from the moment of conception.

An important distinction needs to be made here between what happens naturally and what is caused to happen by human agency. The loss of fertilized eggs from the womb, quite unknown to the mother, is a natural process, but to destroy them in a glass dish is a deliberate act. To lose a child unexpectedly as a result of a miscarriage is a sadness, but to cause it to miscarry requires prior thought and choice. To die at the end of a long and happy life is natural; no moral blame is attached to it. But to cause a person to die is to kill, and penalties may be incurred as a result.

Where abortion is concerned, it is clear that the Church has maintained a consistent opposition from the start. In his paper 'Abortion and Early Christian Thought', the theologian G. Bonner notes that in the early Church abortion was punished by lifelong exclusion from communion, although this was reduced to ten years in 314. Early Roman society had given a father the power of life and death over his children, and exposure or infanticide were within his right. Under the influence of Christianity, however, this practice was finally banned and, in 374, made a capital offence. At that time Basil the Great condemned abortion as murder (Bonner 1985: 107, 94, 97, 98). Since those days official opposition to abortion has continued consistently. In most modern states, including Britain, it has only been permitted, under certain conditions, since the latter part of this century. The Roman Catholic Church continues to oppose the practice with considerable conviction.

Themes

Four themes seem to emerge from these passages about life in the womb in the pages of the Bible. First, **the desire to have children is natural and strong, and where a couple is unable to have a family, they should be helped with all the medical skill available**. Some, today, may be able to bear the sorrow involved in being childless and to seek their fulfilment in other activities, and they are to be honoured and supported in this choice. But such a choice would hardly have been understood in ancient times. Assisting people to conceive and to give birth, to form a family in which love can grow, seems in principle to be consistent with the witness of the Bible.

Secondly, **two alternative approaches to the question of the status of the embryo itself have been developed and need to be carefully understood**. The distinction between them is helpfully described in *Personal Origins*. The first is based on the idea of the 'continuity of the individual subject'. In every individual we can discern 'a "someone" whom we call by a name, who is the bearer of a particular life-history'. This individual history can be traced back as far as fertilization. The second approach is based on the 'attributes which must be possessed by a developing embryo before it can be called a person'. Some people argue that individual development begins at around fourteen days, others that the 'establishment of a functioning nerve-net at around 40 days after conception' is the moment at which this personal life begins. This latter view parallels 'the common acceptance of brain-death (as distinct from, say, heart failure) as the mark of the end of physical life'. On this second view, to be a person is to be a 'subject of consciousness'. The authors of the report conclude, 'We have come (not without difficulty) to recognize in both these approaches the possibility of a scientifically judicious and theologically responsible set of convictions' (Church of England General Synod BSR 1985: 28–30).

Thirdly, **there is no clear indication of when a developing embryo can be said to have the same rights**

197

as a full member of the community. There is a process of development. Each stage has the potential of the next within it, and of all those that will follow. But what is most to be valued and protected is not just the physical cells in themselves, but the capacity for feeling and emotion, for relationship with others, for the use of the brain and the powers of thinking and reasoning, for choice, for creativity, for responding to God himself. This is what makes a bundle of cells into a person. It is all these together that constitute the image of God that is in us, and which is to be given dignity and respect. The life is in the 'spirit' not in the 'blood'.

A growing degree of protection may seem appropriate, therefore, at each of the different stages in this development. We can identify some of them: conception, implantation, sentience or the capacity to feel pain, the beginning of brain activity, quickening, viability or the point when the fetus can survive on its own outside its mother's womb, and birth itself. To give full protection from the moment when the child is born does not necessarily imply giving identical protection from the moment it is conceived.

Fourthly, **where there is a conflict between the life of the embryo or the fetus and that of the mother, the lesser evil is the right course of action to take**. It is no longer a question of whether that life is personal or not; at twelve or twenty weeks the fetus clearly has all the characteristics of a person, albeit as yet only minimally developed. Rather it is a question of how to avoid the greatest amount of suffering in such a situation of conflict.

If the mother's life is threatened by the continued presence of the child, or if her life can be saved by an operation which has an abortion as a secondary effect, it may be justified. A child conceived as a result of the brutality of rape may be an aggressor on the unwilling mother and the cause of intolerable hurt, although the man who attacked her is the main aggressor. A fetus that is very severely handicapped may be saved much suffering if its life is brought to an end, and it is reverently commended to God's greater loving care, as

198

soon as this is discovered, rather than allowing it to linger on in pain. This is the lesser evil.

But in other circumstances, the general obligation to welcome life as a gift from God, and to support the innocent and weak, would seem to prejudice the Christian against abortion. Social abortion, for little more than personal convenience, or as a technique of 'birth control', cannot be justified. The growing child, although totally dependent on its mother, is not just a part of her body for her to do what she likes with, like a kidney or a lung; it is a separate 'subject of consciousness' with its own personal identity, deserving of growing protection as it develops towards full independence at birth.

So Alan and Joan can go ahead with their IVF programme without apprehension. They can feel confident that human skill, implanted by God, is being used to help them fulfil one of the deepest of human longings. Rosie, on the other hand, has to continue to live with the tragic consequences of her holiday fling. If only she had been taught more about sex and contraception, and about the responsibilities of intimate relationships, things might have been different.

SUICIDE AND EUTHANASIA

The ending of life in the womb before it has hardly begun involves conscious decisions affecting other people's lives. But in cases of suicide, and sometimes of euthanasia, people make this decision about their own lives. It may be morally acceptable, in some circumstances, to end the life of others, but is it right to end your own life, or to allow others to do it for you?

Ronald and Hermione, for example, were both in their eighties, and living in secluded retirement in Scotland after a busy academic life. They agreed that as soon as they became an intolerable burden on each other, or on the community, they would commit suicide together. When they judged that the moment had come, they put their affairs in order, and booked the overnight train to London. On arrival they were found dead together. At the memorial service at their college, for neither was a Christian, a passage was read in which the first-century Stoic philosopher Seneca imagines a conversation with Fortune: 'I give thanks for what I have possessed and held. I have managed your property to great advantage, but, since you order me, I give it up. I surrender it gratefully and gladly' (*On Tranquillity of Mind*). Henry, sitting in the congregation, finds it hard to think that such a deliberate, rational, act of surrender could be wrong.

Evelyn, too, in her nineties, longed to die. Confined to bed, humiliated by her incontinence, dependent on drugs to control her pain, she wanted the doctor to bring her life gently to an end. 'I am tired of life like this', she whispered. 'I want the boys to have the money.' A month later, after discovering from her family that she had often talked about this moment, the doctor gave her a large injection of morphine. He was convinced that his duty to relieve pain now outweighed his duty to preserve life. Two days later she was dead.

Death without Dishonour

There are several cases of suicide and of assisted suicide, or voluntary euthanasia, in the Hebrew Scriptures, together with other passages which indicate something of the value of human life. In Genesis, human beings are accountable to God, in whose image they have been created, for what they do with their lives and the lives of others. '*I give you everything,*' God says to Noah, '*with this exception: you must not eat flesh with life, that is to say blood, in it. And I shall demand account of your life-blood, too. I shall demand it of every animal, and of man. Of man as regards his fellow-man, I shall demand account for human life . . . For in the image of God was man created . . .* ' (9:3–6). Human beings are not entirely autonomous agents, accountable to no one but themselves.

The commandment in Exodus, '*You shall not kill*', also gives a basic status to human life (20:13; Dt. 5:17). It is the taking of another person's life by deliberate intention that is forbidden. As Job says in his despair, '*Naked I come from my mother's womb, naked I shall return. Yahweh gave, Yahweh has taken back. Blessed be the name of Yahweh!'* (Job 1:21).

The first case of assisted suicide comes in Judges. During a battle in which he is hit on the head by a millstone thrown by a woman, Abimelech says to his armour-bearer, *'Draw your sword and kill me, so that it will not be said of me that "A woman killed him".'* Abimelech's death is interpreted as retribution for his own sin in committing murder (9:50–56). Samson seems also to commit suicide deliberately in the temple of Dagon. Summoned to amuse the assembled company, he asks to be led to the temple pillars, prays for strength, and shouts, *'Let me die with the Philistines!'* Heaving with all his might, he perishes with the others in the ruins of the building (16:23–31).

In 1 Samuel, Saul commits suicide. Heavily pressed in battle, his sons all dead, he says to his armour-bearer: *'Draw your sword and run me through with it; I do not want these uncircumcized men to come and make fun of me.'* But the man is frightened and refuses. So Saul *'took his own sword and fell on it'*, and the armour-bearer *'fell on his sword too and died with him'* (31:4–5). The motive again is death without dishonour, as it was then understood.

A different version of the story is given in 2 Samuel. Here a young Amalekite tells David of Saul's death. He had come across him *'leaning on his spear'*, surrounded by the enemy, and Saul had called out: *'Come here and kill me. My mind is swimming, although I still have all my strength.'* The young man did what he asked, knowing that *'once he fell he could not survive'*. David's response, however, when he hears this, is to kill the man, *'a resident foreigner'*, for not being afraid to lift his hand to *'destroy Yahweh's anointed'* (1:9–16). The same story is told in 1 Chronicles, omitting the fate of the young Amalekite, and adding the explanation that Saul, too, had died because of his unfaithfulness to Yahweh (10:1–14).

The story of Ahitophel's suicide is told in 2 Samuel. In spite of his good reputation for sound advice on political matters (16:23), his strategy for capturing and killing David is not followed by Absalom. On discovering this, *'He saddled his donkey and set off and went home to his own town. Then, having set his house in order, he hanged himself'*, and was *'buried in his father's tomb'* (17:23).

A further case appears in 1 Kings. Zimri, facing defeat in battle, *'went into the keep of the royal palace, burned the palace over his own head, and died'* (16:18). Again his sin is given as the reason for his death. It is also possible that Job may have been recommended to take his own life. Seeing him in great pain from ulcers, his wife urges, *'Curse God and die'*, though he does not follow this advice (Job 2:9–10).

In the Apocrypha, martyrdom and suicide are mentioned several times. In 2 Maccabees, Eleazar chooses to endure death by torture rather than share in pagan sacrificial meals. *'If I am man enough to quit this life here and now,'* he says, *'I shall prove myself worthy of my old age, and I shall have left the young a noble example of how to make a good death, eagerly and generously, for the venerable and holy laws'* (6:18–31). Seven brothers also prefer torture and death to religious defilement (2 Macc. 7). Razis, a Jew, commits suicide by disembowelling himself (14:37–46). In Tobit, there is a tale of a girl who contemplates suicide but thinks better of it (3:7–17).

In the Christian Scriptures there is one actual and one attempted suicide. In Matthew, full of remorse for betraying Jesus for *'thirty silver pieces'*, Judas *'made off, and went and hanged himself'* (27:3–10; Acts 1:16–19). In Acts, when an earthquake had destroyed his prison, the jailer *'drew his sword and was about to commit suicide, presuming that the prisoners had escaped'*. But Paul shouts out, *'Do yourself no harm; we are all here.'* The conversion and baptism of the jailer and *'all his household'* then follows (16:25–34).

There is also possibly an oblique reference to the idea of seeking death as a form of self-sacrifice in a passage in Romans about the death of Christ on the cross. Paul writes, *'You could hardly find anyone ready to die even for someone upright; though it is just possible that, for a really good person, someone might undertake to die'* (5:7).

The idea, however, that it is God who determines life and death is reflected in a later passage. *'None of us lives for himself and none of us dies for himself; while we are alive, we are living for the Lord, and when we die, we die for the Lord: and so, alive or dead, we belong to the Lord'* (Rom. 14:7–8). In 1 Corinthians, the same theme of dependence on God appears in a passage on sexual immorality. *'Do you not realize,'* Paul writes, *'that your body is the temple of the Holy Spirit . . . ? You are not your own property; you have been bought at a price. So use your body for the glory of God'* (6:19–20).

Active and Passive

No developed theory about the surrendering of life can be built on these texts. In some cases the death is said to be a result of sin, but not the method by which that death is brought about. But these stories do contain the seeds of much of the subsequent discussion about the issues involved. The terms need careful clarification. Suicide means taking your own life, whatever your state of health. The word was artificially made up out of the Latin for 'self' and 'kill', and was first introduced into the English language in 1651. It was a more neutral term than 'destroying, murdering or slaughtering', words in common use for this practice at the time. Euthanasia – *euthanatos* in Greek – means an 'easy or good death'. In *Terminal Choices*, the American Presbyterian philosopher Robert Wennberg defines it as 'taking the life of a person who is hopelessly ill and doing so for reasons of mercy' (Wennberg 1989:3–4).

Further distinctions also need to be made. Suicide involves the deliberate intention to die, when you are not already terminally ill and death but a short way off. A martyr, for example, is not a suicide, because he or she is in full health and the intention is to witness to the faith, whatever may befall. Nor is a soldier rushing headlong into an enemy bayonet. He is a hero, defending his country. Death may be foreseen in both cases, but it is a secondary consequence, not a primary intention.

Euthanasia can be either active, when a lethal drug is administered to hasten a death already imminent, or passive, when drugs are withheld or treatment withdrawn that might have helped to prolong life. It can be direct, to bring about death, or indirect, as a side-effect of a drug whose primary

203

purpose is to relieve pain. If the patient's consent is given, it is voluntary euthanasia. If consent is not given, because the patient is too comatose to make any deliberate decision, or if it is against his or her will, it may be murder.

Shaping Death

The ancient Greeks and Romans adopted a variety of views about the taking of life in these ways. Plato felt that we are 'the property of the gods and are not to desert our post before we are relieved', though he was sympathetic to euthanasia in cases of 'agonizing and debilitating illness'. His pupil Aristotle held a more uncompromising view. 'To quit life,' he said, 'in the face of suffering is an act of cowardice.' On the other hand, Seneca, the first-century Stoic philosopher, writes: 'Against all the injuries of life I have the refuge of death. If I can choose between a death of torture and one that is simple and easy, why should I not select the latter? As I choose a ship in which I sail and the house which I shall inhabit, so I will choose the death by which I leave life . . . Why should I endure the agonies of disease . . . when I can emancipate myself from all my torments?' (Wennberg 1989: 42–43).

The Christian approach, however, has been one of persistent opposition. Robert Wennberg writes: 'The Christian Church, at least from the time of Augustine onward, was firm, uncompromising, and absolutist in rejecting both suicide and euthanasia.' Augustine felt that suicide was worse than murder, for murderers could at least repent and restore their relationship with God, but suicides 'enter eternity in an unforgiven condition'. Thomas Aquinas condemned suicide as a breach of the duty of charity to oneself, for people should naturally love themselves and seek to preserve their lives. He also saw it as a failure of duty to the community, robbing it of a contributing member, and a failure of duty to God, for he alone gives life and takes it away (Wennberg 1989: 40, 55, 65–71). And this has remained the general position in almost every Western country until quite recently.

In 1936, however, an attempt was made in Britain to legalize euthanasia, subject to elaborate safeguards, for people suffering from 'an incurable, fatal and painful disease', but without success. In 1961 suicide ceased to be a crime, though assisting it could mean up to fourteen years in prison.

In 1969 a further attempt to legalize voluntary euthanasia was rejected by the House of Lords. The Bill proposed that a person might be permitted to sign a Declaration containing these words: 'If I should at any time suffer from a serious physical illness or impairment thought in my case to be incurable and expected to cause me severe distress or render me incapable of rational existence, I request the administration of euthanasia . . . ' (Wennberg 1989: 98). The clause would have allowed euthanasia in cases of illness or damage that was incurable, but not necessarily terminal. This extension of the concept seems to have helped to bring about the Bill's rejection by a vote of three to two against.

Some years ago the Karen Quinlan case in America raised the question of euthanasia for people who are so seriously damaged or handicapped by disease or accident that they are in a 'persistent vegetative state', where 'personality, memory, purposive action, social interaction, sentience, thought, and even emotional states are gone' and 'only vegetative functions and reflexes persist' (Wennberg 1989: 164). After being weaned from dependence on a respirator, Karen's heart and lungs continued to function for some ten years, although she had to be kept alive by feeding through gastronasal tubes. In this case death was only kept at bay by artificial means. But reluctance to 'pull the plug' is widespread, and suspicion about what doctors might be 'thought to be up to' may put an unhelpful barrier between patient and physician.

The question about whether to assist, or to hasten, the onset of death is particularly acute where people suffer horrific accidents that disable them severely, or where they face the prospect of a painful, long-drawn-out and frightening death from incurable diseases. The processes of dying may already have begun, though death may not be properly called imminent until the last months or weeks have been reached.

Although resisting euthanasia for those who are not yet terminally ill, Robert Wennberg expresses sympathy for those who are reduced to the vegetative state. He writes:

205

'What is of special value about human life is personal consciousness, which make it possible for the individual to participate in God's creative and redemptive purposes for human
beings . . . It is morally inappropriate to treat what no longer
images God (in acts of intellect, emotion, and will) as if it
did.' In such cases, the 'person' is already dead. By removing
treatment the doctor simply recognizes what has already
happened. For the Christian death may be allowed to enter
'as a conquered enemy who is now to be greeted as a friend'.
Wennberg believes that Christians are committed to 'shaping
a death in accord with a Christian vision of human existence'.
This includes accountability to the creator who is the source
of our being, and accountability 'for the death one elects to
die and for the deaths one elects to cause' (Wennberg 1989:
176, 124, 225). The idea of shaping death, as we shape our
lives, opens up possibilities for much further creative discussion on these matters.

Themes

The themes that emerge from this discussion of suicide and
euthanasia are these: First, it is clear that **human beings are
accountable to God for what they do with their own
lives, as much as those of others**. To claim that we are
autonomous agents, answerable only to ourselves, or to the
community, for what we do with our lives or our bodies, is
not a view that receives support from the Scriptures or the
Christian tradition. Suicide reflects a state of hopelessness
that is in itself tragic. A loving concern for the person and
his or her need for relationship and affection, may well banish
the despair that longs for death. To invite others to bring
your life to an end is to reject the love of self which expresses
itself in the natural will to live, and which lies at the root of
the love of the neighbour.

Secondly, however, **in the cases of suicide and assisted
suicide in the Bible, it is the sense of dishonour and the
denial of human dignity that underlies the desire for
an early death**. To put your affairs in order, calmly and
rationally, and to avoid further burden on the community,

is a responsible act. There seems to be no condemnation of Ahitophel for doing what he did; he is still *'buried in his father's tomb'*. On the other hand, to help Saul to die when his mind was disturbed by an apparently fatal accident and *'once he fell he could not survive'* was an act of mercy as well as one to be punished. It is not only the king who is *'Yahweh's anointed'*; we are all his children made in his image.

Thirdly, **bringing about an early death is a form of doing harm**. It does do damage. The jailer in Acts was a person, able to accept responsibility and to respond to God. In the case of those who have been so severely damaged by accidents, or are so ravaged by progressive diseases that can end only in painful death, the situation is not the same. They no longer have about them the capacities that belong to being a person, and it is no longer so clear that harm will be done if they are helped to slip gently to the end. In these extreme cases technology and medication used to keep them alive are no longer being used in the service of persons made in the image of God. To accept this, and actively to welcome death as a friend, and not as an enemy, may seem right.

But fourthly, **the responsibility to shape our death, as we shape our lives, can be seen as part of the fulfilment of the ancient vision of men and women exercising dominion over life**. The opportunities for this in our own day are much greater than they were in ancient times. We shape our fertility, our relationships, our work, our environment, our political and community life. We intervene in nature to cure disease, to relieve the effects of natural disaster or famine, to replace parts of the body that no longer function well enough. To leave the processes of death, alone, to the unassisted working of 'nature' may be to refuse this responsibility at one of its most crucial points. We are to die well, as we are to live well, for dying is part of living.

Part of this shaping can be done through the preparation of people for death in a supportive and caring context. The hospice movement, for example, has much to teach about the loving management of the last years and weeks of life. Those who are living through this time with cancer, or with Aids, are still members of the community, loved and wanted.

To shape our death itself, so that we die with dignity, can be a loving and responsible act. It can be to act in the image of God himself. If our last hours are lived under our control, without enduring dishonour or humiliation, and if they are lived without burdening others, they can bring glory to God.

So Henry has a point. It is hard to see that what Ronald and Hermione did was anything other than a rational and responsible act. What Evelyn asked for at the end of her life was also an act of responsible moral choice. But shaping the actual moment of death like this would be wrong if it were to be done out of fear, or despair, or under pressure from relatives or the medical profession, or for financial reasons, or as any sort of irrational or wilful choice. The occasions when the conscious and deliberate act of handing one's life back to God in these ways, as an entirely free choice done entirely without pressure from others, are likely to be very few.

8.

LIVING A CHRISTIAN LIFE

The people who have come in and out of this book, helping to root it in the practicalities of everyday life, are all real. By telling their stories I have tried to provide a context in which to think about the complex issues of human behaviour today Of course the names have all been changed and many of the details, too. But the core of each story is true. Every pastor will recognize the reality and the pain in these stories.

These are not exaggerated cases, describing situations that few people actually face. They are ordinary stories from middle-class Britain. It is true that young people live together outside marriage in increasing numbers. More than one in three of all marriages does end in divorce. Gay and lesbian people do experience prejudice and fear from others. Violence and abuse is all too common a feature of domestic life. Women are exploited in our society. Prejudice against African-Caribbean and Asian people is widespread.

Work in a ruthlessly competitive world, together with redundancy and unemployment, does break some people while it makes others. The drive to acquire more money and more possessions dominates most people's waking hours. The poor do die alone, unwanted, and public provision for them is inadequate. The green environment is crumbling under the onslaught of concrete and tarmac, and cruelty to animals continues unabated.

The power of the state stretches into more and more aspects of human life, even when politicians claim it is being rolled back in favour of greater individual choice. Bitter fighting and war continue in Asian and African countries. Even though the communist world has collapsed, weapons systems are being powerfully upgraded. There is still a substantial voice in the British parliament for the return of capital punishment.

Bio-medical processes are moving forward apace. Abortions are performed in large numbers. People commit suicide as a result of economic and other forms of stress. Cancer and progressive diseases still cripple the last years of many people's lives. These matters affect all of us. This is our life today.

But how are we to live as Christians in the midst of all this? How are we to know what God's will is for human living and for human relationships? This book has tried to show how we can begin to answer these pressing questions. I have suggested that, taken together, Scripture, tradition and reason can guide us in living a Christian life based on principle and tempered to reality. It is possible to combine Christian standards and the practical demands of today's world in ways that are both just and loving.

The themes for living well that are set out in this book are based on Christian love. This love looks for compassion, feeling **with** others, giving such a degree of attention to them that our common humanity before God is recognized. It looks for equal regard, for human dignity, for equality in treatment for everyone.

This love looks, also, for a just society in which the values of sharing and mutual respect inform the way institutions work and organizations function. It is as much concerned about the policies that shape national life as it is about you and me in our life together. Christian love is corporate as well as individual, social as well as personal, public as well as private. It affects the structures of society as well as our personal relationships one with another.

A QUESTION OF FAITH

The Hebrew Scriptures speak constantly about the covenant relationship between Israel and Yahweh. The ethic that they set out applies to the internal life of the community of faith.

In the Christian Scriptures this same sense is also to be found. Much that is said applies to the life of the Christian fellowship, to the brothers and sisters. But this concern is not limited to the community of faith alone. We are to love the stranger as well. In any case, the Church is to be an example to the community as a whole. What is right for the one is right for the other. Our God is not just God of the Church, he is God of the whole creation.

The Church today is faced, therefore, with an insistent question about its own internal life and behaviour. Are we a loving community? Do we run our activities, our groups, our organizations, our synods in a way that treats everyone according to these standards of love and justice? And if not, how can they be brought into our life more effectively? What has to be done? What has to change?

The Church is also faced with an equally insistent question about its witness in the wider community. Do we stand up for human dignity, for human rights, for mutual support, for a greater degree of sharing in society? Are we prepared to run practical caring projects to support those in need, and to join in campaigns for certain causes at local, regional and national level? What has to be done to build a just and loving society? What has to change and how?

If a concern about Christian ethics is just left to those who 'like that sort of thing', it runs the risk of being regarded as optional, as something on the periphery, not part of the life-blood of Christian living. It can be marginalized and suppressed.

But if we are to be true to the gospel, we have to love God **and** love our neighbours as ourselves. Christian ethics are not peripheral, they are central to the Christian life. And so they should be central to the life of every church, every congregation, every parish, circuit, district and deanery, every diocese, district and province.

These concerns should have a strong presence in the work and the debates of churches at local, regional and national level, for the issues of Christian behaviour apply to each of these.

It is really a question of faith. We believe in a God who is

211

present in his creation, who works in history, who meets us in our relationships and in the events of ordinary life. Do we really believe this or not? If we do **not**, we reject the witness of the Bible to the nature of the true God, and if we do this we need to repent and be converted. Our eyes need to be opened so that we can see.

This point can be pressed with an example from the world of fine art. In the small eighteenth-century chapel at St Edmund Hall, in Oxford, there is a picture by the Welsh painter Ceri Richards called 'The Supper at Emmaus'. Painted for the chapel in 1958, it depicts in bold colours the moment in Luke when two disciples recognize the risen Jesus in the breaking of bread in their home at Emmaus (24:13–35). On the left, in a shaft of yellow light coming down from the top and forming a cross with the yellow table, is the figure of Jesus, his hand uplifted in blessing. On the right in green is a still uncomprehending disciple, his hands folded in prayer. But in the centre, in vibrant blue and with his back to us, is the other disciple, springing back from the table at the moment of recognition. The figures are those of working men, their hands and feet roughened and worn with toil.

The point is powerfully made in this picture that the Lord is alive and that he is known to us through the material world, through encounter with people as they go about their business, through a world of rough tables and chairs, a jug of wine, a loaf of bread. We meet him and respond to him in the world as it is, and not only in the silence of private meditation or the uplifting experience of corporate worship. I know this picture, because I prayed in that chapel for three years, and Ceri Richards' insight has been with me ever since. Like those early disciples at Emmaus, our hearts need to burn within us along the road, our eyes need to recognize this truth.

A SOCIALLY RESPONSIBLE CHURCH

A church committed to the Christian gospel in the full sense, and following the interpretations set out in this book, will have certain characteristics. It will be trying to become a 'socially responsible' church. It will be involved in programmes of work on each of the subjects I have discussed. It is worth hinting, even if only in the briefest way, at the sort of activity that will play a prominent part in its life and its work. With each course of action mentioned, there is also an organization to contact or a book or a study kit to obtain for further details. Other information should, of course, be available more fully from local sources. But if all else fails, here are some addresses and phone numbers with which to start.

Intimate Relationships

A socially responsible church acting along the lines suggested here will have, for example, a marriage preparation programme for those who come asking for church weddings. Lay people with appropriate experience will be involved in it: a marriage counsellor, a bank manager, a doctor, a child psychologist, a theologian. The elements of a course can be found in *Making Marriage Work* by Margaret Grimer (Geoffrey Chapman 1987), and in *Made in Heaven? Ministry with Those Intending Marriage*, by Peter Chambers (SPCK 1988).

Such a church will arrange for skilled counselling help for couples in trouble in their relationships. This service is offered, for example, in some Anglican dioceses, and is increasingly in demand at a local level. Many clergy do not themselves have the time, or the training, to help members of their own congregations with these problems, and are only too glad to have this professionally qualified, pastoral help from those who do. Some dioceses have Family Life officers who specialize in this form of ministry.

Further details about work with couples and families can be obtained from the Family Life and Marriage Education (FLAME) network (c/o Board for Social Responsibility, Church House, Great Smith Street, London SW1P 3NZ. Tel: 071 222 9011), and from the Catholic Marriage Advisory Council (Clitherow House, 1 Blythe Mews, Blythe Road, London W14 ONW. Tel: 071 371 1341).

213

Such a church will welcome all those who come seeking a wedding ceremony, rejoicing with them at this public expression of their commitment. It will offer support for couples whose marriages have broken down, providing an opportunity for them to think through the experience of divorce and come to terms with it and with their responsibilities towards any children they may have. It will also help them to cope with being alone, and with forming new relationships which may lead to a new marriage. It will conduct second marriages in church, with careful preparation and with on-going support for those involved.

It will also create a climate of understanding and support for homosexual people, encouraging committed and faithful relationships. It will oppose prejudice and homophobia wherever it is found. It may be in touch with the Lesbian and Gay Christian Movement (Oxford House, Derbyshire Street, London E2 6HG. Tel: 071 739 1249) for further information and advice.

Family and Community

A socially responsible church will have an integrated structure of support groups for parents and children. It may use the study kits prepared by the Family Caring Trust with these titles: *The Veritas Basic Parenting Programme, The Teen-Parenting Programme*, and *The Married Listening Programme* (Family Caring Trust, 44 Rathfrithland Road, Newry, Co. Down BT34 1LD. Tel: 0693 64174). The kits have leader's guides, tapes and work-books for participants.

Such a church may be involved in running creche facilities, a play group, a nursery school, a family centre, perhaps in partnership with the local authority and The Children's Society (Edward Rudolf House, Margery Street, London WC1X 0JL. Tel: 071 837 4299). Where it finds evidence of child abuse it may be in touch with the NSPCC (National Society for the Prevention of Cruelty to Children, 67 Saffron Hill, London EC1N 8RS. Tel: 071 242 1626). It may be involved in pressing for a better deal for children nationally, and be in touch with the Child Poverty Action Group

214

(CPAG, 4th Floor, 1–5 Bath Street, London EC1V 9PY. Tel: 071 253 3406).

Prejudice and discrimination against people on grounds of gender or race will be carefully identified and rooted out of church life and church members will be among those active in the community to oppose sexism and racism. Such a church may be in touch with the Equal Opportunities Commission (Overseas House, Quay Street, Manchester M3 3HN. Tel: 061 833 9244), and the Commission for Racial Equality (Elliot House, 10–12 Allington Street, London SW1 5EH. Tel: 071 828 7022) for advice and for help in taking up any grievances that come to its notice. It may also be in touch with local Racial Equality Councils, and with Evangelical Christians for Racial Justice (12 Bell Barn Shopping Centre, Cregoe Street, Birmingham B15 2DZ. Tel: 021 622 6807).

The Council for Social Responsibility in the Diocese of Chelmsford has produced *Equal Opportunities Policy: A Guide for Church Organisations*, setting out the law on these matters and offering detailed guidance on equal opportunities in employment in church organizations, in the provision of services to the local community, such as the letting of church halls to members of other faith groups and in providing appropriately for people living with disabilities (CSR, Guy Harlings, 53 New Street, Chelmsford, Essex CM1 1NG. Tel: 0245 266731).

Inclusive language will be introduced into the forms of worship used in such a church, and its members given careful and sensitive help in understanding why this matters and how hurtful the constant reference to man or him can be to women.

Wealth and Poverty

A socially responsible church will encourage its members to bring the issues and problems of work, redundancy, unemployment, money, social security, debt into its life, to pray about these matters in public, and to support each other in times of stress and need. It will be in touch with industrial chaplains in the area for advice and help. Further details about

215

industrial mission and related activities and organizations can be obtained from the Industrial and Economic Affairs Committee of the General Synod Board for Social Responsibility (Church House, Great Smith Street, London SW1P 3NZ. Tel: 071 222 9011), from Luton Industrial College (Chapel Street, Luton LU1 2SE. Tel: 0582 29374), and from the Catholic Bishops' Conference on England and Wales, Committee for World of Work (39 Eccleston Square, London SW1V 1PD. Tel: 071 834 5442).

Concern about fellowship, sharing, will have an important place on the agenda of such a church. It may put its money, and encourage its members to put their money, in ethical investment funds. It will press the Anglican Church Commissioners, and the financial agencies of other Churches at national level, to do the same. It will seek to avoid investing in products that damage people or the environment and to support human-scale, participative, environment-friendly products and organizational methods.

Such a church may set up a barter scheme among its members, running a toy library, offering help with babysitting, arranging transport to hospital for those who are sick, visiting, gardening and offering other support for elderly people. Its members may grow and exchange produce from the garden and the kitchen, and swap professional, technical, decorating and other skills, in order to develop a greater sense of practical fellowship, of mutual support and care.

A concern about poverty and the poor will play an important part in the life of such a church. It may argue for more adequate social welfare benefits, and for more widely available welfare rights advice. It may be in touch with Church Action on Poverty (Central Buildings, Oldham Street, Manchester M1 1JT. Tel: 061 236 9321).

It may also be involved in schemes to provide temporary housing for homeless people, and flats and houses at affordable rents in urban and rural areas. It may be in touch with Shelter (88 Old Street, London EC1V 9HU. Tel: 071 253 0202), and with CHAS (Catholic Housing Aid Society, 189a Old Brompton Road, London SW5 0AR. Tel: 071 373 4961).

216

It may be pressing for church land to be made available for affordable housing development where the need has been established and where it is welcomed locally. In country areas the local Rural Community Council will have information about this.

Such a church will also be generous in its giving to charitable causes locally, nationally and overseas. It may run a Traidcraft stall, offering Third World goods for sale (Kingsway, Gateshead, Tyne and Wear, NE11 0NE. Tel: 091 491 0591). It may be in touch with Christian Aid (P.O. Box 100, London SE1 7RT. Tel: 071 620 0719), with CAFOD (Catholic Fund for Overseas Development, 2 Romero Close, Stockwell Road, London SW9 9TY. Tel: 071 733 7900), and with other aid agencies.

The Natural Environment

Members of a socially responsible church will be examining the use of their church premises, as well as their activities at home, with conservation in mind. Energy will be saved. Recycled paper will be used for all correspondence, leaflets, posters and magazines. Newspapers and bottles will be recycled, and furniture and machinery repaired rather than replaced. Unleaded petrol will be used in cars. Artificial fertilizers will be avoided in the churchyard and in the garden.

A church with these concerns may invite the local Wildlife Trust to survey the churchyard and devise a management plan to conserve any rare plants it finds there. It may be in touch with the Arthur Rank Centre Church and Conservation Project (National Agricultural Centre, Stoneleigh Park, Warwickshire CV8 2LZ. Tel: 0203 696969), and with Christian Ecology Link (2 Curborough Road, Lichfield, Staffordshire WS13 7NG. Tel: 0543 264074).

Such a church will support local animal sanctuaries, and hold services of animal blessing. It may be in touch with Animal Christian Concern (46 St Margaret's Road, Horsforth, Leeds LS18 5BG. Tel: 0532 583517). Its members will be pressing to see that non-intensive methods are increasingly

217

used on any church-owned farm land, and conservation clauses inserted in new tenancy agreements that are negotiated.

Politics and Violence

A socially responsible church will build relationships with the local authority and with local councillors. It will be in touch with the MP or MPs, and with the MEP, in its area, meeting with them to express support and concern, pressing particular causes on them, and criticizing policies and practices that offend the Christian conscience.

International links with other countries will be built up, particularly with countries in Eastern Europe and the developing countries. Such a church will take part in or arrange exchange visits to churches in other countries in order to increase understanding and a sense of interdependence.

It may develop links with the local Probation Service, and with any prisons or remand centres in the area, encouraging a concern for rehabilitation, visiting people in prison, and working to improve prison conditions. Every time capital punishment is debated in Parliament its members will write to their MP setting out the reasons why this is unacceptable to Christians and urging him or her to vote against its introduction.

Life and Death

A socially responsible church will encourage adequate sex education in local schools, setting intimate relationships within the context of commitment, and helping parents with the difficult problem of raising these matters with their children at home. It may use the Family Caring Trust's *Parenting and Sex Programme* (address above, p. 214).

Information about counselling for those who find themselves unwillingly pregnant, and who are frightened and do not know where to turn for help, will be collected and made available in suitable places, such as the public library or local

218

shops. Places where help can be found by those who grieve after an abortion, perhaps long afterwards, will be identified and details made discreetly available.

Such a church will support the hospice movement in the area. A greater openness about death and how to die well will feature in its study programmes. It may be in touch with St Christopher's Hospice (51 Lawrie Park Road, Sydenham, London SE26 6DZ. Tel: 081 778 9252), and St Joseph's Hospice (Mare Street, Hackney, London E8 4SA. Tel: 081 985 0861), and other local hospices.

The Corporate Life of the Church

These are, of course, only examples of what might be done. But every one is being done in churches somewhere. In summary, a socially responsible church will become an informed centre of study and discussion about Christian ethics. It will introduce a greater sensitivity to these matters in its own corporate life, as well as into the lives of its members and their families, and encourage more effective action on them. It will hold all this up to God in its worship and its prayer, seeking help and guidance and support as it grows in its concern for love and justice in the world.

Such a church will also press the diocese, the province or the district to appoint social responsibility officers, chaplains to industry and commerce, professionally trained counsellors, family life officers and others, who can specialize in these subjects and gain the necessary expertise to develop this aspect of their corporate life.

It will press for debates in synods at local and regional as well as national level on issues of public concern. For some people such debates will be simply educational, as they learn more about what is involved. But for others such debates will be the occasion for a powerful witness to the wider community on issues of Christian concern. They will provide a forum in which Christian opinion and values can be expressed, concern aroused and action set in hand. The secular world is often greatly interested in what the Church has to say about the issues of its own life. It often welcomes involvement by the Church, alongside other community groups, in seeking better provision for human need.

Such involvement in debate and action is powerfully resourced and led by the social responsibility, and church and society boards and committees of the churches at national level, both separately and ecumenically in association with each other. If this witness is to grow and develop it needs continued support at times of financial difficulty in the churches. This work is not a luxury; it is central to the proclamation of the gospel in the modern world.

For the church to be known as a powerhouse of social concern and action effectively commends the gospel to those who look askance at its ideas and activities. A church that is thought to be entirely inward-looking in its concerns, administratively and organizationally unprofessional, and obsessed with curiously antiquated views, harms the spread of the Christian gospel. Actively to love people in these practical ways, on the other hand, is to demonstrate that God exists, that God is a God of love and justice, and that those who believe in him are serious about their faith.

Of course, there is much more that can be done, and should be done. The church is a huge tanker on the high seas; it takes a sustained pressure on the tiller to begin to pull the ship round and to move it in another direction. But to fail to exert this pressure, even if for the moment little change of direction is perceived, is to live a Christian life that is weak in understanding of the faith, unloving, without hope. It is to turn the gospel into a cosy, supportive 'drug' to suppress the pain of real life. It is to turn people **away** from the world, instead of awakening them to God's presence **in** the world. It is to give up on the gospel, to deny the command to love that lies at its heart. A church like that deserves to decline and in the end to die. To press forward, however, in serious engagement with the issues of everyday living is to rediscover faith as a force in life, and to open up a future full of hope.

A COMMUNITY LIKE YOURS

This book is not just one person's story, whatever our six-year-old may have said when I began to write it. In reality it is the story of those whom you have met in its pages. And they are not just isolated individuals, they are a community.

Without giving too much away – and here is the twist to the tale mentioned in the Preface – I can tell you that Stephen and Elaine, living together, are old friends of Tessa, at the school gate. Belinda and Alan, splitting up, live opposite Anne, whom Louise told about little Evie. Sarah, stuck at home, and Jane, worried about her husband's redundancy, send their children to the same school. Maurice, lonely and gay, works for another branch of the same company as Winston, concerned about the Muslim burial ground. John and Christopher, walking in the countryside, live near each other, and Eleanor and Jean are their wives. Stephen is their MP. William meets Christopher for a drink in the pub from time to time. Henry, at Ronald and Hermione's funeral, is one of Charles' friends.

Oh, and there is now a Muslim burial area in the cemetery, with 150 spaces, although few have been taken up. But Alan and Joan are still trying to have a child, and eight months later Robert is still looking for another job.

These people are a microcosm of society. Their lives are inter-woven with each other. The pressures they face individually are also the pressures of their community, for they are all bound up with each other in the bundle of life. Where is this community? That would be to reveal too much, but the truth of the matter is that they are also a community like yours. They live in your town, your village, your neighbourhood. They are among your friends and acquaintances. Their problems are everyone's problems.

To echo the words with which this book began, people in every community face children growing up asking endless questions, and we all struggle to find the right answers. If we do not find some guidelines, at least, by which to live, some idea of God's will for human living, there will be little hope for us or for our children.

If the stories of the people you have met in these pages help you to love your neighbour more fully, more effectively, they will not have been told in vain.

STUDY COURSE AND QUESTIONS FOR DISCUSSION

The material in this book has been presented in such a way that it can be used as a flexible study course. Each section can be used on its own, or in conjunction with any of the others. Five or six sections might be selected, for example, to form a short course, or all eighteen used as an intensive introduction to Christian ethics over a six-month period.

THE STRUCTURE OF THE COURSE

Every session should last about an hour and a half, and have six parts to it taking between ten and twenty minutes each.

Group leaders should watch the clock and keep to time. They should have this book with them, and be ready to read parts of it out as appropriate.

Group members can use their own Bibles. Comparing translations in different versions is often helpful.

The questions suggested for each session have sometimes been put in a provocative form to encourage discussion. There isn't necessarily a right or wrong answer to them.

The purpose of the course is to identify two things: Christian attitudes to adopt, and Christian action to take on each subject studied.

THE SESSIONS

In the **first session** on making moral decisions:
(i) Read the story of the good Samaritan (Lk. 10:29–37).
(ii) Tell your own stories about being 'good samaritans' in the local community. Ask what love and justice require.
(iii) Talk about the relationship between Scripture, tradition and reason as the main 'tools' for making moral decisions. Read the passage about Holbein's painting 'The Ambassadors', and consider how it illustrates the structure of the Bible.
(iv) Talk about the relevance of the Bible for today. Read the passage about the 'experiential' Bible study at the industrial chaplains' conference, and consider whether you could use this method.
(v) Discuss the two questions set out below for this session.

In the **subsequent sessions** on particular subjects:
(i) Read the story which introduces each section and tell each other about your own experience of the issues it raises.
(ii) Bring in the facts and figures quoted that are relevant to your discussion.
(iii) Read out the most important passages from the Bible quoted in each section and talk about them. The group leader should decide which they are beforehand. Use this book to help you interpret their significance, bringing in the ideas from the Christian tradition that are relevant.
(iv) Read out the main points in the 'Themes' that emerge from the material set out at the end of each section and talk about them.
(v) Discuss the two questions set out below for the appropriate session.

In the **final session** on living a Christian life:
(i) Read the passage about Ceri Richards' painting 'The Supper at Emmaus', and consider how it illustrates the way we meet the Lord in ordinary life.

(ii) Read the section headed 'A Socially Responsible Church', and talk about the ideas contained in it. Compare them with what happens in your church now.

(iii) Make detailed plans, and agree on specific action to take, to develop a more effective socially responsible church in your community.

(iv) Discuss the two questions set out below for this session.

(v) Read the final section headed 'A Community like Yours' to round off the course.

THE QUESTIONS

Making Moral Decisions

1 Which is more important: behaving in a loving way towards individuals or struggling for a just and upright society?

2 Who is our neighbour in this area?

Marriage

1 Does sex between single people outside marriage threaten trust and faithfulness between husband and wife inside marriage?

2 How can marriages be supported and protected more effectively at each stage of their development?

Divorce

1 Is a marriage over when the relationship has gone, or only when the contract has been dissolved?

2 Should second marriages be conducted in church?

Homosexuality

1 If homosexuality is natural to some people, has anyone the right to condemn it?

2 If discrimination against people on grounds of gender is wrong, should the Church conduct services of blessing for committed gay and lesbian couples, as it conducts weddings for heterosexual couples?

Parents and Children

1 What makes a family: being linked with others through a blood relationship, or being linked through a commitment to support and care for them?
2 Which is more important: telling your children what is right, and disciplining them when they disobey, or allowing them to make their own choices and supporting them when things go wrong?

Women

1 Should women be subordinate to men at home, at work, in society, and in the Church?
2 Do men and women complement each other, or are they equal and different?

Race

1 Are you proud to belong to a particular nation, or is nationality irrelevant in the world as it is today?
2 How can greater understanding and tolerance between people of different cultures and different faith be encouraged?

Work

1 Is work more likely to give people dignity and enable them to develop their talents, or to wear them down, and exploit and degrade them?
2 In a plural, multi-faith society should everyone have the same day of rest each week?

Money and Possessions

1 Is it possible to get rich without being corrupt?
2 Which is better: compulsory sharing of wealth through a system of taxation and welfare benefits, or voluntary sharing by personal giving in response to immediate human need?

The Poor

1 If people are poor is it their own fault, or is it the result of greed and selfishness on the part of the rich and powerful?
2 How far should concern for the poor extend: to our families alone, to other people in our own country, or to people in the world as a whole?

Ecology

1 If human beings are to show a proper respect for nature, even though it may cost money, what changes in lifestyle are required in our family, our community, and our church?
2 Which is more important: building houses, roads and new factories, which many people want, or preserving green open spaces and natural species, whether people want them or not?

Animals

1 If human beings are to be partners with animals, is it right to hunt them, experiment on them, or use them for entertainment?
2 Should Christians give up eating meat and become vegetarians, or vegans?

The State

1 Should the law be obeyed even if we fundamentally disagree with it?

2　How far should the Church go in getting involved in politics?

War and Peace

1　Can modern warfare, with its terrifying destructive power and accuracy, ever be considered just?
2　What should be done, on an international scale, to make peace more effectively between countries, and to reduce dependence on armaments?

Capital Punishment

1　What is the main purpose of punishment: to give criminals what they deserve, to stop others doing the same, or to reform offenders and return them to normal society?
2　Given that judges and juries sometimes make mistakes, could it ever be right to use the death penalty for any crime?

Life in the Womb

1　Should human embryos have the same degree of protection under the law from the moment they are conceived, as children have from the moment they are born?
2　What should be done to reduce the demand for abortion?

Suicide and Euthanasia

1　Is it more dignified to seek to die before we become incapable of looking after ourselves, or to wait until we die naturally, whatever the pain or the burden on others?
2　What should be done to prepare people for death more effectively, and to care for them as they die?

Living a Christian Life

1　What needs to be done if our church is to become a socially responsible church?

2 What issues should we take up locally, regionally and nationally to help build a socially responsible society?

Bibliography and References

This is not a complete list of publications on the subjects discussed in this book. This bibliography does contain, however, all the books and reports referred to in each section, as well as those found to be most helpful in its preparation. They are set out according to the Harvard referencing system, putting author and date first and then other details. Further literature is listed in the bibliographies contained in these publications themselves.

MAKING MORAL DECISIONS

Atkinson, David (1989), *Pastoral Ethics in Practice*, Eastbourne: Monarch.

Birch, Bruce and Rasmussen, Larry (1976) *Bible and Ethics in the Christian Life*, Minneapolis: Augsburg Publishing House.

Boff, Leonardo and Boff, Clodovis (1987), *Introducing Liberation Theology*, Tunbridge Wells: Burns & Oates.

Bonino, José Miguez (1983), *Toward a Christian Political Ethics*, Philadelphia: Fortress Press.

Brown, David (1983), *Choices: Ethics and the Christian*, Oxford: Basil Blackwell.

Brunner, Emil (1945), *Justice and the Social Order*, London: Lutterworth Press.

Central Statistical Office (1992), *Social Trends 22*, London: HMSO.

Fletcher, Joseph (1966), *Situation Ethics: The New Morality*, London: SCM Press.

Gill, Robin (1985), *A Textbook of Christain Ethics*, Edinburgh: T. & T. Clark.

Hauerwas, Stanley (1981), *A Community of Character: Toward a Constructive Christian Social Ethic*, London: University of Notre Dame Press.

Hebblethwaite, Brian (1981), *The Adequacy of Christian Ethics*, London: Marshall Morgan & Scott.

Higginson, Richard (1988), *Dilemmas: A Christian Approach to Moral Decision-making*, London: Hodder & Stoughton.

Houlden, J. L. (1975), *Ethics and The New Testament*, London: Mowbray.

Jones, Richard G. (1985), *Groundwork of Christian Ethics*, London: Epworth Press.

Langford, Michael J. (1985), *The Good and the True: An Introduction to Christian Ethics*, London: SCM Press.

Meeks, Wayne (1987), *The Moral World of the First Christians*, London: SPCK.

Newlands, George (1985), *Making Christian Decisions*, Oxford: Mowbray.

Niebuhr, Reinhold (1979), *An Interpretation of Christian Ethics*, New York: The Seabury Press. First published 1935.

Ogletree, Thomas W. (1983), *The Use of the Bible in Christian Ethics*, Oxford: Basil Blackwell.

Oppenheimer, Helen (1983), *The Hope of Happiness: A Sketch for a Christian Humanism*, London: SCM Press.

Outka, Gene (1972), *Agape: An Ethical Analysis*, London: Yale University Press.

Preston, Ronald H. (1983), *Church and Society in the Late Twentieth Century: The Economic and Political Task*, London: SCM Press.

Rowland, Christopher and Corner, Mark (1990), *Liberating Exegesis: The Challenge of Liberation Theology to Biblical Studies*, London: SPCK.

Rowlands, John (1985), *Holbein: The Paintings of Hans Holbein the Younger*, Oxford: Phaidon Press.

Sanders, Jack T. (1986), *Ethics in the New Testament: Change and Development*, Second impression with new preface, London: SCM Press.

Schrage, Wolfgang (1988), *The Ethics of the New Testament*, Edinburgh: T. & T. Clark.

Stott, John (1990), *Issues Facing Christians Today: New Perspectives on Social & Moral Dilemmas*, Second edition, London: Collins/Marshal Pickering.

Temple, William (1976), *Christianity and Social Order*, Foreword by Edward Heath, Introduction by Ronald Preston, London: Shepheard Walwyn/SPCK. First published 1942.

Tillich, Paul (1959), *Theology of Culture*, London: Oxford University Press.

White, R. E. O. (1979), *The Changing Continuity of Christian Ethics, Vol. 1, Biblical Ethics*, Exeter: The Paternoster Press.

231

White, R. E. O. (1981), *The Changing Continuity of Christian Ethics, Vol. 2, The Insights of History*, Exeter: The Paternoster Press.
Wink, Walter (1990), *Transforming Bible Study*, London: Mowbray.

INTIMATE RELATIONSHIPS

Bagot, Jean-Pierre (1987), *How To Understand Marriage*, London: SCM Press.
Brett, Paul (1991), *Rethinking Christian Attitudes to Sex*, Colchester: Centre for the Study of Theology in the University of Essex.
Central Statistical Office (1992), *Social Trends 22*, London: HMSO.
Chambers, Peter (1988), *Made in Heaven? Ministry with Those Intending Marriage*, London: SPCK.
Church of England General Synod Board for Social Responsibility (BSR) (1979), *Homosexual Relationships: A Contribution to Discussion*, London: Church Information Office.
Church of England General Synod House of Bishops (1991), *Issues in Human Sexuality*, A Statement, London: Church House Publishing.
Church of England General Synod Marriage Commission (1978), *Marriage and the Church's Task*, London: CIO Publishing.
Church of England General Synod Standing Committee (1988), *An Honourable Estate*, London: Church House Publishing.
Coleman, Peter (1989), *Gay Christians: A Moral Dilemma*, London: SCM Press.
Countryman, L. William (1989), *Dirt, Greed & Sex: Sexual Ethics in the New Testament and their Implications for Today*, London: SCM Press.
Dominian, Jack (1987), *Sexual Integrity: The Answer to AIDS*, London: Darton, Longman and Todd.
Dominian, Jack (1991), *Passionate and Compassionate Love: A Vision for Christian Marriage*, London: Darton, Longman and Todd.
Fuchs, Eric (1983), *Sexual Desire and Love: Origins and History of the Christian Ethic of Sexuality and Marriage*, Cambridge: James Clarke.
Grimer, Margaret (1987), *Making Marriage Work*, London: Geoffrey Chapman.
Heron, Alistair (Ed.) (1963), *Towards a Quaker View of Sex: An Essay by a Group of Friends*, London: Friends Home Service Committee.
Mortimer, R. C. (Chairman) (1966), *Putting Asunder: A Divorce Law for Contemporary Society*, The Report of a Group appointed by the Archbishop of Canterbury, London: SPCK.
Nelson, James B. (1978), *Embodiment: An Approach to Sexuality and Christian Theology*, Minneapolis: Augsburg Publishing House.

Oppenheimer, Helen (1990), *Marriage*, London: SPCK.

Spong, John Shelby (1990), *Living in Sin? A Bishop Rethinks Human Sexuality*, San Francisco: Harper & Row.

FAMILY AND COMMUNITY

Anderson, Ray and Guerney, Dennis (1985), *On Being Family: A Social Theology of the Family*, Michigan, Grand Rapids: William B. Eerdmans.

Beauvoir, Simone de (1972), *The Second Sex*, Harmondsworth: Penguin. First published 1949.

Borrowdale, Anne (1989), *A Woman's Work: Changing Christian Attitudes*, London: SPCK.

Borrowdale, Anne (1991), *Distorted Images: Christian Attitudes to Women, Men and Sex*, London: SPCK.

Central Statistical Office (1992), *Social Trends 22*, London: HMSO.

Church of England General Synod Board for Social Responsibility (1990), *Ageing*, Report of the Social Policy Committee, London: Church House Publishing.

Equal Opportunities Commission (1991), *Women and Men in Britain 1991*, London: HMSO.

Fiorenza, Elizabeth Schuessler (1983), *In Memory of Her*, London: SCM Press.

Grant, Paul and Patel, Raj (Eds.) (1990), *A Time to Speak: Perspectives of Black Christians in Britain*, Birmingham: Community and Race Relations Unit and Birmingham: Evangelical Coalition for Racial Justice.

Hampson, Daphne (1990), *Theology and Feminism*, Oxford: Basil Blackwell.

Hill, Clifford S. and Matthews, David (1968), *Race: A Christian Symposium*, London: Victor Gollancz.

Leech, Kenneth (Ed.) (1985), *Theology & Racism 1*, London: General Synod Board for Social Responsibility Race, Pluralism and Community Group.

Leech, Kenneth (1988), *Struggle in Babylon: Racism in the Cities and Churches of Britain*, London: SPCK.

Loades, Ann (Ed.) (1990), *Feminist Theology: A Reader*, London: SPCK.

Runnymede Trust (1991), *Race and Immigration*, July/August 1991 Bulletin, London: Runnymede Trust.

Walrond-Skinner, Sue (1988), *Family Matters*, London: SPCK.

Witherington III, Ben (1990), *Women and the Genesis of Christianity*, Cambridge: Cambridge University Press.

WEALTH AND POVERTY

Avila, Charles (1983), *Ownership: Early Christian Teaching*, London: Sheed & Ward.

Bleakley, David (1983), *Work: The Shadow and the Substance: A Reappraisal of Life and Labour*, London: SCM Press.

Boerma, Conrad (1979), *Rich Man, Poor Man – And the Bible*, London: SCM Press.

Central Statistical Office (1992), *Social Trends 22*, London: HMSO.

Church of England, Archbishop of Canterbury's Commission on Urban Priority Areas (1985), *Faith in the City*, London: Church House Publishing.

Church of England General Synod Board for Social Responsibility (1979), *Work and the Future: Technology, World Development and Jobs in the Eighties*, A report from the Industrial Committee, London: CIO Publishing.

Church of England General Synod Board for Social Responsibility (1986), *Not Just for the Poor: Christian Perspectives on the Welfare State*, Report of the Social Policy Committee, London: Church House Publishing.

Clarke, Roger (1982), *Work in Crisis: The Dilemma of a Nation*, Edinburgh: The Saint Andrew Press.

Forrester, Duncan B. (1985), *Christianity and the Future of Welfare*, London: Epworth Press.

Forrester, Duncan B. and Skene, Danus (1988), *Just Sharing: A Christian Approach to the Distribution of Wealth, Income and Benefits*, London: Epworth Press.

Gonzales, Justo (1990), *Faith and Wealth: A History of Early Christian Ideas on the Origin, Significance and Use of Money*, San Francisco: Harper & Row.

Griffiths, Brian (1982), *Morality and the Market Place*, London: Hodder & Stoughton.

Griffiths, Brian (1984), *The Creation of Wealth*, London: Hodder & Stoughton.

Gutierrez, Gustavo (1974), *A Theology of Liberation: History, Politics and Salvation*, London: SCM Press.

Handy, Charles (1984), *The Future of Work: A Guide to a Changing Society*, Oxford: Basil Blackwell.

Hartropp, Andrew (Ed.) (1988), *Families in Debt: The Nature, Causes and Effects of Debt Problems and Policy Proposals for their Alleviation*, Research Paper No. 7, Cambridge: Jubilee Centre Publications.

Haughey, John C. (1989), *The Holy Use of Money: Personal Finance in Light of Christian Faith*, New York: Crossroad.

Hengel, Martin (1974), *Property and Riches in the Early Church*, London: SCM Press.

Jerome, Jerome K. (1957), *Three Men in a Boat*, Harmondsworth: Penguin Books. First published 1889.

Mealand, David (1980), *Poverty and Expectation in the Gospels*, London: SPCK.

Mullin, Redmond (1983), *The Wealth of Christians*, Exeter: The Paternoster Press.

Pope John Paul II (1981), *Laborem Exercens*, Encyclical letter on Human Work, London: Catholic Truth Society.

Pope John Paul II (1988), *Solicitudo Rei Socialis*, Encyclical letter for the Twentieth Anniversary of *Populorum Progressio*, London: Catholic Truth Society.

Pope Leo XIII (1891), *Rerum Novarum*, Encyclical letter on the Condition of the Working Classes: the Workers' Charter, London: Catholic Truth Society.

Pope Pius XI (1931), *Quadragesimo Anno*, Encyclical letter on Reconstructing the Social Order, London: Catholic Truth Society.

Richardson, Alan (1963), *The Biblical Doctrine of Work*, London: SCM Press.

Ryken, Leland (1987), *Work and Leisure in Christian Perspective*, Leicester: Inter-Varsity Press.

Sayers, Dorothy L. (1947), 'Why Work?' in *'Creed or Chaos? And Other Essays in Popular Theology'*, London: Methuen.

Schumacher, E. F. (1979), *Good Work*, London: Jonathan Cape.

Tawney, R. H. (1938), *Religion and the Rise of Capitalism*, Harmondsworth: Penguin Books. First published 1926.

Townsend, Peter (1979), *Poverty in the United Kingdom: A Survey of Household Resources and Standards of Living*, Harmondsworth: Penguin Books.

Weber, Max (1976), *The Protestant Ethic and the Spirit of Capitalism*, Second edition, London: George Allen & Unwin. First published 1930.

THE NATURAL ENVIRONMENT

Bradley, Ian (1990), *God is Green: Christianity and the Environment*, London: Darton, Longman and Todd.

Carpenter, Edward (Chairman) (1980), *Animals and Ethics*, A Report of the Working Party convened by Edward Carpenter, London & Dulverton: Watkins.

Cooper, Tim (1990), *Green Christianity: Caring for the Whole Creation*, London: Spire.

Fox, Matthew (1983), *Original Blessing*, New Mexico, Santa Fe: Bear.

Linzey, Andrew (1987), *Christianity and the Rights of Animals*, London: SPCK.

Linzey, Andrew and Regan, Tom (Eds.) (1988), *Animals and Christianity: A Book of Readings*, New York: Crossroad.

Lovelock, James (1979), *Gaia: A New Look at Life on Earth*, Oxford: Oxford University Press.

McDonagh, Sean (1986), *To Care for the Earth: A Call to a New Theology*, London: Geoffrey Chapman.

McDonagh, Sean (1990), *The Greening of the Church*, London: Geoffrey Chapman.

Moltmann, Juergen (1989), *Creating a Just Future: The Politics of Peace and the Ethics of Creation in a Threatened World*, London: SCM Press.

Porritt, Jonathon (1984), *Seeing Green: The Politics of Ecology Explained*, Oxford: Basil Blackwell.

Regenstein, Lewis G. (1991), *Replenish the Earth: A History of Organised Religion's Treatment of Animals and Nature – Including the Bible's Message of Conservation and Kindness to Animals*, London: SCM Press.

RSPCA (1984), *Policies on Animal Welfare*, Horsham: Royal Society for the Prevention of Cruelty to Animals.

Secretary of State for the Environment and others (1990), *This Common Inheritance: Britain's Environmental Strategy*, London: HMSO.

POLITICS AND VIOLENCE

Anglican Consultative Council (1988), *The Truth Shall Make You Free: The Lambeth Conference 1988: The Reports, Resolutions & Pastoral Letters from the Bishops*, London: Church House Publishing.

Barclay, Oliver R. (Ed.) (1984), *Pacifism and War: Eight Prominent Christians Debate Today's Issues*, Leicester: Inter-Varsity Press.

Bennett, John C. (1958), *Christians and the State*, New York: Charles Scribner's Sons.

Bonino, José Miguez (1983), *Toward a Christian Political Ethics*, London: SCM Press.

Chester, Andrew (1989), 'The Concept of Peace in the Old Testament', in *Theology* Vol. XCII, November 1989, No. 750, London: SPCK.

Church of England General Synod Board for Social Responsibility (1982), *The Church and the Bomb: Nuclear Weapons and the Christian Conscience*, The Report of a Working Party under the Chairmanship of the Bishop of Salisbury, London: CIO Publishing.

Church of England General Synod Board for Social Responsibility (1988), *Peacemaking in a Nuclear Age*, The Report of a Working Party, London: Church House Publishing.

Church of England General Synod Board for Social Reponsibility (1991), *Crime, Justice and the Demands of the Gospel*, G. S. Misc. 359, London: General Synod Board for Social Responsibility.

Cullmann, Oscar (1957), *The State in the New Testament*, London: SCM Press.

Ferguson, John (1973), *The Politics of Love: The New Testament and Non-violent Revolution*, Cambridge: James Clarke.

Hoyles, J. Arthur (1986), *Punishment in the Bible*, London: Epworth Press.

Kaye, B. N. and Wenham, G. J. (1978), *Law, Morality and the Bible: A Symposium*, Leicester: Inter-Varsity Press.

Macgregor, G. H. C. (1953), *The New Testament Basis of Pacifism*, Revised edition, London: The Fellowship of Reconciliation.

Niebuhr, Reinhold (1966), *The Children of Light and the Children of Darkness: A Vindication of Democracy and a Critique of its Traditional Defense*, New York: Charles Scribner's Sons.

Ramsey, Paul (1961), *War and the Christian Conscience: How shall Modern War be Conducted Justly?* Durham, N. C.: Duke University Press.

Roman Catholic Church U.S. Bishops (1983), *The Challenge of Peace: God's Promise and Our Response*, Pastoral letter on War and Peace in the Nuclear Age, London: Catholic Truth Society/SPCK.

Speller, Adrian (1986), *Breaking Out: A Christian Critique of Criminal Justice*, London: Hodder & Stoughton.

Temple, William (1976), *Christianity and Social Order*, Foreword by Edward Heath, Introduction by Ronald Preston, London: Shepheard Walwyn/SPCK. First published 1942.

Yoder, John Howard (1972), *The Politics of Jesus: Vicit Agnus Noster*, Michigan, Grand Rapids: William B. Eerdmans.

LIFE AND DEATH

Berry, Dr Caroline (1987), *The Rites of Life: Christians and Bio-medical Decision Making*, London: Hodder & Stoughton.

Blacker, Russell (1992), 'Euthanasia', in *Crucible*, Part I January–March 1992, Part II April–June 1992, London: General Synod Board for Social Responsibility

Bonner, G. (1985), 'Abortion and Early Christian Thought', in Channer, J. H. (Ed.) (1985), *Abortion and the Sanctity of Life*, Exeter: The Paternoster Press.

Cameron, Nigel M. de S. (Ed.), *Death Without Dignity*, Edinburgh: Rutherford House Books.

Church of England Church Assembly Board for Social Responsibility (1965), *Abortion: An Ethical Discussion*, London: Church Information Office.

Church of England General Synod Board for Social Responsibility (1975), *On Dying Well: An Anglican Contribution to the Debate on Euthanasia*, London: Church Information Office.

Church of England General Synod Board for Social Responsibility (1985), *Personal Origins*, The Report of a Working Party on Human Fertilisation and Embryology, London: CIO Publishing.

Donald, Professor Ian and Others (1985), *Test Tube Babies – A Christian View*, Second edition, Oxford: Becket Publications and London: Unity Press.

Glover, Jonathan (1977), *Causing Death and Saving Lives*, Harmondsworth: Penguin Books.

Higginson, Richard (1988), *Whose Baby? The Ethics of 'In-vitro' Fertilisation*, Basingstoke: Marshall Pickering.

House of Lords (1988), *Report of the Select Committee on the Infant Life (Preservation) Bill [H.L.]*, London: HMSO.

O'Donovan, Oliver (1984), *Begotten or Made?*, Oxford: Clarendon Press.

Rogerson, J. (1985), 'Using the Bible in the Debate about Abortion', in Channer, J. H. (Ed.) (1985), *Abortion and the Sanctity of Life*, Exeter: The Paternoster Press.

Singer, Peter and Wells, Deane (1984), *The Reproduction Revolution: New Ways of Making Babies*, Oxford: Oxford University Press.

Trowell, Hugh (1973), *The Unfinished Debate on Euthanasia*, London: SCM Press.

Warnock, Dame Mary (Chairman) (1984), *Report of the Committee of Inquiry into Human Fertilisation and Embryology*, Department of Health & Social Security, London: HMSO.

Wennberg, Robert (1989), *Terminal Choices*, Michigan, Grand Rapids: William B. Eerdmans.